French Politics

STUDIES IN HISTORY AND POLITICS

French Politics

Edited with an introduction by

Martin Harrison

University of Keele

D.C. HEATH AND COMPANY

A DIVISION OF RAYTHEON EDUCATION COMPANY

Lexington, Massachusetts

Library of Congress Catalog Number 68-3128

COPYRIGHT © 1969 BY RAYTHEON EDUCATION COMPANY

PRINTED IN THE UNITED STATES OF AMERICA

Table of Contents

Introduction

Traditionally France has long been one of that fairly limited group of countries studied in the comparative government courses of colleges and universities throughout the world. This is true, perhaps, because of France's historical great-power status and the cultural prestige of the French, combined with the decidedly optimistic assumption that France was the one foreign country about which students could be reasonably expected to read documents in the original language. If based on these reasons, the traditional prominence of France in the syllabuses would look decidedly shaky. But beyond routine and tradition, other more compelling considerations make France a particularly relevant and engrossing subject to study.

Sharing many of the political values of countries such as Britain and the United States, France's profoundly different historical experience, particularly during the last two centuries has produced not only an administrative structure and tradition which is notably in contrast with theirs, but also a quite distinctive pattern of political development. This is an old country which, like so many of the emergent nations, has still to resolve the basic problem of political legitimacy, where there exists no continuing consensus on either the rules of the political game or the distribution of power between organs of government and political forces, and where political disagreements may rapidly turn into a challenge to the fundamentals of the system. Here a constitution is not a venerable document nor a set of understandings, but one of the ways by which the side which comes out on top in any major political upheaval seeks to consolidate its ascendancy. Alongside the historical assertion of liberty, equality, fraternity, invariably so difficult to conciliate with one another, have flourished attitudes inimical to healthy democracy—the survival of authoritarian and revolutionary traditions, the respectability of the absence of civic consciousness known, untranslatably, as *incivisme*—the legacy of individualism and historical divisions.

All of these problems have been evident in recent years as France has been passing through yet another phase of institutional upheaval and constitution-making and prolonged constitutional controversy. Even now the nature of her long-term political structure remains in question. Despite periods of relative stability in recent years, the near collapse of the régime in 1968 showed clearly that the problem of finding political institutions appropriate to her economic and social structure is far from solved. France remains a country where some of the basic dilemmas of political community are unresolved, where the attempt to reconcile stable and effective government with democracy proves peculiarly difficult—in short, a country still struggling with a longdrawn crisis of political modernization. These are some of the problems which lend the study of French politics a particular interest, and on which this collection sets out to shed light.

Few of the items which follow assume a detailed knowledge of French political structure of history. They are designed in fact to be read by someone equipped with the kind of background that might be derived from textbook treatments of French politics and history—indeed the collection is largely designed to add an additional dimension to the more formal and institutional accounts. I emphasize the desirability of both historical and political background, since this volume reaches back only occasionally before 1945. A full understanding of the present political system of any country clearly requires at least a general conception of what has gone before; this is particularly true of France where one finds oneself being reminded of the link between past and present more than in many other countries. Superficially, there is the traditional fondness of French orators for interweaving their speeches with references to the "night of August 4," "December 2," "February 6," "May 13" (the year being invariably omitted), the *Versaillais* or the *communards*—alluding thus to major turning points in the history of France—a custom which may well flatter the political memory of ordinary apolitical Frenchmen. More substantially, as the work of scholars such as André Siegfried and François Goguel have amply demonstrated, the divisions in French society which underlie the persistent fragmentation of the party system, and consequently the chronic tendency towards political instability, are deeply rooted in the history of the last two centuries, and even before.

Generally, extracts in this volume tend to presuppose this broader historical context but certainly do not dismiss it, though several of the earlier pieces do in fact relate the nature of the Fifth Republic's heritage to the underlying socioeconomic structure and inherited political attitudes. If inadequate historical perspective is one pitfall to be avoided, the danger of a collection of contemporary material being merely speculative and ephemeral is surely the other. Nowhere is the difficulty greater than in writing about France where politics are seemingly in a perpetual state of "becoming." Items have therefore been deliberately selected with an eye to conveying both the elements of change and tradition which uneasily coexist in this political and social system, and which will aid in understanding the future, irrespective of the specific character of the régime. Naturally, descriptions of some events, such as elections, include allusions peculiar to a particular political context—but even behind these there lies a general illustration of what France's political campaigns, very slow to change, are like. The attention given to the views of President de Gaulle is certainly no exception to this broad approach. Plainly no collection of readings on the Fifth Republic could avoid giving prominence to the man who, more than any other, has molded and dominated it since its birth. His comments on parties, the state and the presidency are today basic documents. Yet even in the post-gaullist period it will be years before the political system can be fully understood without reference to the gaullist experience and the General's conception of political action. Thus the collection is conceived so as to make it relevant to both the gaullist and post-gaullist phases.

Inevitably the make-up of a volume like this reflects the nature of the available material as much as the editor's personal approach to political analysis. Since the Fifth Republic is still young, the amount of published work on the policy-making process, on the working of the President's and Prime Minister's office, and on consultative procedures remains limited. But the tendency of the book to tilt towards a more classical institutions approach, rather than to stress processes, arises as much from the character of French political discourse as from the nature of recent published work, for debate on the country's political institutions has a far more central place in everyday political debate than it would in the United States or Britain, where organs of government are more often taken for granted than debated.

Thus in putting together this collection I have tried as far as possible to convey something of the distinctive feel of French politics, and French political argument. As far as possible I have presented the views of Frenchmen addressing themselves to their fellow-Frenchmen and most particularly of actual participants in the political system, whether arguing about it or simply describing their experience with it. I have called on French authors particularly frequently, partly because their work is rather less accessible than the standard British-American authors, but also to present some impression of the way the French themselves discuss their political system. I have tried to provide the materials by which the reader can get to grips with the views of both de Gaulle and the leading critics of the régime, rather than having to rely on the pemmicanized analyses of the commentators. In the more descriptive sections it may seem occasionally that beneath some of the mildly exotic trappings of some of the activities described, there lie attitudes and behavior which have parallels closer to home. This is no coincidence. While so much of French political life in these pages is clearly distinct from that of other western democracies, it is as well to be reminded of the many similarities between politicians there and politicans generally.

Finally, the book has been constructed in such a way as to provide as much internal dialogue as possible, by offering contrasting analyses or descriptions of the problems or institutions discussed. French politics suffer such fragmentation that one cannot reproduce the views of every faction on every problem, but as far as possible the main lines of agreement and disagreement have been documented. Needless to say, then, this is not one of those symposiums in which every word reflects the views of the editor; in fact I differ profoundly with quite a number of my contributors. Throughout, the aim has been not to grind axes, but to allow the reader the maximum access to opposing views, to present the fairest and most comprehensive survey possible, within the space available, of the distinctive character of politics in contemporary France, as a guide not only to the present but as a basis for understanding the continuing struggle for political stability and modernization which has still to be won.

Glossary

Bourbon.   Palais-Bourbon — meeting place of the National Assembly

Centre démocrate.   a center; center-right party since 1962; now moribund

Community.   The grouping of France and her colonies created by the 1958 Constitution, of little practical consequence since the colonies became independent, but still formally in being

Elysée.   Palais de l'Elysée — official residence of the French President

Entente Démocratique.   a center and center-left grouping in the Assembly, mainly to 1962

Federation.   i.e., Fédération de la Gauche Démocrate et Socialiste — alliance of left-wing parties and clubs led by François Mitterrand

FLN.   National Liberation Front (Algerian nationalist organization)

GPRA.   Provisional Government of the Algerian Republic

18 June 1940.   Date of de Gaulle's appeal to continue fighting the Germans

Liberation.   Liberation of France from German occupation, 1944/5

Luxembourg.   Palais de Luxembourg — meeting place of the Senate

Matignon.   Hôtel Matignon — official residence of the French Prime Minister

13 May 1958.   Date of insurrection in Algiers which overthrew the Fourth Republic

MRP.   Mouvement Républicain Populaire — Christian Democratic Party now in suspended animation

ORTF.   Office de Radiodiffusion-Télévision Française

PCF.   Parti Communiste Français

PDM.   Progrès et Démocratie Moderne — center-right grouping in the Assembly formed after 1967 elections

PSU.   Parti Socialiste Unifié — small left-Socialist party

Rassemblement Démocratique.   A center and center-left grouping in the Assembly, mainly 1962–7

RI.   Républicains Indépendants — a moderate right-wing party uneasily allied with the UNR

RPF.   Rassemblement du Peuple Français — Gaullist party under the Fourth Republic

SFIO.   Section Française de l'International Socialiste — Socialist Party

UD-5. Union des Démocrates pour la Cinquième République—a new name for the Gaullist party

UDT. Union Démocratique de Travail—Left-Gaullists

UNR. Union pour la Nouvelle République—name of Gaullist Party under the Fifth Republic until 1967

I. Society and Politics —
The French Political Problem

1940 . . . 1944 . . . 1958. Three times within their own lives mature Frenchmen have seen their country's political system overthrown and drastically remodelled. In 1940, the moribund Third Republic abdicated to the authoritarian rule of Vichy in the hour of military defeat. Vichy in its turn was swept ignominiously away at the Liberation. High hopes that the Fourth Republic would usher in a new political era faded, and when short-lived and irresolute governments proved incapable of resolving the crisis of decolonization, the Fourth Republic succumbed to the Algiers revolt of 1958, which brought General de Gaulle back to power. Since then France has entered a period of relative political stability. And yet the Fifth Republic has been so closely identified with its founder, President de Gaulle, that its ability to survive his passing without substantial change is inevitably in doubt. The transition to yet another political system — possibly the Sixth Republic — may thus lie ahead. Why has the search for stable political institutions proved so difficult in France? This must inevitably be one of the first questions one asks in attempting to understand not only the recent past in France, but also the prospects for the future. Consequently this opening section explores the roots of political instability. Appropriately enough it opens with Philip Williams' discussion of the breakdown of the Fourth Republic which, like so many excerpts in this book, shows the tensions arising from both tradition and change.

Philip Williams

SOCIETY AND THE STATE IN MODERN FRANCE

The Fourth Republic lasted less than a dozen years, but during that brief period French economy and society changed more quickly than it ever had in the preceding century. Economic modernization and new means of mass communication reduced the old differences between regions and classes, but brought new tensions between

From Philip M. Williams, *Crisis and Compromise: Politics in the Fourth Republic*, Archon Books, third edition, 1964, pp. 444–449. Reprinted by permission of Archon Books and of Longmans Green, Ltd.

those who gained and those who lost. In so conservative a country, this pace of progress imposed severe strains — greatly accentuated by the external crisis which began before the Fourth Republic but reached a climax under it. For men humiliated in 1940, who had rapidly rebuilt and increased the absolute strength of their country, were called on to adjust to a sharp decline in its power relative to its rivals and former subjects. Within Europe, France made her adjustment to the new conditions more readily than Britain; outside Europe, far less readily. The tensions born of simultaneous progress at home and retreat abroad came to a head over the Algerian problem, which first paralysed the working of government and then threatened political liberties.

These problems were dealt with by new men working a new constitution. The parliamentary personnel of the Fourth Republic was largely recruited through the Resistance and the Free French movement, and inspired by outraged patriotism and impatient exasperation with the manoeuvres, compromises and evasions of the prewar politicians. Yet the new men quickly resumed the practices they had once roundly condemned. The regime was remade in 1946 in order to destroy the bad old ways; but before long the System reappeared. This return (not persistence) of traditional attitudes and methods suggests that the problem of adapting the political mechanism to social change lay not in the faults of character of two very different sets of men, or the institutional weaknesses of two constitutions devised for quite different ends, but deep in the history and social structure of France.

In twentieth-century French politics the cleavages of the past remained as wide as those of the present day. France had her incomplete industrial revolution before the political victory against authoritarianism had been won. No consensus had been found about the objectives of political action, and no rules agreed for the tenure and transfer of power, when industrial civiliza-tion raised the stakes of the political game by provoking demands for governmental protection of the producer against domestic or foreign competition, the capitalist against the claims of labour, the worker against the pressure of his employer.

The French industrial revolution was itself localized, incomplete and stunted. Over most of the country the old order of self-sufficient peasants and artisans survived, and they used their disproportionate political influence to protect their own interests and those of their rich allies at the expense of the industrial workers. An overcrowded tertiary sector, above all in commerce, offered the traditional outlet for the many who sought a precarious and unreal economic independence. A majority of voters wanted the diffusion of wealth and power, and resisted speed and standardization, mass production and large-scale organization, plenty and instability — in a word, Americanization. Through her thwarted economic development, France acquired the social problems of industrialism without its material benefits. Two distinct types of politics coexisted there: a revolutionary class struggle, dominant in most industrial areas, and a traditional ideological conflict which prevailed mainly in backward regions. Politicians had to shape their attitudes to the needs and demands of both, and the diversity of issues and alignments created many parties and factions: the reflection, not the cause, of the absence of an electoral majority.

The old political fabric was torn asunder by the sweeping social changes of the post-war years and the governmental policies which encouraged them. For the first time for over a century the birth-rate rose. The traditional domination of the family by the older generations was upset. New age-groups pressed impatiently on the heels of their elders, acceding to responsibility — in business, politics, agriculture, the civil service — far younger than in the past. They called for expansion to accommodate the growing numbers of Frenchmen, invented new voluntary associations for common purposes, and insisted on a wider conception of governmental activity than the mere preservation of *situations acquises*. A new attitude to risk-taking and modernization soon spread from industry to agriculture. The industrial structure was transformed by the growth of large plants and of specialized skills, which broke up the old uniformity of the working class and created in the newer industries a common interest in stability between management and worker. Under the impact of material prosperity, labour shortage, and the reforms of 1936–37 and 1945–46, labour relations and even class divisions gradually began to lose some of their old bitterness. The rapid growth of towns upset the country's social and geographical balance, until one Frenchman in four lived in an urban area of over 100,000 inhabitants. The old self-sufficiency of the village disappeared; prosperity and paid holidays brought townsmen to the countryside, while agricultural mechanization and the decline of the artisan reduced employment in rural areas.

New social conditions broke the old lines of political communication. The small-town newspaper declined as a political force, but neither the regional nor the Paris press took its place—except for *Le Monde*, which soon acquired the status of a republican institution. Even broadcasting had far less political importance than in Britain or the United States, and television arrived too late to play a significant role in Fourth Republican politics—though within its narrow geographical range it contributed to a growing uniformity of tastes and interests.

As urbanization spread and regional differences waned, the ancient quarrel between Church and *Université* lost its former virulence. The *curé* was withdrawn from some parishes, and where he remained he might well champion progress, not conservatism. The new and radical grassroots organizations were often founded and manned by young Catholic laymen, products of the flourishing Church youth movements. On social and especially colonial questions many Catholics were active reformers—and some anticlericals from the traditional Left took up conservative or reactionary stands. When the Algerian war revived the passions of the Dreyfus case, the alignment was new and unexpected: in 1900 Church and army had stood together against the indignant protests of the teachers and intellectuals, but now the angry officers found many of their former allies in the opposite camp, along with the *Université*. As the clergy withdrew from militant opposition to the regime, and as political power shifted from the countryside to the towns, fewer village schoolteachers regarded themselves as the embattled missionaries of the Republic. Every year diminished the large fund of accumulated mistrust which still remained for political exploitation, and with its decline the two great corporations lost their central place in political organization and conflict.

Other factors helped to promote the nationalization and modernization of political life. With the abolition of small single-member districts and the growth of official and semi-official regional institutions, the prefect became less of a focus for political activity and the deputy lost some of the social standing he had formerly enjoyed in his constituency (if not in Paris). Wider horizons and stronger parties weakened the authority of the individual politician, though less than was expected in the first post-war years. The traditional notables, the professional and business class of the small town, lost their dominating influence over their fellows as education became more general, modern communications made the country more uniform, and the tiny autonomous unit, after falling behind its big competitors in industry and then in agriculture, began to lose ground even in its last strongholds: commerce and politics. The state, traditionally feared and restricted, exercised so powerful and pervasive an influence throughout the economy that the old contrast between the *pays légal* and the *pays réel* came to seem meaningless even to extreme conservatives. The new

3

professional organizations—of labour, business, the peasantry and various middle-class groups—rapidly acquired an altogether new solidity and influence during or just after the war. While after 1948 the trade unions lost most of the ground they had gained, the other confederations survived to play a growing role in politics. But since they usually acted by pressure from without, rather than directly in the electoral or parliamentary struggle, these new corporations did not replace the old decaying political mechanisms.

Indeed, in the short run better organization merely allowed the conflicting groups to express more vigorously their unanimous conviction that others were being favoured at their expense. The hungry occupation years had been a godsend to the peasantry, and the black market and inflation were the shopkeeper's golden age; both resented the return to normality which cost them their privileged positions. The social reforms of the Popular Front and the governments issuing from the Resistance did not wholly reconcile the industrial workers to the regime, but they did alarm employers whose power was challenged. Yet the state on which all these pressures converged was poorly armed to resist them, for the politicians who were eager to expand its functions economically were afraid of strengthening the executive politically. Historic fears of reaction and revolution imposed "the paradox of a weak government with a strong state"; and the administration's Maginot Line against the invading pressure-groups could often be turned by an attack on its unfortified parliamentary flank.

Some groups fought for their interests in the old ways; and any effort to impose taxes on peasants or collect them from small businessmen, cut the alcohol subsidy or make railwaymen work beyond the age of 55, would cause a political storm and provoke the party whose clients were threatened to overturn the government. Some sections of the new middle class, concerned for modernization and efficiency and dis-satisfied with the traditional parties, contributed to a floating vote far larger than before the war and gave emphasis to the fluctuations of public opinion. Other victims, finding the old lines of communication inadequate, resorted to disorderly and extravagant forms of protest. Some felt wholly cut off from their political representatives. Suspicious of a government whose processes they could not understand and whose policies they abhorred, and convinced that occult forces had captured the state for their own nefarious ends, they inspired outbursts as furious and irrational, though not as dangerous, as those of the Third and Fifth Republics.

At home the growth of the economy aroused resentment among those who lost by it or who benefited little; identifying the misfortunes of their class with those of their country, they clamoured for diehard resistance to change both abroad and at home. Poujadism, the rebellion of static France against the economic ascendancy and progress of the advanced regions, was also a protest against any concession in the empire. But the new psychology which underlay the expansion in "modern France" was partly a product of revolt against the collapse of 1940, and for many modernizers the very purpose of this economic progress was to rebuild the power of the French state even more than the prosperity of individual Frenchmen. The crucial decisions on atomic development were taken by Fourth Republican premiers, including Mendès-France—whose eloquent appeals for national resurgence made him for a time a hero of the Gaullists. Men from the Resistance and Fighting France, who against all prudent calculation had entered upon a struggle against overwhelming odds in 1940, were often unimpressed by appeals to historical inevitability or demonstrations that France had not the strength to hold her place in the new world. Thus economic progress gave rise to exasperation as well as satisfaction when the country, feeling a new internal strength and vigour, found itself faced with a steady decline in its external power.

It was therefore not surprising that the familiar problem of reconciling France's ends and her means was not always discussed in purely rational terms. In 1945 only the Socialists stood out against the policy of crushing Germany on which nationalists and Christian democrats, Gaullists and Communists agreed; and many Frenchmen seemed to find Soviet Russia a more congenial diplomatic partner than democratic America. But within five years France was committed, despite violent opposition, to the Atlantic alliance; and many Resisters, whose proven patriotism under Nazi occupation gave them a clear conscience, had taken up the old themes of intelligent defeatists like Caillaux and Laval and were preaching Franco-German reconciliation. In 1954 a revolt of neutralists and nationalists defeated the European army plan after a furious battle which divided Resisters as well as Vichyites, and Left as well as Right. But the new perspective of European unity had caught the imagination of many able and idealistic young Frenchmen, and after the EDC struggle which seemed to purge the old hatred of Germany, the adjustment to a new constellation of forces in Europe was accepted without friction—even by its former opponents when they came to power in 1958.

Elsewhere the change was harder to tolerate. Progressive internationalists in France had always fought for equal rights for the colonial peoples, not for independence. Nationalist conservatives who had painfully accepted reality in one sphere found it all the harder to abandon their remaining illusions. So the business defeatists like Raymond Cartier, who attacked the Algerian commitment as too expensive, found no hearing in the Fourth Republic. Instead, on Left and Right alike, old conservatives and new nationalists combined to silence the liberals and the realists until it was almost too late in Tunisia and Morocco, much too late in Indo-China and Algeria. Their task was the easier because the colonial bureaucracy was as conservative as the

economic bureaucracy was progressive; and above all because France, alone among colonial powers, had a mass Communist party. Neither politicians nor voters were prepared to pay the price for its support; and while without it the decolonizers were outnumbered, with it they were discredited. Social reformers at home faced the same dilemma, and the housing and educational opportunities of the poor remained shamefully inadequate. But there desirable measures could be deferred without immediate disaster. Overseas, time was fast running out.

Despite the obstacles, parties and people slowly accepted the need for change, and by 1958 the diehards commanded only a quarter of the National Assembly and a minority of the public. At this point the struggle moved to a new plane, for the humiliations and retreats of twenty years had had their deepest effect on the men who had borne the brunt of them, the army officers. More democratically recruited and less traditionalist in outlook than ever in the past, they had been taught in 1940 that there were higher duties than obedience to the legal government. One defeat in Indo-China reinforced their determination not to tolerate a second in Algeria. For two years fear of military insubordination helped to paralyse ministers, who abdicated to the army while publicly proclaiming confidence in its fidelity. So the Fourth Republic was destroyed at last, like most previous French regimes, by a foreign failure; its own servants repudiated it, and an indifferent people no longer felt sufficient loyalty to come to its defence. Unhappily, the circumstances of the collapse made the twin problems of legitimacy and authority more acute than ever. For if the Fourth Republic had shown the perils of weak political authority in its lifetime, its death reminded Frenchmen that revolutionary violence still seethed not far below the political surface, and that dangerous hands were waiting to grasp the levers of a strong governmental machine.

Bâtonnier Toulouse

THE DILEMMA OF OBEDIENCE AND LEGITIMACY

A political system's legitimacy becomes a matter for public discussion only when the nature or existence of the state is challenged. In Britain, Switzerland, or the United States since the Civil War, legitimacy has ceased to be a matter of practical debate. The experience of France is different. Every political regime since the Revolution has had its legitimacy challenged by some section of the community. At times of revolutionary change such as 1940 and 1958 particularly, rival "legitimacies" clash and appeal to men's loyalties. Something of the confusion that can be caused by these struggles emerges in this extract from the address by defense counsel on behalf of Generals Challe and Zeller, during their trial for their share in the "generals' revolt" of April 1961—an attempted takeover led by four generals based in Algiers, which challenged directly de Gaulle's Algerian policy and, at least by implication, the very existence of the Fifth Republic.

But, they tell me, you are mistaken. Gentlemen, in such a matter as this anyone who claims to represent truth is indeed presumptuous. In the course of time History will tell us, though none of us will know her judgment—which doubtless will be revised again in the further course of time.

But suppose, *Monsieur le Procureur-Général*, that our clients were mistaken. In that case, I turn to my judges and say: is it a crime to be mistaken when one's aim is to serve France and defend her flag?

I can hear the reply already: all the Army has to do is obey. There is the word at last: obedience! Of course one does not mean by this, *Monsieur le Procureur-Général*, the sort of discipline I learned when I was myself a soldier, in which lay the chief strength of the armed forces, and by which I was put under the orders of my corporal who was in turn under his sergeant. The obedience of great military leaders . . . (and I have the honor, gentlemen, to plead before great military leaders), this question is one they must often face and settle with their conscience. The obedience of great military leaders . . . . The tragic events which have assailed France since 1940 and which have led to a great many governments who spoke or claimed to speak in her name, have put the spirit of our great military leaders to a harsh test, for disobedience by these leaders was considered in turn treasonous or glorious.

Monsieur le Procureur-Général, just now you alluded to the precedents of the Occupation and the Liberation. Gentlemen, I have had the redoubtable honor of defending many great leaders before every High Court set up in France during the last twenty years, their names and composition varying with the period. The crime was always the same—treason—only the defi-

Editor's translation.

nition varied. I pleaded, gentlemen, before the Riom Court during the Occupation. We were defending leaders who trusted de Gaulle—and because they trusted de Gaulle they had disobeyed and they were prosecuted for having disobeyed. These great leaders were told: Marshal Pétain represents France; you must obey Marshal Pétain and those who obey orders from outside (from de Gaulle) have disobeyed and must be punished.

And so, gentlemen, those who, through fidelity to de Gaulle had disobeyed Pétain were condemned.

And then, at the Liberation, I defended more great leaders before the High Court: this time for obeying the Marshal. As I was trying, gentlemen, though without success, to uphold just those rules of obedience which, it seems, are inflexible, and was saying that they had obeyed the Marshal, this is what we heard from the lips of one of the judges, in words borrowed from the Declaration of the Rights of Man: Insurrection is a duty.

On 13 May 1958, gentlemen, the great military leaders disobeyed. On 13 May 1958 they had received a categorical order from the government. The minister told them: "If any failure of discipline comes to your attention you are to punish it immediately and report to me immediately."

I also have before me the solemn appeal to general officers issued by the President of the Republic, Commander in Chief of the armed forces. Listen to it, gentlemen:

As guardian of the unity of the nation, I appeal to your patriotism and good sense not to add to our country's trials that of division of the French people in the face of the enemy. Any failure in discipline," the Chief of State said, "can only benefit those against whom we are fighting. As Commander-in-Chief, by virtue of article 33 of the Constitution, I order you to do your duty under the authority of the government of the French Republic.

And what happened? They disobeyed. All these generals disobeyed. They disobeyed because obedience commanded them to be at the orders of what they thought were the Nation and the Country. And these same generals now appear before you because (in April 1960) disobedience was held against them as being insurrectionary.

They failed, you will tell me, *Monsieur le Procureur-Général,* I know; when a movement fails it is called a riot; when it succeeds it is a revolution. But, turning to you gentlemen, I ask you, does justice judge men's actions by their results? Does that mean, *Monsieur le Procureur-Général,* that the basis of our laws and morality has now become success? If there was confusion in the minds of the chiefs, recognize as I do that the responsibility is not theirs alone.

Laurence Wylie

THE ORGANIZATION OF FRENCH SOCIETY

As Philip Williams has argued, the roots of political instability in France lie less in the quality of her leaders or the nature of successive constitutions than in her history and social structure. Continuing with this theme, Laurence Wylie discusses some of the characteristics of French social organization which have had repercussions on the working of the political system.

Reprinted by permission of the publishers from Stanley Hoffman et al., *In Search of France,* pp. 216–224. Cambridge, Mass.: Harvard University Press, Copyright, 1963, by the President and Fellows of Harvard College.

The first feature is the weight of the past. By its very existence, the social organization is a conservative element blocking social change. We have already considered a number of changes which have taken place in France in the last fifteen years, and in every case the structure of that portion of the social organization in which the change has been observed has itself limited the rate and the extent of the change. Today the farmer in France has the opportunity to modernize his operation, but the way in which a French farm is traditionally cut into many dismembered bits notably limits the usefulness of modernization.

Once rules and habits and relationships are established, inertia if nothing else would tend to preserve them. But besides this force there are others. The fear many people have who identify the values for which they live with the social organization through which those values are expressed tends to maintain the *status quo*. It also takes time for social change to assume a form that is in harmony with the existing value system. A state-planned economy may be generally resisted if it is thought of as the result of *dirigisme,* or of the manipulations of the privileged group called the "two hundred families," but it becomes acceptable if it is thought of as *planification* carried out by trained functionaries trying to improve the whole social system. The planners of the new French economy seem less alarmingly revolutionary if they are called "neo-Colbertists" or Saint-Simonists.

An example of the conservative effect of an existing organization is the obsolete political structure of the *départements* in France. Their present boundaries were established in the eighteenth century so that a citizen could travel from his home on the periphery of the *département* to the capital and back in one day. Now the round trip can be made in two hours at the most. The same general problem exists for every commune. The village of Chanzeaux was at one time a social, economic and political entity. With the transformation of communication facilities and the consequent integration of Chanzeaux into a wider regional unit, the original function of the village as an economic and cultural necessity has disappeared. Administratively, however, Chanzeaux remains a relatively autonomous entity; and its functions could certainly be carried out more efficiently if the village were officially integrated into the larger area.

The ways in which the past impinges on the present in France may be either real or imaginary. In the case of the administrative organization of the departments and communes the effect is concrete. So is it concrete in the school system in Chanzeaux, where two hundred children crowd the two Catholic schools and are taught by teachers who can barely live on the funds raised by the community. In the same village a public school with a well-trained teacher stands almost empty; only the seventeen children of social deviants of the community attend it. The age-old argument between Church and State continues to exert its influence.

The second feature of French social organization that hampers change is the sharp way in which all of its elements are defined. Every function, attribute, responsibility, right, or relationship of the individual has been spelled out in either legal or official terms, or in tacit but clearly understood codes. The individual knows exactly how society expects him to behave in any situation. To a degree, of course, this is true in any culture, but it is particularly characteristic of France. The manner in which a criminal is punished, the way children ought to spend their time in recess, the specific responsibility one has for the material welfare of his parents, the procedure *boules* players should follow in the rare event a *boule* should split during a game, and the correct complimentary close to use in a letter to one's prospective mother-in-law—all these contingencies are foreseen by an item in some code or other.

These clearly stated definitions may well follow from the stress which in French education is put on the necessity for detailed and rational planning. They are perhaps also an outgrowth—or corollary—of the emphasis the French place upon limiting human behavior to protect an individual from hostile action by other people. In that case rules governing behavior would be intended as limits to unexpected actions, but in restricting human initiative they also inhibit social change.

The notion of the family as a clearly-defined cell remains powerful in France. A friend from Roussillon often comments that going into another person's house is like "crossing an invisible frontier." Another French friend once told me that in spite of the fact that he had played all during his childhood with the children living next door, as far as he could remember his playmates were never once in his house, and it was only for a single emergency during the war that he had ever been inside their house. "We preferred neutral ground, the street in front of the houses."

The clear definition of the family cell is formally strengthened by law. The Civil Code defines exactly what constitutes the family, what its relationship to society is, and the rights and duties of its members to each other. Little by little the definition has been altered but the extent of the alterations has been bound by the very clarity and formality of the original definitions in the Civil Code. The *Code de la Famille*, the social security system, the *statuts du fermage* have all been justified mainly on the ground that they help preserve the traditional family cell. Legal changes come slowly and, as often as not, only give official sanction to a transformation that has already taken place.

A third feature of the social organization in France that hinders change is the rigidity of the political structure. This may come as a surprise to those who see France as a land of political chaos, with new constitutions and a succession of governments. These phenomena are not to be denied, but their spectacular character and the common ignorance of the way the government of France really works often blind us to one of the most conservative institutions in the French social system: the vast, well-organized, and hierarchically controlled corps of government employees who are in charge of public services. The cabinet officers and elected officials come and go, but the corps of *fonctionnaires* remains. The members of the *Conseil d'Etat*, of the *Inspection des Finances*, of the prefectorial system, of the national police, and so on, are the men who actually govern France.

At every level in the political hierarchy there are appointed counterparts for the elected officials. The elected officer is considered temporary; the *fonctionnaire* has tenure. The elected officer has official responsibility as well as the right, in principle, to make policy; he is well-known to the public and takes the praise or blame for turns of events. But his counterpart, the *fonctionnaire*, has actual responsibility. He is not well-known to the public but his power is real. Since in principle and by definition the *fonctionnaire* is not responsible for policy, he is neither praised nor blamed, but it is thanks to him that government goes on even when governments continually fall. . . .

In most activities there is a line of authority and interest that runs from the local community through the *département* and the regional center to Paris. This form of organization can be a force for change if, as in the case of *planification*, the hierarchical authorities transmit orders calling for change. In the nineteenth century the provinces saw the strength of the hierarchy and complained that all the revolutions took place in Paris and were then imposed on the rest of France. Today, however, the usual effect of the domination of France by its many hierarchies is strongly conservative. The long lines of command are filled by *fonctionnaires* who have an established interest in keeping things as they are. Initiative comes from the top and deadens initiative at the lower levels. People cannot act without orders from above; so unless they can exert influence at the top they must resign themselves to complaining about a situation without hope of changing it.

It should be pointed out that the hierarchical structure of French society is also an example of my earlier point that because the elements of the French social organization are so clearly defined, social change is limited. French officials are notorious for their awareness of the precise limits of their responsibility and for their consequent reluctance to take even the slightest chance of doing something which does not lie within the precise limits of their duty. Every visitor to France has come away with at least one story of the *fonctionnaire* behind his grill whose only reaction to a repeated plea was: "The law is the law . . . This is not my responsibility . . . You'll have to go to some other office . . . How should I know which one? . . . I can do nothing about your case . . . Go talk to my superior if you like."

Every person in the hierarchy must avoid understanding too much about the individual problems of the public, for, according to the old French proverb, *"tout comprendre, c'est tout pardonner"* ("to understand is to excuse"). The public official must remain aloof, on a level at which *"ne pas comprendre, c'est tout condamner"* ("not to understand permits one to condemn everything"). Only thus can the hierarchy be preserved. An official of a prefecture once said to me: *"Si le public dit du mal de moi, je l'emmerde sereinement. Cela ne fait que prouver la valeur de ma section et de mes méthodes. Plus le public est emmerdé, mieux l'Etat est servi."* The incivility and sometimes tyranny displayed by its "public servants," the French seem to accept as natural and inevitable manifestations of an effective civil service.

The French have not completely given in to the power of the hierarchy and its civil servants, however. Officially and ostensibly there is acceptance, which indeed limits the possibilities for progress in the development of the social organization. Unofficially and not quite openly a whole system of escape hatches has been worked out. Just as the individual escapes the limits placed on his personal behavior by openly accepting various codes but privately living in the world of his imagination, so society has found an escape from the limitations placed on it by a too-rigid hierarchy.

The *Système D* consists of any devious and usually ill-defined means by which an individual can take initiative in spite of the restrictions imposed on him by society. Earlier, in discussing the French attitude toward the reality of man-made rules, we saw how the *Système D* favored social change by allowing the individual to by-pass the strangling mass of official red tape. In avoiding these entanglements of hierarchical red tape, however—for essentially this is the aim and accomplishment of the *Système D*—time and energy are wasted and the social organization itself is kept from evolving. Ironically, the rigidity of the political structure is increased because its rules are ignored at the same time they are accepted.

The French acceptance of hierarchy—even though the acceptance may be punctuated with cries of outrage or an escape into the devious paths of *Système D*—points to a further characteristic of the French social organization which acts as a brake on social change. Each clearly defined unit within a hierarchy is aware of its rights and responsibilities in relation to other units in the system, and it is generally understood that one of the important functions of any superior authority is to protect the rights of his subordinates. Assured of this protection from above, every group barricades itself behind its "acquired rights" (*droits acquis*) and resists all movements for change; at the suggestion of a threat an organization is formed which invariably takes the name "Association for the defense of the rights of the . . ." In the blank space one may substitute the name of any group which feels its rights are under attack—"peasants," "middle classes," "savings bank investors," "taxpayers," "independent distillers," and on and on. . . .[1]

A corollary to the existence of *droits acquis* in French society is the necessity which is felt to give equal treatment to parallel elements within the social organization. Within a hierarchy a responsibility of every member is to respect and preserve equality among subordinates belonging to the same rank. This is a concept which permeates most of French life. The principle of equality was a motivating force of the Revolution,

one ideal of which was to suppress legal privileges of favored sections of the population such as first born children who were favored by primogeniture. Many of the elaborate plans for the modernization and economic encouragement of the less favored regions of France have been justified by the principle of giving equal opportunities and thus establishing a more harmonious equilibrium of the country. The second and third terms of the national motto, *liberté, égalité, fraternité*, consecrate the principle of equal rights for similar elements within the social organization.

[1]These examples are taken from the appendix of Jean Meynaud, *Groupes de pression en France* (Paris: Colin, 1958), p. 359 ff.

Laurence Wylie

TRADITIONAL ATTITUDES TO AUTHORITY: A CASE STUDY

It is easy to lose sight of the everyday realities which underlie the generalities and abstractions inherent in discussions of entire social or political systems. Laurence Wylie provides here this much-needed additional dimension by describing how the village of Roussillon in southwest France viewed the outside world. His sketch of attitudes towards the state, authority and politics is based on direct observation when he and his family lived there in the early fifties.

When Madame Arène says, "They (*ils*) have raised the price of coffee on us again," she is not referring to the *ils* of the village, but to a more dangerous set of *ils*. She means the *ils* within Roussillon are a nuisance, but since they are specific individuals whom one knows and sees every day, one can guard against them. The *ils* outside Roussillon are dangerous because they are anonymous, intangible, and over-powering. Against the outside *ils* an individual has little defense, and yet from them come the greatest evils that beset the people of Roussillon: inflation, taxation, war, legal restrictions, administrative red tape. It

is the outside *ils* who are blamed for raising the price of fertilizer, for forcing young men to spend eighteen months in the army, for preventing a farmer from planting as many wine grapes as he wishes, for taking a substantial portion of the family income in the form of taxes, for complicating existence with waiting-room queues and forms to be filled out.

The identity of the outside *ils* varies. The term may refer to Big Corporations or to Newspapers or to the *Syndicat d'Initiative d'Avignon*. It may refer to the French People or to the Americans or to the Russians or to People in general. Usually, however, it refers to the French Government in all its manifestations, for it is the Government which collects taxes, makes war, controls the wine production, and employs impersonal civil servants.

This attitude is in direct conflict with what the children are taught in school. In their civics books they read that the Government is simply the concrete manifestation of the State, which is the political personality of *La patrie*. They learn by heart such sentences as:

1. The French nation has a body formed by the soil and the men who live on it; a soul formed by the history, language, tradition, and symbols.

2. When men feel love for their nation it becomes a *patrie*.

3. The State is the nation organized and administered.

4. The Government is the directing organism of the State.

5. A good citizen always seeks to become educated. He respects the law, pays his taxes loyally, accepts the military obligation, and defends his *patrie* when it is threatened.

6. A good citizen possesses the spirit of cooperation and mutual aid.

7. Politics too often arouses distrust, disdain, and even disgust.

8. Politics should not be an excuse for furthering private interests and above all it should not unleash our passions.

9. Politics should be a great public service, the art of bringing about more justice and happiness among men."[1]

The children have no difficulty in accepting the concept of *la patrie*, for at home and throughout the village they hear *la patrie* spoken of only with love and respect. One of the most hallowed spots in the village is the *Monument to Those of Roussillon who Died in Defense of the Patrie*. Several

times a year they see the men of the village temporarily forget their personal differences and march together to lay a wreath at the foot of the monument. The children know that France is a country favored above all others—"Sweet France" of the marvelous hexagonal shape. They know that the French language is the language of Civilization and that Civilized People everywhere consider France as their second *patrie*. Culturally, emotionally, geographically, aesthetically, the people of Roussillon feel they are an integral part of *la patrie*. They recognize also that officially, legally, statistically, they are a part of the State, which they respect but do not love.

Unfortunately, *la patrie* and the State must be translated into human terms, and it is at this point that the people of Roussillon refuse to accept the "beautiful sentences" of the civics textbook. Theoretically, Government may be an alter ego of *la patrie*, but in point of fact it is made up of men—weak, stupid, selfish, ambitious men. It is the duty of the citizen *not* to cooperate with these men, as the civics books would have people do, but rather to hinder them, to prevent them in every possible way from increasing their power over individuals and families.

This is a point on which everyone in Roussillon would agree: a man with power over you is essentially evil. They readily admit that a man may be virtuous when he goes into politics, but they would deny that he can remain virtuous if he attains power. Except for a few supporters of the MRP, the voters of Rousillon say that the heads of their parties and of all other political parties, are "a pile of bandits." Even people who are not in politics but in government administration are tainted by the corrupting force of power. They become insensitive to the feelings of others.

In preaching civic virtue to the school children, the authors of the civics book

---

1. These sentences are taken from the sections entitled "Retenons par coeur" of chapters 26, 36 and 37 of Ballot and Aveille, *Education morale et civique. Classe de fin d'études* (Paris: Charles-Lavauzelle, 1952).

recognize that their precepts describe an ideal rather than an actual state of things. They warn:

Many honest and intelligent people, who could be the best guides in public life, avoid politics, and condemn it harshly.

1. Indeed, politics arouses much *distrust*. People avoid talking about it in family gatherings, in friendly professional or social groups. It is excluded from the army, which must remain impartial (*la grande muette*), and from the judiciary branch of the government. It must be kept out of school. This phrase is almost always found in the constitutions of clubs and societies: "All political and religious discussions are formally forbidden." Thus, distrust seems general.
2. The *disdain* in which politics is held is no less great. "Politics is a specialty which I am willing to leave to the specialists," says the writer Georges Duhamel. Thus he expresses the *disdain* which many intellectuals feel for what one of them calls "the housework of the nation."
3. Hence the distaste for politics and for politicians who are often portrayed as men of little morality, of slight merit, incapable of making their way honestly and serving usefully.

The authors of the civics text then go on to preach a different and democratic ideal to the students, but in these paragraphs they have described the reality that the children have witnessed. They constantly hear adults referring to Government as a source of evil and to the men who run it as instruments of evil. There is nothing personal in this belief. It does not concern one particular Government composed of one particular group of men. It concerns Government everywhere and at all times—French Governments, American Governments, Russian Governments, all Governments. Some are less bad than others, but all are essentially bad.

Of course, much of the talk against Government and politicians must not be taken too seriously. People do not mean all they say. They recognize the necessity of a certain amount of civic spirit. However, when they are confronted by the frustrations caused by these outside *ils*, they fulminate against them. The outside *ils* are like the weather: they are necessities which one must accept, because "that's the way it is." It makes a person feel better to curse the weather and to curse the outside *ils*. We should be naïve to take much of the cursing seriously, but still we should be equally naïve to ignore the cursing. The hostility towards government is real and it is deep.

Michel Debré

THE CAUSES OF FRANCE'S POLITICAL ILLS

Contributors so far have explained the difficulty of achieving political stability in France primarily in terms of the underlying social and economic structure. Michel Debré would not deny that the many divisions of France make her inevitably a difficult country to govern. Nevertheless, for him the heart of the problem lies precisely in the political system. He sees the political malady as the consequence of the tradition of identifying democracy with the ascendancy of parliament rather than accepting the need for a strong executive. Essentially, the problem is first one of the conception of authority, then of political machinery. Whether one accepts this analysis or not, it derives additional importance from

From Michel Debré, *Au Service de la Nation* (Paris: 1963), pp. 191–194. Printed by permission of Editions Stock. Editor's translation.

the fact that views such as this inspired Debré when he was supervising the drafting of the current constitution — precisely as a cure for political ailments.

Since the very beginning of the Republic the seat of power, and therefore of political authority, has been Parliament. The constitutional tree planted by the Versailles Assembly in 1875 rapidly bore precisely the fruit that was to be expected. Terms like "separation of functions" and "balance of powers," to which worthy professors have devoted so much of their teaching over the last half century, bore no relation to reality. The constitution-makers were set on having a sovereign parliament. Their successors have been too.

Originally the powers granted to the Senate and the President of the Republic created an illusion. But this illusion was rapidly swept away. Those constitution-makers who wanted a sovereign parliament won, and their successors have extended their victory. As was logical, the assembly elected by universal suffrage became the expression of parliamentary power, while the second assembly (the Senate of 1875 or the Council of the Republic of 1946) acted as a moral guardian or brake — at first a significant rôle but later severely weakened. The President of the Republic was not and could not be a chief of state. The way in which he was elected and his powers — or rather his lack of them — all prevented this. As for the government, the logic of the system reduced it to being a mere committee of delegates of the parties composing the "majority" — a majority made up of disparate elements who had of course not the least intention, rare moments of crisis apart, of subordinating themselves to a leader or of setting any curb to personal ambitions. Neither in 1875 nor in 1946 was any constitutional limit set to parliament's powers.

Another factor contributed to the character of this structure: access to a political career lay through parliament and only through parliament. The desire to serve has, as its goal, a place in the government.

But for this a twofold success was needed: first success with the electorate in order to enter parliament, and then success within parliament itself, the sole source of authority . . . This was inherent in the situation. There is no democracy without parties, without groups of men brought together by a shared ideology or platform, seeking to ensure that they prevail and accordingly delegating some of their number to positions of responsibility. In any free political system the parties are the normal intermediaries between the government and public opinion.

The republican system therefore had a sovereign: the Chamber of Deputies of 1875, the National Assembly of 1946. The change of name is an expression of the persistence of an ambition: to represent the nation to the extent of arrogating to oneself its sovereignty. The beneficiaries of this takeover are the parties. This rapidly became *the* problem of our political life: the confiscation of sovereignty by intermediaries who were exceeding their proper function. *Scrutin d'arrondissement*, with its two ballots, and even the proportional representation system, skillfully confirmed the stranglehold of the parties — who were allies and enemies in turn — on the machinery of the state. This omnipotence of the parliamentarians, dominating the legislature, the executive, the administration, and even on occasion the judiciary, was subject to only two real checks: the continual need for compromise between partners whose political evolution was soon such that no one would cherish the hope of forming a governmental majority; and the intervention of pressure groups and organizations of all kinds whose strength was inevitably greater because the government was so feeble. There is no need to go on. The picture is only too familiar and has been commented on in detail many times already.

During the last few years confusion and

incompetence became even worse. Difficulties abroad, among which colonial problems must be included, the activities of a Communist party which proportional representation had granted a key rôle in the parliamentary game, the new violence of the "pressure groups" with their skill at bringing their weight to bear on political decisions, and seeking either to identify themselves with a party or to set different parties competing for their support. All these factors condemned the sovereign to impotence and the country with it.

The sickness was deep-seated. Mere tinkering could not provide a cure. For the cause was not to be found in some mild excess or taking a wrong turn but in the basic principle of the system: the sovereign parliament. Our political system, handed down from the nineteenth century, bore all the marks of an age when governments were not obliged to take a multitude of wide-ranging decisions. In those days the principles on which society was founded did not seem seriously threatened either internally or externally. The maintenance of law and order and defense apart, the State intervened only in a limited range of matters to make the necessary legal provisions. Of course weakness in the State was dangerous — it always is — but the rôle of the State was limited. A parliament theoretically qualified to do absolutely anything but in practice incapable of either foresight or command was appropriate to such a conception of the State. The development of the world after the First World War should have opened people's eyes. It did not. The Second World War should have made even the blind see. It did not.

But today a completely different approach is required: the twentieth century cannot be satisfied with the institutions of the nineteenth. Whether one thinks of the choices that must be made in foreign affairs or those needed in the domestic field, the State must clearly take many and frequent decisions. The State not only cannot be weak, it can no longer play a limited rôle. It must be as effective in everything it undertakes as it was when its tasks were limited to public order and defense. Today's world lets no nation stand still; it is merciless to those which are unable to decide on or maintain the efforts essential for adaptation and development. Finally, the freedoms that are proclaimed so as to ensure the finest flowering of the human spirit and guard it against the arbitrary practices of princes have, with that ease with which virtue gives birth to vice, become a means by which occupational, economic and social interest groups attack the sovereign in the hope of subjecting it to their grasping, clamorous desires. Respect for freedom is indeed a mark of democracy — but the national interest must be respected too.

The lesson of this new situation is clear: the nineteenth-century institutions which had already shown themselves to be outdated after the First World War now looked positively dangerous because they did not provide the nation with a means of taking decisions which were both rapid and legitimate. In the Anglo-Saxon democracies election of the chief of state by universal suffrage, or electoral systems favoring only two parties made possible an evolution producing an authority capable of taking decisions without any drastic modifications in their system. But in France our political divisions, the opportunist manoeuvering of the parties — including the scheming of the Communists — emphasized the inadequacies of institutions inherited from the previous century.

The gulf between the nation and its sovereign, which was already evident in the thirties, became more unmistakeable and deeper than ever after the restoration of the old system in 1946. How was it that the men who were then our leaders failed to recognize that collapse was inevitable? While the nation, which was steadily more aware of the quality of its government lost confidence in a sovereign whose morals, methods, alliances and even language were increasingly foreign to it, the princes who governed us, prisoners of their own mythology — that is, wedded to the interests of their parties—refused all real reform. They even refused to grasp the need for it. They stood by, helpless accomplices, at the death of the republican state.

This deep-seated sickness had to be treated at its source. Another sovereign had to be brought into being, and powers balanced in such a way as not to constitute a negation of power. The 1958 revision was decisive, as was the 1962 addition to it.

Maurice Bourjol

STABILITY AND INSTABILITY—A COMMUNIST VIEW

Discussion of the nature of France's political ailments tends all too frequently to remain cosily confined within the conventions of liberal-democratic assumptions. And yet France is a country where one voter in five votes communist. Despite the pedestrian and hidebound approach of the French Communist Party to constitutional matters since the war, its arguments constitute a fundamentally different challenge which cannot reasonably be ignored. This analysis of the question of stability from the party's theoretical monthly journal both challenges previous contributors' arguments and indicates the party's general angle of attack.

It is time to put an end to the use of "governmental stability" as an argument to justify the most anti-democratic concoctions. The myth of governmental stability, so ardently preached by everyone from the UNR to the Socialists does not stand up to serious examination. On this criterion Guy Mollet should be holding up the Franco and Salazar regimes as an example because of their exceptional stability. Governmental stability can be a blessing or a curse depending on whether the government in question governs in the interests of the people or is reactionary.

In reality, the apparent "instability" of the Fourth Republic cannot mask the *continuity* of the reactionary policy pursued after 1947 when the communist ministers were evicted from the government. Quite apart from the fact that the same people simply shifted from one office to another—to give just one example; from November 1954 (Mendès-France government) to May 13 1958 (Gaillard government) the policy was to make war in Algeria. Similarly the apparent stability of the Fifth Republic cannot hide the ministerial merry-go-round (five ministers of Education, four of Information, three of Finance, Agriculture, and Justice, the Interior, and Posts & Telecommunications) occurring under the Debré government, any more than it can hide the difference between the triumphant Debré and *"Algérie française"* of 1959 and the choleric Debré of the "governmental declaration" on Evian in 1962.[1] All the technical remedies, whether it be "one-government-per-legislature" or "contracts between the parties of the majority" cannot mask this reality: the only successful "recipe" by which governments will achieve stability is for them to rest on the people, represented by an elected Assembly and not—as with the system of *gouvernement de législature* —for the birth of a conflict between the

[1]This declaration, following the Evian negotiations with Algerian nationalist leaders, announced the settlement leading to Algerian independence. [Editor's Note.]

From "Gaullisme et Démocratie," *Cahiers du Communisme*, September 1962. Printed by permission of the publisher. Editor's translation.

government and the Assembly to lead to the dismissal of the latter. When a government refuses to apply the policy laid down by the Assembly it is the government which should withdraw.

And that is just where the shoe pinches. Leo Figuères has recalled the two essential causes of governmental instability are "the fact that there is too often a divorce between governors and elected representatives and the aspirations of the people," and "the determination to ignore political reality, the place which the Communist party holds in the life of the nation."

Can anyone be unaware that if the proposals of the French Communist party had been carried out in 1940 for the struggle against the Nazi invader, in 1947 for Indochina, in 1954 for Algeria, France would have been spared the occupation, seven years of war in Asia and eight years of war in Africa!

But unfortunately some people on the Left refuse to end the anticommunist ostracism which so far has only played into the hands of the Right. That ostracism echoed by M. Duverger writing in *Le Monde*: "In talking of the Left one does not imply a governing coalition of all the left-wing parties. The communists will doubtless remain a special case for a long while yet." It is no consolation to find him adding "That will scarcely be any change in French tradition for, excepting the Jacobins of 1793–4, the first provisional government of 1848, the Popular Front of 1936 and tripartism in 1944–6 we have never known anything different." Just so! The only periods of democracy France has known were those when the people were associated with power. No doubt the reactionaries of the period attacked the Jacobins for being in the pay of foreign powers and the socialists of 1848 for being "splitters," but popular pressure was so great that it was impossible to eliminate them.

All these cunning calculations to discover how to square the circle and achieve governmental stability are intended solely to ensure the continued exclusion of the com-

munists and prevent any return to the days when the people really exercised power. In reality, as Lenin said in his speech to the Second Congress of Soviets: "For the bourgeoisie a State is strong only when it can use the full weight of governmental power to hold the masses where the bourgeois leaders want them. Our conception of force is totally different. For us, the strength of the State lies in the consciousness of the masses; it is strong when the masses know everything, when they can judge everything, and when they are constantly involved in action."

Only a genuine democracy will make it possible to carry through the programme whose adoption the communists are recommending, and which is simply the "old" programme of the National Council of the Resistance in an up-to-date form: extension of local liberties; the democratization of the administration; genuine nationalization, separation of Church and State.

Moreover it is amusing to note that the "technocrats" of both Right and Left who talk about "modern democracy," the "rationalization of parliamentarianism," or "the personalization of power" draw only on procedures and institutions inherited from archaic systems of personal power. Doubtless they are banking on forgetfulness and ignorance, but behind their frail reasoning one can see the financial powers which control them. The Communists know that the State is an instrument of class; but because they are supporters of socialist democracy, the broadest and most genuine form of democracy, they defend democratic freedom and struggle for it to be widened. Because they do not support a policy of all or nothing, because they are the heirs of the democratic tradition of 1789 and the Communards, they advocate a solution which draws its inspiration from the revolutionary tradition of their country.

As Jacques Duclos writes in *L'Avenir de la Démocratie*, it is the Communists' wish that "even before socialism is established, the working class should have the chance to take part in the conduct of public affairs." Moreover, they know that socialism can be achieved by parliamentary means, through developing the activity of the masses, but that implies reestablishing the rights of the Assembly elected by the peo- ple. As in 1944, this programme can unite all republicans and all whose illusions have been shattered by four years of personal power and eleven years of disillusion under the Fourth Republic.

Nathan Leites

THE FLIGHT FROM RESPONSIBILITY

Where governmental instability becomes as institutionalized as under the Fourth Republic it inevitably becomes a major element conditioning the behavior of the participants in the political game. Nathan Leites is attempting here to schematize the operational rules and understandings which tend to develop in such circumstances. What he says is most nearly true of the declining years of the Fourth Republic—and even then isolated individuals stood above the System he describes. With these qualifications, he provides a telling insight into the price of instability and its translation into political behavior.

Since the life of a government is very short (a phenomenon which makes one sometimes overlook the fact that the average presence of a minister in a given post lasts noticeably longer), it is very often possible to affirm that the life of a certain policy extended over several governments; why, then, pick on any one of them? The actions which it took may have been rendered inevitable by those of its predecessors; and it may have done nothing more than maintain an already established "groove."

The possibility of having recourse to such arguments constitutes one of the many advantages of governmental instability, advantages which are, of course, rarely mentioned, but which contribute to perpetuating this instability despite its universal condemnation in public statements, and in the face of the intermittent onslaughts of reformers.

Thus, to take a minor instance, a parliamentarian can conclude a speech with these words: "I have shown that all organizations for the unification of Europe have been permitted to be inactive for years. Thus I have no particular criticism to address to the present government. . . .

"Those whom I cannot claim as accomplices, as it were, because they have preceded me in power, are often implicated by the stands they have taken." Thus the politician's code continues. A few weeks after the agony of Dien Bien Phu, and in the middle of that of his own government, Joseph Laniel ascended the rostrum. "Before examining the way in which the government . . . has conducted the war in Indochina or tried to make peace," he wanted to issue a reminder:

"I should like to recall that four candidates for the premiership have, on the occasion of the last crisis taken a stand on Indochina before I did. Three among them, Messieurs Reynaud, Bidault and André Marie, agreed to enter my cabinet, in which they are associated with all important decisions. As to the fourth, M. Mendès-

Reprinted from *On the Game of Politics in France* by Nathan Leites, pp. 43–49, with the permission of the publishers, Stanford University Press. © 1959 by the RAND Corporation.

France . . . he did not on that occasion enumerate aims which were different from those stated by the three personalities whom I have just named."

In an even more direct fashion, the politician can justify his own actions by generously granting absolution to his predecessors. Admitting that the military budget for 1958 failed, like previous budgets, to show the revolutionary changes often promised, the minister in charge indicated why this could not be helped and added:

"During the last ten years . . . every one of my predecessors have recognized the necessity of preparing for the future. But . . . first Indochina and then Algeria absorbed so much time and such large resources, so many cadres and men, that it has until now not proved possible to orient our military establishment toward the future . . . Speaking as I do, I believe that I am acting toward my predecessors not only in a spirit of courtesy but also in one of equity."

But was the minister's generosity to those who came before him not also advantageous to himself?

It is imprudent to give in to the inclination which pushes those in power to "draw up the balance sheet" of those who came before them. Sooner, rather than later, one will need their support in a world in which the various sectors of the political class are almost all "condemned to live together." It is thus of the greatest importance to avoid antagonizing anyone. . . .

In addition, the sharing of responsibilities by so many gives those who are attacked excellent possibilities for replying effectively. They can answer with a *tu quoque*, pointing out that the imprudent critic has, in fact, implicated himself, too. "Since the war," a parliamentarian recalled, "we have lost Indochina, the French establishments in India, the Fezzan, Tunisia, the Saar and Morocco. In addition, a revolutionary war is now being conducted against us in Algeria." He added: "Who is responsible? Nobody. If you pronounce one name, the one you have designated protests immediately and cites in his turn the names of two or three of his predecessors. . ."

When Mendès-France as Premier spoke of the responsibilities for the unfortunate outcome of the war in Indochina, Georges Bidault could answer: "I have heard it said . . . that the policy pursued at present succeeds eight years of errors. This, I must say, involves many governments and many ministers. Among them are perhaps some who are members of the present government. . . ."

To supplement this handling of the past, the politician tries to ensure that he will be in appropriate company when he proceeds to a "delicate" action — an elementary maneuver which is hardly distinctive of French politics, but also a concern which perhaps is especially acute in France. One of the worst things that might happen to a politician is to find himself alone in taking a stand that might arouse antagonism . . .

It is, of course, precisely his most dangerous rivals and enemies whom the politician must induce to become his "sureties." If they refuse to do so, he will not venture out by himself. In the words of an observer, "When sacrifices are demanded of an assembly . . . every political group turns toward its most dangerous electoral neighbor and declares: 'With him yes, without him no. . .'"

The politician may even abandon the pretense of judging issues or men solely on their merit. On November 12, 1957, the finance committee of the Assembly voted on the question whether it should take as a basis of its discussion the financial proposals of the government.

M. Boisdé (Moderate) was the first to announce his vote: against. M. de Tinguy (Christian Democrat) declared himself in favor, but added, "I reserve the right of rectifying my vote," wanting in this fashion to indicate that he would renounce voting for the proposal of the government if the Moderates . . . were to refuse their votes. M. Courant (Moderate) announced in his turn: "The same vote as M. de Tinguy."

But as M. Guy Petit (Moderate) voted against, the Christian Democrats changed their vote to abstention; the Moderates who had voted in favor then did the same . . . and M. David (Socialist) declared that in these circumstances his friends, while desiring to vote in favor, did not wish to be the only ones to support the government and would also abstain.

Thus the proposal of the government seemed doomed to fail when M. Courant asked for a suspension of the meeting. A few minutes later the Moderates . . . announced that they would vote in favor of taking the proposals of the government into consideration. A vote was taken again, and this time it was favorable: 30 against 14 . . .

It often appears prudent to those who want to rise to the upper levels of power not to take a stand on even the limited number of important problems which are publicly posed and discussed. One derives greater advantage from being "reserved" than from proposing "solutions". To take any public stand may "mark" a man and thus become the reason for a veto raised against him by some individual or group at a crucial juncture. "One becomes Premier by the force of one's silence," stated a satirical journal, which attributed the following complaint to an unsuccessful candidate for the presidency of the Republic: "But how could he have done less than I did?". . .

When a difficult ministerial crisis was about to begin (in the spring of 1957 after the fall of Guy Mollet), "I prefer not to be around during the crisis," declared Edgar Faure, taking off for China.

If one does not absent oneself one can al- ways abstain. This happens so frequently that the various proposals for a revision of the constitution in early 1958 were in good measure directed to making this attitude impossible on the occasion of important votes. At present, a parliamentarian recalled, "it is just as easy to assemble a single majority against a proposal of the government as it is difficult to marshal against it . . . an absolute majority."

Similarly, a government may try to survive by taking a safe stand on the most explosive problems of the hour, namely, by the obligatory abstention of its members. This happened in the case of the law granting subsidies to Catholic schools in 1951 and in the case of the treaty establishing EDC in 1954. A parliamentary group in danger of disintegrating may attempt to preserve itself in the same fashion. On the occasion of the vote on a candidate for the premiership (Antoine Pinay, in the fall of 1957) a journalist said about the Christian Democrats, "It was easy to obtain the abstention of the large majority among them. That position had the advantage of preserving the unity of the group." And about the Radicals: "Trying to make the group adopt a common attitude, M. Daladier proposed collective abstention. . . ."

When it does not seem appropriate to abstain, it may at least be possible not to speak; or else the leaders of a group may remain silent, leaving it to the rank-and-file to explain their position. Thus a government is often "strangled by the dumb slaves of the seraglio," as Clemenceau called his Radical enemies.

II. *The State and Politics: The Gaullist Conception*

Charles de Gaulle

LEADERSHIP

This meditation upon the nature of leadership, so self-revealing as to amount to anticipated autobiography, was published by de Gaulle when he was an almost unknown army major in 1932. Written with a candor which has not always characterized his more recent political utterances, this document, together with the Bayeux speech which follows, is essential reading if one wishes to understand de Gaulle's views on the nature of authority, the character of the ordinary citizen, and the techniques of wielding political power.

These are hard days for authority. Current custom attacks it; legislation tends to weaken it. In the home and in the workshop, in the State or in the street, it arouses impatience and criticism rather than confidence and obedience. Rudely assailed from below every time it shows itself, it is beginning to doubt itself, to be tentative, to assert itself inopportunely—either too little and with reticence, excuses and extreme caution or else to excess with harshness, roughness and unimaginative formalism.

This decay follows the decline in the moral, social and political order which has held sway for centuries in the nations of old Europe. Whether by conviction or calculation men have long held that power has an origin and the elite has rights, thus justifying the emergence of hierarchies. But the whole fabric of these conventions is now collapsing from the cracks that have opened it. With their wavering beliefs, their bloodless traditions, and their exhausted loyalties, our contemporaries no longer have either a sense of deference or respect for those rules of conduct which were observed in the past. *"Nos Dieux sont décrépits et la misère en tombe."*

Such a crisis, however general it may appear to be, cannot last indefinitely. In their hearts men can no more do without being told what to do (*dirigés*) than they can live without food, drink and sleep. These political animals have a need for organization, that is for order and for leaders. If authority totters on its shaken foundations, the natural equilibrium which is the nature of things will sooner or later provide it with new ones which may or may not be better but which are at all events appropriate to the establish-

From Charles de Gaulle, *Le Fil de l'Epée* (Paris: 1962), pp. 73–89. Reprinted by permission of Berger-Levrault. Editor's translation.

ment of a new discipline. Better still, the foundations of this new discipline can be discerned even now: the value of individuals and the ascendancy of a few men. What the masses once granted to office or birth, they now reserve only for those who can assert themselves. What legitimate prince was ever so blindly obeyed as the dictator who at the beginning had nothing beyond his own audacity? What established authority ever left such a mark on an endeavour as does today's engineer with his technical skill? What conquerors were ever so widely acclaimed as our athletes whose success springs from their personal efforts alone?

This transformation of society cannot fail to have its effect on military discipline. In the army, as elsewhere, it is said that "respect is disappearing." But in fact it is finding a new focus. The man who commands, at whatever level, should be proud that he is obeyed less for his rank than for his own worth. We must no longer confuse power and its external signs.

That does not, of course, mean that discipline now owes nothing whatever to the things in which it was at one time steeped. Men do not change so quickly or so completely, and human nature does not move forward in jumps. The exercise of authority over others still depends to a large extent on the aura conferred by rank and seniority. Conversely, the personal ascendancy of the master has long helped him to secure obedience. But in these unsettled times, within a society whose framework and traditions have been so violently disturbed, the conventions of obedience are growing progressively weaker, and the personal prestige of the leader is becoming the mainspring of command.

* * *

Authority (*prestige*) is a matter of feeling, suggestion and impression, a kind of instinctive attraction inspired in others. It depends primarily on an elementary gift, a natural aptitude which defies analysis. The fact of the matter is that authority flows from certain men virtually from birth, although it is impossible to say exactly how

this comes about. It can surprise even those who are under its influence. This is something which has much in common with love, which is inexplicable apart from the effect of an attraction that words cannot express. Furthermore, the authority exercised by certain individuals may not correspond in the least to their intrinsic worth. We find men of the highest intelligence and valor who have no impact on those around them, while this quality may be vested in others less endowed in mind and heart.

But though this authority contains an ingredient which cannot be acquired, which comes from the depths of a person's being and varies in each, certain constant and necessary elements can nevertheless be discerned. These can be acquired or at least developed. The true leader, like the great artist, must have an innate quality which is moulded by his experience in his craft.

Above all, there can be no authority without mystery, for familiarity breeds contempt. All religions have their holy of holies and no man is a hero to his valet. In the aims and manner of a leader, and in the working of his mind, there remains a certain "something" which others cannot quite fathom, which baffles them, moves them and keeps them in suspense. That is not to say that he should shut himself away in an ivory tower, ignoring his subordinates and inaccessible to them. On the contrary, if one is to hold sway over men's minds one must observe them and let each one believe that he has been singled out from among his fellows. But only on condition that his practice is combined with the habit of giving nothing away, with the resolve always to keep in reserve as a surprise some secret which can be brought forward at any moment. The latent faith of the masses will do the rest. Thereafter, once the leader has been judged capable of adding the weight of his exceptional personal qualities to the effective normal handling of a situation, hope and confidence in their mysterious way enhance his standing.

Such an attitude of reserve will normally

imply corresponding words and gestures—outward signs no doubt but it is on these that the crowd forms its opinion. And, after all, is it wrong to do so? Is there not some relationship between a man's inner force and his outward aspect? Thus, no fighting man has ever underestimated the importance of physical appearance. And while, among military commanders, lesser men are concerned simply to behave correctly before their men, the greatest arrange their interventions carefully. They make an art of this, as Flaubert realised very well; in *Salammbô*, he depicted for us the effect produced on flagging troops by Hamilcar's carefully calculated arrival on the scene. Every page of the *Commentaries* shows us how Caesar weighed his every movement in public. We know what thought Napoleon took, always to show himself in such a way as to impress those who saw him.

Sobriety of speech lends emphasis to an already striking manner. Nothing enhances authority more than silence. It is the crowning virtue of the strong, and the refuge of the weak; the modesty of the proud and the pride of the humble; the prudence of the wise and the wit of fools. The man who is moved by desire or by fear is naturally likely to look to words to divert him from such anguish. If he yields to such temptation he is compromising with his desires or fear. Moreover, speech waters down one's thoughts, lets one's ardor flow to waste, in short dissipates one's strength when for action it needs to be concentrated. Silence and order are necessarily interrelated. "Attention!" is the command when troops are to be put to work. And, since everything that comes from the leader is highly contagious he creates calm and alertness providing he keeps his silence. Thus men instinctively mistrust a master whose words flow too freely. *Imperatoria brevitas*, as the Romans said. Regulations have always laid down that orders should be concise, and we are only too well aware today how authority is undermining itself with its floods of paper and torrents of words.

However, the systematic reserve practised by the leader makes no impression whatever unless it is felt to be cloaking the decisiveness and zeal within. We can all think of men whose impassiveness brings them, first, a temporary reputation for sphinx-like wisdom but later they are considered half-wits. Ascendancy is born of the contrast between inner power and self-control—just as style in a gambler lies in his ability to appear calmer than ever when he is raising the stakes, and an actor makes the greatest impact on his audience in giving the appearance of restrained emotion. Barrès had only to look at the statues of Alexander in which passion and serenity, the august and the terrible combine, to grasp what was the source of that authority which, for thirteen years, amid unspeakable trials, maintained order among jealous underlings and unruly troops, and imposed Hellenism on a corrupt and savage world.

Moreover, the ability to dominate events, to make his mark on them, and to take responsibility for the consequences: this above all is what is expected of a leader. The elevation of a man above his fellows is only justified if he gives an impetus and the guarantee of his character to the common task. After all, considering the privilege of command, the right to give orders, pride at being obeyed, the thousand-and-one attentions, praises and privileges which go with power, the honour and glory which so largely accrue to the leader—why should he receive these without any return? And how else can he pay for them except by taking personal responsibility upon himself? Obedience would not be tolerable if the man who called for it put it to no good purpose. And how could he do this without daring, deciding and acting? . . .

The plan to which the leader devotes himself must bear the stamp of grandeur. For he must answer the secret wishes of his followers, who in their weakness seek perfection and, limited by their natures, cherish boundless hopes and, recognising the smallness of their own stature, agree to collective action only if it has some great purpose. Mastery depends on touching this secret spring. Anyone who is to lead the masses must be skilled in using it. It is the foundation of eloquence: every orator must know how to clothe the slimmest of cases in the most grandiose of arguments. It is the key to business success: every banker's prospectus rests on progress. It is the starting point for political parties—all of which are ceaselessly talking of universal bliss. The leader's commands must tend therefore toward some elevated aim. He must aim high, have a broad vision, in sharp contrast with the limited scope of ordinary debate. He must be a symbol of contempt for mere everyday contingencies, while the masses are committed to everyday cares. He must eliminate the mean and shabby from his behaviour, where lesser men would cease to be cautious. This is not a matter of virtue; evangelical perfection never brought a man to ascendancy over his fellows. The man of action is almost inconceivable without a strong dose of egotism, pride, harshness and cunning. However, allowances are made for all this, and he stands out even more sharply if he uses these as a means to achieve great things. Thus, by satisfying the secret desires of everyone, by this compensation for the constraints he imposes, he wins the loyalty of his subordinates and, even if he should fall on the way, he holds in their eyes the prestige arising from the peaks to which he sought to lead them. But if he limits himself to mundane matters, and is soon satisfied—he's finished! He may be a good servant but he will never be a master, to whom men turn in faith and hope.

Aloofness, character, greatness: these are the qualities necessary for authority, and which lay on those who wish to attain them a burden from which most men shrink. The unrelenting self-discipline, the constant taking of risks, try a man to the depths of his innermost being. There results, for those who subject themselves to this course, a constant inner struggle which is more acute or less acute according to the individual temperament, but which never, for a single moment, ceases to wound his spirit, as the hair shirt torments the penitent. Here we find the real reason for so many ill-explained withdrawals, of men going from success to success amid public acclaim, who suddenly lay the burden down. Moreover, in keeping himself in isolation from his fellows, the leader must turn his back on the simple pleasures of relaxing self-restraint, of easy relationships, and even of friendship. He commits himself to that loneliness which is, as Faguet puts it, "the affliction of superior beings." The state of satisfaction, tranquility, and unpremeditated joy which go by the name of happiness are denied to those who lead. The choice must be made: it is a cruel one. From it comes that trace of melancholy which is inseparable from majesty whether in men or in things. One day, as Napoleon stood before an old and noble monument, someone said "How sad it is!" "Yes," came the reply, "as sad as greatness."

Charles de Gaulle

THE BAYEUX SPEECH: AUTHORITY AND THE STATE

Delivered at Bayeux on June 16, 1946, when the constitution of the Fourth Republic was under discussion, this speech foreshadows many of the institutional relationships which were eventually embodied in the 1958 constitution

---

Editor's translation.

of the Fifth Republic. But beyond its significance as the adumbration of the current régime, this remains a classic exposition of de Gaulle's analysis of the modern state and the nature of political power and authority. There is the belief in the power of leadership and strong institutions to prevail over the inherent tendency of a divided society to instability; the dislike of parties and the tepidness towards parliament, the final position of which remains elusively vague; and finally the rejection of the risks and crudity of dictatorial rule combined with the assertion of the imperative need for unity, order, and a Chief of State ruling as a republican monarch above the political strife.

Here, in our glorious, mutilated Normandy, Bayeux and the countryside around witnessed one of the greatest events in history. We can testify that they were worthy of the occasion. It was here that, four years after France and her allies met their first great disaster, the final victory of the allies and France began. And it was the events which took place here which gave the conclusive justification to the efforts of those who had never yielded, and around whom, after June 18th, 1940, the spirit of our nation had rallied and the power of France had re-formed.

It was here that, at the same time, the State reappeared on the soil of our forebears. The State: legitimate because it rested on the interest and the feelings of the nation. The State: whose true sovereignty had been borne away to the camp of war, freedom and victory, while the camp of servitude retained merely its outward trappings. The State: with its rights, dignity and authority safeguarded in the midst of vicissitudes, penury and intrigue. The State: capable of rebuilding the unity of the nation and of the empire around itself; of mustering all the forces of the country and the French Union; of carrying the war through to victory together with the allies; of dealing with the other great nations of the world as equals; of preserving public order; of seeing justice done, and of beginning the task of reconstruction.

But these great achievements were carried through outside the former framework of our institutions, for these had not met the nation's needs; they had abdicated when the storm struck. Salvation had to come from elsewhere. It came first from an elite, which sprang spontaneously from the depths of the nation and which, far above any concern with party or class, devoted itself entirely to the liberation, the renewal, and the grandeur of France.

A feeling of moral superiority; an awareness of exercising a sort of ministry of sacrifice and example to others; a passion for risk and venture; scorn for unrest, pretension and demagogy; supreme confidence in the strength and cunning of its powerful conspiracy as well as in victory and the future of the country: such was the psychology of this elite which began with nothing and which, despite heavy losses, was to sweep the whole of France and the Empire along behind it. Yet this elite would not have succeeded without the assent of the great mass of the French people who, in their instinctive will to survive and triumph, had always seen the disaster of 1940 as merely one of the vicissitudes in a world war in which France served in the vanguard. Though many were forced to bow to the circumstances, the number of those who accepted them in their hearts was literally infinitesimal. Never did France believe that the enemy was anything but the enemy, or that salvation lay anywhere but in the camp of freedom. As the veils were steadily torn away, so the real, deep-seated feeling became evident.

Everywhere the cross of Lorraine appeared, it brought the collapse of the scaffolding of an authority which was merely imaginary even though it had the appearances of being constitutionally founded. It is true indeed that political institutions are valuable in law and practice only if they are in harmony with the highest interests of the country and rest on the confident support of its citizens. Institutions built on anything else are built on sand. That way lies the danger of seeing the edifice crumble once again at one of those crises to which our country is, in the nature of things, so often exposed.

That is why, once the safety of the State had been ensured by victory and the maintenance of national unity, one task was urgent and essential above all others: the establishment of new political institutions for France. Therefore, as soon as it was possible the French people were invited to elect a Constituent Assembly, precisely limiting its mandate and reserving the final decision to themselves.

Then, once the train had been put back on the rails, I withdrew from the scene, not only in order not to involve in the political battle what I may symbolize in virtue of events, for this belongs to the entire nation, but also so that no personal considerations regarding a man who was running the state should in any way falsify the legislators' work.

Yet the nation and the French Union are still waiting for a constitution which is made for them and to which they could give their joyful approval. However, though we may regret that the building has yet to be built, we can all agree that a somewhat belated success is preferable to speedy but unsatisfactory completion.

During a period no longer than twice the lifetime of a man France has been invaded seven times and has experienced thirteen regimes. . . . All these shocks have built up poisons in our public life, fomenting still further the old gallic propensity for quarrels and divisions. The unparalleled trials through which we have just passed have naturally aggravated this state of affairs. The present world situation in which the powers between which we lie confront each other behind opposing ideologies, is con-stantly introducing an element of impassioned agitation into our political struggles. In short, party rivalries in our country reach right down to fundamentals, continually calling them all into question, and all too often blurring the highest interests of the country. This obvious fact arises from national temperament, from the vicissitudes of history and from the commotions of the present; it is indispensible for the future of the country and of democracy itself that our institutions should take account of this and protect themselves in order to maintain respect for law, governmental cohesion, efficient administration, and the prestige and authority of the state.

For disorder in the State inexorably breeds disaffection towards its institutions among its citizens. And then, given its chance, the threat of dictatorship will appear. Particularly since the rather mechanistic organization of modern society makes it day by day more desirable and necessary for the controls to be in good working order and the machinery to operate smoothly.

How and why did our First, Second and Third Republics come to an end? How and why did Italian democracy, the Weimar Republic and the Spanish Republic give way to other regimes?

And yet what is dictatorship but a gamble? No doubt it seems advantageous at first. Amid the enthusiasm of some and the resignation of others, with the strict order it imposes and the aid of a glittering decor and one-sided propaganda, it at first takes on a dynamic air which contrasts sharply with the preceding anarchy. But dictatorship is destined invariably to overreach itself in what it undertakes. As impatience with compulsion and regret for the freedom they have lost spread among its citizens it must at all costs offer them vaster and vaster successes in compensation. The nation becomes a machine which its master accelerates with ever-increasing frenzy. Whether in foreign or domestic plans its aims, risks and efforts gradually exceed all measure. At every step a host of obstacles rise in its path at home and abroad. At last the mainspring breaks. The grandiose structure collapses in blood and tribulation. The nation is shattered more gravely than before the adventure began.

We need only mention all this to understand just how essential it is that our new democratic institutions should, by themselves, be able to offset the effects of our perpetual political effervescence. What is more, in the world and the century in which we must live this is a matter of life and death for us, for clearly the position, independence and even the very existence of our country and the French Union are at stake.

It is, of course, the very essence of democracy for opinions to be expressed and for their advocates to seek, by way of the franchise, to bring legislation and the decisions of the various organs of the state in line with their views. But equally, principles and experience alike require that the arms of government—legislature, executive, judiciary—be clearly separated and fully balanced, and that rising above political contingencies there should be set an arbiter of the nation, providing continuity amid the intrigues.

It is clear, and beyond dispute, that the final vote on laws and budgets should lie with an assembly elected by direct universal suffrage. But the initial impulses of such an assembly are not necessarily wholly clear-sighted or serene. There must therefore be a second assembly, elected and made up differently, with the task of publicly examining matters that have been considered by the first, and of framing amendments and putting forward proposals. Now, if the main political currents will naturally be reflected in the Chamber of Deputies, local life has also its political tendencies and its rights.

These rights exist in metropolitan France. They obviously exist too in the overseas departments which are connected to the French Union by very varied ties. The future of the 110 million men and women who live under our flag lies in an organization of federal form which time will little by little spell out, but a beginning should be made by organizing its development in our new constitution.

All this leads us to set up a second chamber whose members will, essentially, be elected by departmental and municipal councils. This chamber will complement the first by inducing it, where necessary, to revise its own proposals or to consider others, and by seeing to it that in the law-making process due weight is given to those administrative considerations that a purely political body tends inevitably to neglect. It would also be reasonable to include in it representatives of economic, parental and intellectual organizations, so that the voices of the country's main activities should be heard within the State itself.

Meeting with the elected representatives of the local assemblies in the overseas territories the members of this assembly will form the great council of the French Union, empowered to consider laws and problems concerning the Union: budget, external relations, internal affairs, national defense, economic matters and communications.

It is self-evident that executive power cannot emanate from a parliament which has two chambers and exercises legislative power without the danger of producing a jumble of powers in which the government would soon be merely a collection of delegations. Doubtless during the present transitional period it has been necessary for the National Constituent Assembly to elect the head of the provisional government since, because we were starting from scratch, there was no other acceptable procedure for choosing him. But that can only be a temporary measure. For the unity, coherence and internal discipline of the government of France must be considered sacred, on pain of seeing the country's leaders rapidly becoming powerless and unable to act. How can this unity, coherence and discipline be maintained for any length of time if the executive power was an emanation of the other power to which it should act as a balance, and if members of the government —which is collectively responsible to all the representatives of the nation — held their posts as mere party proxies?

Executive power must therefore emanate from the Chief of State, who is placed above the parties, elected by a college embodying Parliament but much broader than it and so composed that he is both President of the Republic and of the French Union.

The Chief of State would see to it that in the choice of men the general interest was reconciled with the orientation emerging in Parliament. He would appoint ministers, notably of course the Premier who will have to direct the policy and work of the government. He would promulgate laws and issue decrees, for these bind citizens to the entire State. He would preside over meetings of ministers, bringing to bear the influence of continuity, with which no nation can dispense. He would act as an arbiter above all political contingencies, normally through the council [of ministers], but in moments of grave confusion by inviting the country to make its sovereign decision known through elections. And, should the country be in peril, it would be his duty to guarantee both the treaties concluded by France and the independence of the nation itself.

Some Greeks once asked wise Solon, "What is the best constitution?" He replied: "First, tell me for what people and for what age." Today we have in mind the French people and the peoples of the French Union, and a time which is very hard and very dangerous. We must take ourselves as we are, and take the century as it is. Despite immense difficulties we must carry through a profound renovation which will lead every man and woman among us to an easier life, security and happiness, and which will make us more numerous, more powerful and more fraternal.

We have to preserve the freedom that was saved at the cost of so much suffering. We have to make the destiny of France sure amid all the obstacles which arise in her path and the path of peace. Among our fellow men we must show what we can do to aid our poor and aged mother Earth. Let us be clearsighted and strong enough to give ourselves and to keep rules of national life which will tend to draw us together when we are ceaselessly given to divisions among ourselves. Our entire history is made up of the alternation of immense sufferings by a fragmented people and the fruitful grandeur of a free nation grouped under the aegis of a strong State.

Douglas Johnson

DE GAULLE: POLITICS AND THE PEOPLE

Views such as those expressed by President de Gaulle in the two preceeding extracts tend to arouse attacks or support rather than sympathetic analysis and explanation. Writing with considerable charity Douglas Johnson comments here on some of the salient characteristics of de Gaulle's approach to domestic politics.

Everywhere in de Gaulle's writings and statements, one finds underlined the need for a strong state. It is this which has caused some to compare de Gaulle's thought to that of various European Fascist parties of the pre-1939 period. The symptom of the decline of France between the two world wars was the weakness of the French state,

From Douglas Johnson, "The Political Principles of General de Gaulle," *International Affairs* (October, 1965), Vol. 41, Reprinted by permission of *International Affairs* and of the author.

unable to take effective action when danger threatened. De Gaulle's political experience of these years brought him into contact with the ineffectiveness of French institutions. When the Germans were defeated in the Second World War, this did not mean that danger had disappeared. The whole trend of modern existence represents danger, the whole trend of contemporary developments is to increase that danger. Both supporters and opponents of General de Gaulle associate him with crisis and with disaster. He himself saw his legitimacy as being latent in a period without anxiety, but it would be invoked "as soon as a new laceration threatened the nation."

Gaullists of all sorts insist that the times in which one lives are exceptional. Soustelle asks when, since 1940 or since 1914, have times been normal? De Gaulle has always emphasized "the overwhelming fact" that France is in perpetual danger of sudden death and therefore must have some permanent authority which can take the necessary decisions (14 January 1963). "Politics is action, an *ensemble* of decisions which are made, things which are done, risks which are taken" (23 July 1964).

This being so, the government of a country cannot be entrusted to an assembly. An assembly cannot ensure a strong state. It exists for debate and deliberation, it does not exist in order to take decisions. Assemblies, despite their fine speeches, are, according to de Gaulle, governed by fear of action. And although de Gaulle — like other critics of the French parliamentary system — was personally attracted by the Assembly, as he recalls in his *Memoirs*, and as was noticed by observers during his appearances before the Chamber in the 1958 crisis, he has never varied in his opposition to the Assembly as the source of government. He has recognised that his insistence upon a head of state is in direct opposition to the fundamental principle of the French parliamentary regime, which de Gaulle has characterised as "let no head show above the trenches of democracy," indicative of a timorous, anonymous system.

In order to make France a strong state, in order to promote change, one man must lead the country, must make decisions and give direction. In a striking and revealing passage in his *Memoirs*, de Gaulle describes his return to the Ministry of War in liberated Paris, and his impression that nothing had changed there since he and M. Reynaud had left on the night of 10 June 1940. Gigantic events had overturned the world, the French army had been annihilated, France had virtually collapsed, but at the Ministry of War the look of things was the same. Nothing had been disturbed. "Soon I was to learn that this was the case in all the other buildings in which the republic housed itself. Nothing was missing except the state. It was my duty to restore it: I installed my staff at once and got down to work."

Therefore the task of the head of state is to find means of effecting change and reform: and governmental methods have to be examined in the light of this principle rather than that of ideologies. "Like everyone else," as he puts it, he realised that in our time technology dominated the universe, and the great debate of the century was whether the working classes would be the victims or the beneficiaries of this technical progress. Hence the need for profound and rapid social change. Hence the need for technicians and administrators who would answer the aspirations and fears of the masses, and, by implication, remove the need for the various political banners — liberal, marxist, Hitlerian — which floated over the battlefields. Such a policy as nationalization does not exist because it is inherently just or desirable, but because through nationalization economic change can be promoted. Much of the insistence on military and defense projects can be interpreted as ways of promoting economic change. The referendum has been indicated as a means of effecting reform. Yet the task of the leader is not merely that of providing the decision-making machinery whereby the state will be strengthened. His function exists in relation to the principle of the nation-state. As has recently been re-marked, nationalism is nothing else but the desire to bring together the juridical reality which is the state and the sociological reality which is the national group. De Gaulle sees the leader as effecting this coincidence. There is the people; the people is sovereign. The source of power lies with the people, and although he writes of the occasional value of a temporary period of dictatorship, and of the temptations of dictatorship, yet his conclusion is simple, "no man can substitute himself for a people."

His practice followed his theory. As he boasted, on 19 May 1958, he could have imposed his dictatorship with the Liberation; instead he restored the republic. His resignation in January 1946 may have been a miscalculation, but he never attempted to organise a coup against the Fourth Republic. During the crisis of 1958 all the initiatives which he took were based upon the assumption that he could assume power legally. "I cannot consent to receive power from any other source than the people, or at least its representatives."

And this contact with the people has to take place directly, and without intermediaries. The intermediaries pervert and corrupt the relations between the leader and the people. Intermediaries tend to mean elites and de Gaulle has always been suspicious of these. He believed, even before the war, that the old elites in France were losing their value, and that while men could not dispense with being governed and directed, the respect which had formerly been shown to birth and position was not being accorded to those who showed ability. It has been said that de Gaulle showed a rare perspicacity in realising that the Republic of "the notables," the product of the French Revolution, was destroyed with the victory of 1918. His experience in 1940 confirmed his impression. The elites failed to support him, and none of the eminences of France condemned the armistice. With the Liberation came the realization that the elites had betrayed France, and de Gaulle's realization, at a meeting at the Palais de Chaillot, that his dealings with the professional politicians would be complicated, and that he must seek his support from the people. . . .

Among the elites which were to be mistrusted are, above all, the political parties. De Gaulle's contempt for their limitations is well known: he invited Edouard Herriot to help him in the reconstruction of France, but the reply was that he was rebuilding the Radical Party. His mistrust for their sectarianism, for their tendency to represent particular rather than national interests, is allied to the conviction that in modern times there is bound to be a decadence of political parties and of their ideologies.

Nothing in de Gaulle is more striking than his alliance of theory and practice, his confidence in the people, his realization of the value of modern techniques, his insistence that "this is something between each man and woman of you and me." Into this there enters an element of personalization, of auto-intoxication, comparable perhaps to that of Malraux's heroes who experience *"un vaste frémissement de fraternité!"* in the night at Canton, but all the deeper because it represents the collusion of theory and reality.

And along with this dialogue between the leader and the people, there is another principle. Harmony is necessary to the state. In his earliest book, on the subject of the German defeat in the First World War de Gaulle expresses the view that the harmony of the German state was destroyed when military power invaded civilian power. In the preface he writes: "In a French garden, no tree tries to suffocate the others by its shade." In his account of the recent past he strives to establish this harmony. Darlan, who was to scuttle the French fleet, is condemned because he saw things exclusively from the standpoint of the French navy. The communists are treated as dangerous because they seek to control a national movement. The trial of Marshal Pétain is regretted because it became the condemnation of a part of France, whereas it should have been the condemnation of an act, the armistice. The Resistance was not to be allowed to dominate liberated France: France was greater than the Resistance. The Roman Catholic Church should not be allowed to suffer unduly, and the exclusion of Cardinal Suhard from the Liberation mass was regretted by de Gaulle. It is not unreasonable to suppose that de Gaulle was influenced, after 1958, by the same desire not to see the harmony of the country upset, when considering his attitude to the settlers in Algeria, or his policy towards the army.

The general has two fundamental and contradictory beliefs. That France is united, that there is a fundamental unity; that France is diverse and multiple, with many spiritual families. The contradiction is resolved in great moments of crisis and drama. It disappears when de Gaulle, at the Liberation, stands at the Arc de Triomphe and sees the population massed around him. It reappears when the tension slackens. De Gaulle might well have been thinking of his own position when he wrote of Winston Churchill, "His countenance, etched by the fires and the frosts of great events, had become inappropriate in the era of mediocrity."

Michel Debré

THE NEW CONSTITUTION

No man had a greater impact on the 1958 constitution in its final written form than Michel Debré. De Gaulle himself showed the effect of Debré's constitutional views upon him as early as the Bayeux speech of 1946. As Minister of Justice in de Gaulle's 1958 government, Michel Debré was in charge of the working party which prepared the first draft of the new constitution, and he was closely associated with every succeeding stage of its preparation. Later, as Prime Minister from 1959 to 1962, he was to take an important part in implementing it in a sense which diverged progressively from its original conception. But here, in his speech to members of the *Conseil d'Etat* on 27 August 1958, the eve of the adoption of the constitution by a massive majority at a referendum, he makes the classic exposition and defense of the new system. This is the opening section in which Debré explains why government by an omnipotent assembly and presidential government are equally inappropriate for France. It should be read in conjunction with the two succeeding extracts in which Debré's exposition of the presidency, first in 1958 and then in 1962, are set side by side.

With unprecedented rapidity the unity and strength of France have deteriorated in recent years, our essential interests have been gravely menaced, our existence as a free and independent nation put in jeopardy. Many causes have contributed to this major political crisis. The bankruptcy of our [political] institutions is doubly to blame: our institutions were no longer suitable, to say the least, and their unsuitability was aggravated by a political immorality that they proved unable to correct.

The purpose of the constitutional reform is therefore clear.

Editor's translation.

It is, first and foremost, to try to reconstruct governmental authority without which there is neither State nor democracy, that is, as far as we are concerned, neither France nor Republic.

It is next, in the highest interest of our security and of the equilibrium of the world, to safeguard and renovate that *ensemble* we traditionally call overseas France.

The Constitution alone does not enable us to attain these two objectives. But it must be constructed in such a way that it will not be an obstacle, but will, on the contrary, be a powerful help.

One determination dominates this draft: to rebuild the Republic's parliamentary system. A second determination has led us to detail how a Community could be established around France:

Giving France Parliamentary Government

The government was determined to renovate the parliamentary system. I am even tempted to say that it wants to establish it, because for a number of reasons the Republic has never succeeded in setting it up.

The reason for this choice is simple. Government by an assembly (*le régime d'assemblée*) or by a convention, is both impracticable and dangerous. Presidential government (*le régime présidentiel*) is at present incapable of working in France.

The Impossibility of Government by Assembly

Government by an assembly or a convention in which the totality of power is held in law or in fact by a Parliament—or to be more exact—a single Assembly. The Assembly not only has legislative power and budgetary control, it determines policy and the "government," whose authority is drawn from it and who is dependent on its arbitrary discretion, is merely its clerk. Its decisions can be criticized by no one, even if they are contrary to the Constitution. Their extent is unlimited and the entire range of public authorities is completely subject to their will.

The way the Assembly operates enables it to shoulder this task: sessions which have almost no end; a host of powerful committees; proxy voting which allows the multiplication of sittings and ballots.

Do I need to go on with the description? This system is the one under which we have been living. They tried to remedy its failings by revising the Assembly's rules. Wasted effort! Any changes in the rules which are incompatible with the operation of government by convention are either not applied or of no avail. They tried a new nostrum in increasing the powers of the second assembly. Wasted effort again! The division into two chambers is a good rule for a parliamentary system because it allows an independent government to find in the second chamber assistance which is useful against the first; in government by convention, however, the arbitrary power of one assembly is neutralized, or rather reduced, by the other without there being any real authority. Finally, they sought a remedy in coalitions or pacts between parties. Still more wasted effort! Understandings between factions cannot withstand the feeling of irresponsibility that assembly government gives to each of them and to their members.

The Main Difficulties of Presidential Government

Presidential government is the form of democratic government that is the opposite of government by assembly. It is characterized by the amount of power given in law and in fact to a chief of state elected by universal suffrage.

In such a system the powers are not intermingled. On the contrary, they are very strictly separated. The legislative assemblies are deprived of all governmental influence: their domain is the domain of the law, which is very clearly defined. They approve the budget and, normally, treaties. If there is a dispute, the president has at his disposal such arms as the veto or the power of automatic promulgation to resolve it. The judiciary has a special and usually privileged place in order to ensure that private citizens are protected against such a powerful leader and against the consequences of an agreement between him and the assemblies.

The virtues of presidential government are obvious. The state has a leader, and democracy has power. After having suffered from the anarchy and impotence which result from government by convention there is a great temptation to seek refuge in the order and authority of presidential government.

Neither Parliament, which showed its determination to reform by the law of June 3,[1] nor the government in presenting and then applying that law, succumbed to this temptation, and I believe this was wise. Democracy in France presupposes a Parliament endowed with political power. One can imagine two assemblies which were simply legislative and budgetary—that is to say subordinate. But we must recognise that this conception does not coincide with the image of the Republic which is traditional and in many respects legitimate.

In addition to this legal reason two practical considerations are each decisive.

The President of the Republic has overseas responsibilities; he is also president of the Community. Can one envisage an electorate including every single man and woman in metropolitan France, in Algeria, in Black Africa, in Madagascar, and in the islands of the Pacific? That would not be reasonable and would be likely to be harmful both to the unity of the whole and to the respect which is due to the head of state.

Again, let us look at the situation here in France and consider questions of policy. We are determined that France shall be strong.

Is it possible for authority to rest on so deeply divided an electorate? Can one forget that a sizeable part of the electorate, gripped by the difficulties of past years, adopts an attitude of revolt towards the sovereignty of the nation, and that a certain party[2] forcefully organizes them for ends which statesmen and governmental leaders cannot accept?

The case seems proved to me. It is, at present, dangerous to put presidential government into operation.

The Conditions of Parliamentary Government

Rejecting government by convention, rejecting presidential government, the way ahead is narrow—it is the way of parliamentary government. To the jumbling of powers within a single assembly, to the strict separation of powers with the chief of state pre-eminent, is to be preferred the collaboration of powers—chief of state and Parliament separated and, encompassing a government issuing from the first and responsible to the second, the division of powers between them being such as to give each a similar importance in the operation of the state, and providing the means of resolving those conflicts which are, in any democratic system, the ransom of freedom.

This draft constitution which is submitted to you aspires to create parliamentary government. It does this by four measures or series of measures:

1. Strict regulation of parliamentary sessions
2. An effort to define the domain of the law
3. A thorough-going reorganization of legislative and budgetary procedure
4. An overhaul of the juridical mechanisms which are indispensable to the equilibrium and proper operation of political functions.

[1] M. Debré is referring to the last act of the Fourth Republic Assembly which was to authorise constitutional revision. [Editor's note.]

[2] i.e. the French Communist Party. [Editor's note.]

III. *The Style of the Fifth Republic*

Pierre Viansson-Ponté

GAULLIST RITUALS

We have already seen what importance de Gaulle has always attached to the style of political leadership. Every public appearance, every important communiqué, and every detail of protocol on state occasions is weighed and calculated with infinite care and concern for its political impact and implications. In studying any political regime or period we will find that much of its distinctive flavor lies in its characteristic political rituals and styles, but in France today such rituals are also a fruitful source of insights into the very nature of the régime. Of the descriptions which follow, two—on the way the General receives his visitors in audience, and on the provincial tours which were such a regular feature of the early years of his presidency—are essentially self-explanatory. But the further implications of the semiannual press conferences, as described here by Pierre Viansson-Ponté, merit further emphasis. Not only are these carefully contrived occasions quite unlike the White House press conference or question time in the House of Commons, but they fit into a wider picture in which, unlike his American or British counterparts, President de Gaulle in the end never finds himself obliged to explain and defend himself in uncontrolled public questioning, with the possible exception of a seven-yearly presidential election. This exceptional degree of insulation is what enables him to exercise far greater discretion over how much of himself he chooses to reveal, and to retain the tactical advantages of silence and ambiguity on which he set so much store in *Le Fil de l'Epée.*

THE PRESS CONFERENCE

This is the choral high mass, the great ceremonial rite, endowed with all the pomp of high days and holy days. It begins with a rumour spreading like wildfire: it could well be, the initiates say, that perhaps, before too long, the general will break his silence. . . . The initiates in this case are simply those clever enough to foresee the moment when he will wish to make known his views and when the inherently brief

From Pierre Viansson-Ponté, *Les Gaullistes* (1963), pp. 35–36, 38–41, 46–48. Reprinted by permission of Editions du Seuil. Editor's translation.

and restricted medium of the broadcast talk will seem too limited.

Once the announcement has been made the calculations begin: will he, won't he say . . .? Two or three days before the appointed date there is a sudden hardening of the forecasts, if not about what will be said, then at least about the subjects that will be touched on. This does not mean that light has suddenly dawned in a number of minds, but, more prosaically, that the Elysée's press service has begun to distribute to "journalists" the questions they are to ask the general. There should be no misconceptions on this score: any journalist who puts a question to de Gaulle at a press conference and receives a lengthy reply has agreed in advance to play a role. One can easily tell a question which is really unexpected—and the answer shows it.

Finally, the great day arrives. A huge banqueting hall has been turned into a sort of theatre with a thousand seats. The ministers have taken their places on the speaker's right, and members of the President's *cabinet* and secretariat on his left. Facing him are six hundred journalists and two or three hundred guests—people in important semiofficial positions, diplomats, members of parliament, supporters—have taken their places under the chandeliers with their thousand crystals. The television and news cameras have been set up on the stage and in the four corners of the hall. It is three o'clock. The red curtain parts and the general appears.

The procedure at the press conference has suffered a major alteration in the last year. Until then, questions were put one at a time and answered at once. In practice, the general had before him a rough diagram of the hall with red crosses marking approximately the seat occupied by each of the cooperating "journalists." With the aid of this plan, as he finished one reply he could turn to the section of the audience from which the next question was due. The person concerned rose, waved his hand, and was given the floor and his question heard.

However, there were hitches. Sometimes people who should never have put a question managed to insinuate themselves between two official questioners and caused embarrassment. At other times a subject was expected and an answer prepared, but the question was not asked, making it necessary to pretend, amid laughter, "I believe somebody put a question about Ben Bella." Nobody was deceived. A new method was introduced to remedy these disadvantages. All the questions are put at the beginning in no special order. The general then arranges them by subject and states that consequently he will deal first with this topic and then with that. Then, before embarking on each new chapter, the "authors" of the questions dealing with the subject which is about to be dealt with are invited by name to ask them a second time. Only the "right" questions are repeated and considered. This way there are no mistakes.

The television team peacefully carries on with its job, switching its cameras from the questioners to the questioned, lingering on the audience and on the ministers, though avoiding André Malraux, who tends to fall asleep at the first question and who is no light sleeper. It is warm. The cameras drone on, as does the general. The peroration merges into applause, scandalizing the journalists—the genuine ones, that is—who came to listen, not to acclaim.

Slowly and regretfully, after the last sally and the studied courtesy of the closing thanks, everyone disperses, discussing every shade of intonation. The cloakroom is taken by storm and overwhelmed. Francois Mauriac frets over an allusion, ponders over a reticence. Late that evening the Elysée will distribute the full official text, carefully reread, its form and sometimes its substance changed.

Such is the magic of the press conference that in January 1960 the mere announcement that one was to be held brought about the barricades insurrection—barricades which, moreover, were to collapse in the wake of a speech a week later. Born of words which had not been spoken, the riot was thus quieted under a barrage of words. In this respect the press conference is the régime's absolute weapon.

This is a formal yet good-natured visit by the supreme governor to the simple citizen, designed to set up a bond of direct personal allegiance between the two which subsequently it will be impossible to evade. It is deemed to be so important that, despite the time it takes up and the fatigue it involves, it has been carried through systematically from department to department to the end. Even Paris, where the Chief of State lives eleven months out of twelve, is called on to welcome him arrondissement by arrondissement, and its suburbs are not forgotten, however politically red they may be.

The protocol, method, and organization are by now completely run in. The composition of the cortège is unvarying; it is hemmed in by the security detail, with its various outriders and bodyguards; the programme is laid down in detail, minute by minute, each day filling ten or twenty pages of the little booklet marked "Secret" which is tirelessly consulted by ministers, civil servants and journalists, and the police escort: the order of stops between lunch (which is always at the sub-prefecture) and dinner (which is always at the prefecture, with its menu drawn up in Paris three weeks earlier); the stops of one to five minutes in villages and hamlets where the *conseil municipal*, presented by the mayor, who has himself been presented by the prefect, has no time to deliver its compliments before the stereotyped reply, the bouquet from the little schoolgirl, the handshakes and the car door which is already slamming while the gendarmes bustle about, anxious and exhausted; the lightning visit to the little town decked with bunting; the unsuccessful wait for an incident involving members of the labor unions, who after all come and applaud; the presentation of all the local officials and notabilities, the mayors

—"Ah! *messieurs les maires*, tell me about your water supply situation"—parliamentary and departmental representatives; the visit to the town hall, the university, the sterilizing plant, the museum; mass at the cathedral with a sermon by Monsignor, who is deeply moved; and always the crowd which is handled, embraced, provoked, exhorted, come rain, wind or snow. . . . The provincial tour is like a great procession of pilgrimage, with the Holy Sacrament, banners flying in the wind, clergy and pious crowds, devout maiden ladies bellowing out republican canticles after the sermon. . . .

A Few Words to the Inhabitants

The detailed programme of a presidential journey in the provinces indicates a dozen or so times during each day: "9.32 The general will address a few words to the inhabitants". These "few words" are, by definition, of purely local interest and object. In these circumstances no great national problem is touched on, except possibly by denying that it is being touched on. The model is unchanging and takes on the following pattern: "The welcome given by your delightful locality goes straight to the heart of the man who is speaking to you and who bears the responsibilities you all know. In the majestic shadow of your chateau (or "at the foot of your moving basilica;" or, failing that, "beside this smiling river") I can feel the encouragement and support this message brings me. I shall often look back to it, and in the hours which still lie before him, if God grants him life, General de Gaulle will draw the greatest comfort from the affection of (Montagules-Herbiers, Vandoeuvre-sous-Domecy, Hérissey-le-Petit). *Vive la France.*" Applause. The *Marseillaise* (one verse and chorus), a few more handshakes, then off again.

Short Speeches

These are reserved for the small towns, for third-class sub-prefectures. Unlike the "few words," which are spoken in village squares on the same level as the audience, the short speech is delivered either from the balcony of the town hall or from the top of its main steps, or from a rostrum—a makeshift platform which is difficult to mount and is sometimes shaky and rickety.

The short speech lasts about three to six minutes. It includes a local opening, a first section tinged with regionalism, allusions of varying length to the national situation and an optimistic conclusion looking to the future, youth and hope. Having saluted "beautiful and noble Pézenas," its first citizen and his councillors—"with such men at your head I have no worries for your future"—rustic wisdom and the skill of the winegrowers of lower Languedoc—"Yes, yes, I know your difficulties and your worries"—come Africa, the two great powers, or The Thing[1], according to the needs of the moment.

The phrases have already been aired and re-aired sixteen times; the pretended confidences tried out on at least ten occasions; the cadences rounded to perfection over the passing miles. The time is carefully measured. Then the return to essentials—renovation, recovery, which are grounds for a hope which is all the greater and more solidly founded "since we have our fine younger generation, so many of whom I see among you here" (adding, if there have been a few seditious cries, "and which is so very much alive.") Yes, they will receive our heritage in taking up the burden when we are no longer here. Yes, indeed, "Vive Pézenas, Vive l'Hérault, Vive la République, Vive la France!" Note that the last two terms are always uttered in that order and never reversed.

The Speech

At the beginning of de Gaulle's presidential term, the prefects and officials responsible for these official journeys invariably chose the largest open space in a city to erect the rostrum from which the general would speak, unless he was appearing at the balcony of a public building dominating that space. There were hitches; little by little, particularly if the weather was bad, the big squares were too large and seemed more than half deserted. Believing it was best, or determined to take no risks, the security men prevented all access by the crowd and allowed only carefully selected guests into the reserved area, armed with cards checked ten times over, and even then planted a respectful distance behind barriers. On the television news the general seemed to be speaking to a few hundred only; it looked dreadful. There had to be a change of policy.

From then on the main square was often passed over in favour of a smaller area. Specialists in mass demonstrations have long known that 5000 people packed into an area adequate for half that number look like 20,000 while 20,000 gathered in a place which could hold 50,000 seem to be only 5000.

The speech lasts, on average, 20 minutes. It is local, regional, national and international. It is addressed to supporters and opponents, to young and old, to pillars of the local community and the man in the street. It serves to launch phrases and try out ideas. It always includes one or two written passages on the essential points, intended to be quoted verbatim by the press and often distributed in duplicated form even before they have been uttered. It requires applause at the right places and not the wrong moment, and a prolonged ovation at the end. It provides material for exegesis and often the significance of an apparently unremarkable phrase only becomes evident later.

The Bath in the Crowd

This is an extraordinary and in some ways excessive spectacle. There is always a moment between the reception at the prefecture and the speech, before or after a ceremony or a visit, on arrival or departure from a town, when the general makes contact with the inhabitants. One sees him then, leaving his troop of officials standing, pushing the police to one side and throwing himself into the thickest part of the crowd like a rugby player.

To say he mingles with the crowd is an understatement; he plunges into it, wallows in it, positively melts into it. The eye can follow him less because of his size than because of the movement stirred up around his track. He disappears here, reappears for a moment there, vanishes again for a long submarine journey, surfaces like a diver at the other end of the street, frees himself and crosses to the other side for a further bout. He has been known to move forward in this manner down the narrow streets of old towns at a speed of ten feet a minute for a solid half hour while the procession marked time, the bodyguards panicked and the police were overwhelmed by the crowd.

He has been known to emerge with the sleeve of his uniform torn, three buttons ripped off, his hands scratched, his *képi* awry—and his eye gleaming with pleasure, joyful and happy to be alive. He has offered this choice spectacle to inhabitants of London and Hamburg, Milan and Dakar, Lille and Perpignan. In the streets along which he was going to pass the police have arrested Algerians with serrated knives, activists with loaded revolvers and even madmen armed with hypodermic syringes. It matters little to him; he believes in his destiny (*baraka*); he needs contact with the crowd as a continuing demonstration of his invulnerability, as the proof of his ascendancy, as a bath in the Fountain of Youth.

AN AUDIENCE WITH THE GENERAL

Invariable duration, half an hour. If it lasts longer than this, it is an event in itself. Request: presented to the secretary-general of the Elysée or to the *directeur du cabinet*. Summons: three days or six months after the request. Sometimes never. Date and time: indicated by mail as soon as the audience is granted; confirmed the day be-fore; final reminder the same morning. Cancellations and postponements: extremely rare.

It is advisable to be a little early (but not too early); to be armed with the summons and means of identification to show the guards; to make sure in advance—unless you are an official person of the first magnitude—that the *cabinet* has passed on the number of your car to the guard at the gate, otherwise the gates would remain obstinately closed and you would have to make a humiliating entry on foot.

After the customary check on his identity, the person who has been granted an audience is held in reserve first in the small waiting room which adjoins the offices of the *directeur de cabinet* and the general, and then with the *aides de camp* when the previous visitor has been taken in. In his turn, he is guided in and announced by the *aide de camp*, who quietly closes the door. The *tête-à-tête* begins. It can take one of three clearly distinguishable forms.

The Monologue

Scarcely is the visitor seated when the General begins to speak—and goes on speaking. The visitor has come to make a request, to explain a situation or the state of some problem, or to sound out the General's intentions. It matters little. His appearance, his name, a memory he calls to mind, or the assumed object of his visit sets off a monologue interwoven with allusions which are either kindly or have a didactic intent, with personal recollections or broad historical references and summary judgments. Sometimes the intention is quite simply to prevent the visitor, who dares not interrupt, from presenting a petition which is either known or guessed—and which is judged unacceptable. In other cases it is to bestow a confidence or to think aloud to some privileged visitor. Or, again, to try out on a single witness an idea, a phrase, a proposal which may perhaps be produced later before larger audiences. The thought is developed, broadens, the flights of eloquence succeed one another. The minutes pass; the audience ends. A last phrase as the door opens. The *aide de camp* is there. The visitor departs. He has been unable to put in a single word.

A certain general, a worthy man but of a highly self-effacing and modest disposition, found this surprising reproach conferred upon him at the door after a dazzling monologue: "You see, my dear comrade, what will always come between the two of us is YOUR colossal pride." A certain politician reported to his friends, "I told the General that. . . . I pointed out to him that. . . . I replied 'Oh! no, *mon général*, you have no right to say that!,'" miming an animated and argumentative conversation. On hearing of this account, de Gaulle simply shrugged his shoulders, not without satisfaction, "And to think I didn't even hear the sound of his voice."

Le Silence de la Mer

The visitor has prepared his case well. Brief opening, outline: the reasoning follows closely, the remarks are apposite; the conclusion is set out. The General seems to be listening. He does not interrupt; he makes no comment. Has he heard? It is far from clear. To clear the matter up, and since he must conclude, the visitor strengthens his voice and ends with a series of questions. In these circumstances, might I know what you have in mind? In the event of this explanation seeming convincing to you, would you consent to give the necessary instructions? Can I hope? Nothing. Still nothing. Silence. . . .

The visitor coughs and returns to his questions. His tone is more directly interrogative, more anxious and expectant. But one cannot go on indefinitely repeating the same questions in different terms indefinitely. He waits. Nothing. Still nothing. After an interminable moment the General rises. He says "Good," or he mutters and there seems to be distinguishable "Will see . . . will consider. . . ." In any case, he indicates that the audience is at an end.

He accompanies his visitor to the door. And there, as if gripped by remorse, he launches a phrase of utter finality. Most often it is a brutal dismissal. The secretary-general of a major political party, who came to seek his help and complain about the gaullists, was sent on his way with the following parting shot: "Let me tell you what you represent, Sir. You are an empty till, into which money is put which you don't even know how to use. Good day, Sir!"

The Dialogue

If this develops, it is disjointed, elliptical, jumping from one point to another. The general enquires, interrupts, asks another question, returns to a previous one. Often, disconcerted, the visitor launches into an explanation which is at once stopped short by an incongruous confidence or another request for enlightenment. True discussion or even real conversation are quite impossible except with particularly strong or experienced figures. It is a game consisting either in leading the visitor to contradict himself and give himself away so that the gap which has been opened in his argument can be enlarged pitilessly, or in pressing the lemon until it has given up its last drop of juice before casting it, exhausted, into outer darkness.

In some cases, when the general wants to captivate and dazzle, he offers the visitor a demonstration of his extraordinary memory. An important financier came to discuss a difficult but important technical problem with him. He prepared his remarks with the greatest care, drawing on the advice of his closest assistant. The text, polished and closely argued, had been learned by heart, rehearsed with a tape recorder. Introduced, invited courteously to sit down and explain himself, the banker developed his eleven points according to plan. Scarcely had he finished when the general spoke in turn. One by one, without forgetting or misstating a single one, he took up each of the eleven points and replied no less methodically. These were, it should be repeated, very detailed technical questions which were not conducive to improvisation. The visitor emerged overwhelmed and permanently won over.

Apart from these attempts to captivate, and also the frequently kindly remarks which are scattered through the audience—for if he wants to be the general can be agreeable, solicitous, full of humour, friendly, almost affectionate—the visitor most often leaves nursing his anxiety: Has he been listened to, understood? Has he been heard? There is nothing to show he has been. He has obtained neither the reply nor the approval nor even the tacit assent he was expecting. He will only know from the outcome of his visit—if it has one. Or perhaps a few days or months later will come a public speech or remark in which the visitor will recognize a phrase, expression or idea of his, even though he had come to think that nothing had been heard of his remarks. Such are the chances and risks of audiences.

SAYINGS OF THE GENERAL

One clue to the way a man sees himself and is seen by others lies in the anecdotes that circulate about him. Those centering on de Gaulle are legion, and only he could sort out the accurate from the apocryphal. The most one can say about the selection of incidents involving the General and politics which follows is that all of them *could* have happened. They not only show the General's preoccupation with himself as a historic personage, and his mordently ironical humor, but they add counterpoint to the loftier expression and analysis of his political views in earlier pages.

One day the former prime minister René Mayer asked de Gaulle, "what is your point of view on this question, *mon général?*" To which came the reply, "The most elevated. It is the least congested. . . ."

In wartime London, the General decided that the commissioner for foreign affairs in his wartime government was far too pliable. The unfortunate man was summoned and received a full volley of forceful language. Eventually he bridled at the criticism and sarcasm: "*Mon général*, you have no right to say that! I am as French and as patriotic as you are!"

The General was suddenly calm, and in a softer voice went on, "I know that you are as patriotic as I am, and that you are as French as I am. But I also know (and his voice suddenly swelled) that you are no longer commissioner for foreign affairs."

The General's contempt for danger has always made his aides tremble. His way of mingling with crowds during official journeys keeps them awake nights. One day one of the boldest among them picked up the courage to say, "But, *mon général*, the risks you take are enormous and . . ."

He was interrupted sharply. "Get one thing into your head," the General replied, "De Gaulle interests me only as a figure in history."

Editor's translations.

Soon after his return to power in 1958, de Gaulle received a delegation of labor leaders, one of whom remarked, *"Mon général,* as we have frequently explained to your predecessors . . ."

At which the General interrupted him. "Gentlemen, you have the wrong man. De Gaulle has no (and his voice sank in scorn) pre-de-ces-sors."

In 1958 the leaders of the UNR pleaded with de Gaulle to come out in support of their candidates in the parliamentary elections. Back came the reply, "Gentlemen, you ought to know that General de Gaulle belongs to no one." (There was an angry silence.) "And most particularly not to his supporters."

The referendum of April 1962 approving the Algerian settlement had just resulted in a 90 percent victory for de Gaulle. His Prime Minister, Michel Debré, rushed to the Elysée to hymn the victory.

"Just fancy," said the General, "ninety per cent of the votes. . . ." There followed a long, brooding silence. Then, suddenly, "But really, this country has gone *soft.*"

A month after joining the Pompidou government in April 1962, the MRP left it in protest at de Gaulle's attack at a press conference on the supporters of European integration. Immediately the political world proclaimed the disintegration and imminent collapse of the régime. Everyone waited with bated breath to see what de Gaulle's reaction would be. The following Wednesday, when the cabinet met, de Gaulle opened the proceedings thus: "Gentlemen, you are not unaware of recent incidents. (Silence.) Your ranks have been clarified. So has the situation. Now let us get on with the routine business on the agenda."

Received in audience by the General, one of his ministers, a political veteran, set out to undermine the position of one of his younger colleagues, deploring his lack of scruples and intellectual honesty, even his moral character.

Suddenly the General interrupted him. "All this is extremely reassuring. I had thought that ministers were capable of nothing. It is quite a change (and an icy glance fell on the accuser) to find one who is capable of anything!"

"The French think of nothing but increasing and increasing their standard of living. Steak and fried potatoes are fine. A family car is useful. But all that does not add up to a national ambition."

In September 1958, the Union for the New Republic was formed; its founders were unable to reach agreement on the nature of this new political party. Was it to be a party of the right, the left, the center, the center-left or the center-right? In despair they decided to consult the General himself.

The oracle handed down judgment: "Your party claims to serve de Gaulle?"

An approving and deferential murmur arose from the assembled loyalists.

"Then all this is completely meaningless. De Gaulle is not on the left. (A menacing silence fell.) Or on the right. Or in the center. De Gaulle is *above.*"

During the Algerian war a group of UNR deputies was foolhardy enough to ask the General why certain once fashionable slogans such as *"Algérie française"* and "integration" had been abandoned. The reply came, "A policy cannot be made out of regrets or slogans. Policy is firstly a matter of will (*silence*), and then of realities. . . ."

IV. *The Presidency*

J. E. S. Hayward

TRADITIONAL ATTITUDES TOWARDS THE PRESIDENCY

The present argument in France about the theory and practice of the presidency may owe much to the personality of President de Gaulle, but it is also rooted in differing views of politics in general and the office of president in particular which reach well back into French history—and indeed much of the history of France in the last century and a half has turned on them. J. E. S. Hayward here briefly summarizes the main strands in the continuing debate.

The economic and social harbingers of mass society in France, with its corollaries of the increasing use of the mass media and the increasing personalization of political leadership, met stubborn resistance. To appreciate some of the obstacles to change, particularly in relation to the Presidential office, let us look at the four major alternative attitudes to the Presidency since 1789. Because the parties are often divided within themselves on this issue, these approaches are attributed broad acres of the political spectrum.

Firstly, there is the traditional Jacobin and extreme left-wing view that a President of the Republic, in addition to a Committee of Public Safety or a Prime Minister elected by the National Assembly, is at best an unnecessary duplication and at worst a Conservative device to restrain the democratic process. At the end of the Second World War, de Gaulle briefly united the functions of head of state and head of the govern-

ment, but the Left's attempt to perpetuate this combination of functions in the Constitution of the Fourth Republic by eliminating the Presidency in favor of the Prime Ministership was defeated at the Constitutional referendum of May 1946.

Secondly, there is the traditional Bonapartist and extreme right-wing view that there should be a single head of the Executive, the President of the Republic, who would approximate as closely as possible to an absolute Monarch or dictator. The Vichy regime of Pétain represented an attempt to resuscitate such a system. Strong government, identified undiscriminatingly with authoritarianism, was for long regarded as essentially right-wing, but there has always been an important tradition in socialism and as this standpoint dislodged liberalism as the ideology of the Left, it became increasingly accepted that the Left, when it ceased to be in opposition to the government and actually controlled it, should be

From J. E. S. Hayward, "Presidentialism and French Politics," *Parliamentary Affairs* (1964–1965), XVIII, no. 1. Reprinted by permission of The Hansard Society for Parliamentary Government and of the author.

institutionally in a position to use it effectively to carry out its policies. In the 1950s, the inadequacies of the Fourth Republic, which was subsiding into a caricature of government by Assembly, led left-wing constitutional lawyers and political scientists like Professors Vedel and Duverger to advocate a popularly and directly elected President or Prime Minister as the sole head of the executive.

Thirdly, the Radical Left-Center has generally preferred a dual executive, with the President, as head of state, being markedly less powerful than the Prime Minister, as head of the government. The President would not be elected by universal suffrage as was Louis-Napoleon under the Second Republic but by Parliament in joint session as under the Third and Fourth Republics. However, in the French multi-party context, the President would not merely have the ceremonial and formal functions of a British Constitutional Monarch, but in a political system in which government instability was endemic, he would have the very delicate and influential function of selecting the Prime Minister. During the inter-war years, the tendency for the political complexion of the government to change from Left-Center to Right-Center in the life of each legislature, can be attributed in part to the finesse with which successive Right-Center Presidents manoeuvred at each governmental crisis.

Lastly, the Conservative Right-Center has traditionally also wanted to preserve a dual executive, but one in which the Head of State was more powerful than the Prime Minister. The Constitution of the Fifth Republic seemed originally an attempt to recapture this type of political system, of which the clearest examples were the Restoration and July Monarchies of the first half of the nineteenth century and the early years of the Third Republic—the *République des ducs* as Daniel Halévy described it—until the resignation of President MacMahon in 1877. In the inter-war years, Presidents Millerand and Doumergue made unsuccessful attempts to steer the Third Republic in this direction but both failed conclusively, despite the support of constitutional theorists such as Carré de Malberg and politicians such as Tardieu.

After being indirectly chosen as President of the Fifth Republic by an electoral college in which were collected about 80,000 predominantly Conservative members of that political class of 'intermediaries' for which he has always expressed the greatest contempt, de Gaulle decided that a future President would require the stamp of democratic legitimacy if he was to escape the ignominious fate of MacMahon. To the surprise of the party politicians of all shades of opinion who united to prevent the direct election of the President by universal suffrage and fought to preserve their position of privileged mediators of the popular will in an indirect or representative democracy, the proposal was sufficiently popular to lead to a Gaullist triumph in the Referendum of October 1962 and general election of November 1962. Their experience of the Third and Fourth Republics had convinced most Frenchmen that they could not trust their political elite to reform their ways and give up the past practice of making and unmaking governments within the walls of the *Palais Bourbon* without reference to the wishes of the electorate. The lack of the stable alliances based upon agreed programmes which in other Continental countries have helped to provide representative and effective coalition governments, despite their multi-party systems, has cut the link between electorate and government which alone gives the people the feeling of being represented. Power had fallen into the hands of the Parliamentary middlemen and the ability to participate directly in the choice of the head of the executive thus won the support of many Frenchmen of Right and Left-Center views for the Presidentialist orientation which de Gaulle was giving to the Fifth Republic. The changing style of French politics in which, as in the U.S.A. and Britain, images tend to obscure issues—a trend that is sometimes confused with 'depoliticization'

—has led to the establishment of an ersatz brand of direct democracy in which Presidential press conferences, plebiscites and provincial tours replace parliamentary pronouncements as the focus of political activity.

Michel Debré

THE CONCEPTION OF THE PRESIDENCY, 1958

As we have seen already, to Michel Debré the aim of the 1958 constitution was to provide France with stable parliamentary government; outright presidential rule was dismissed as inappropriate and even dangerous. In this further excerpt from his address to the Conseil d'Etat, Debré outlines his views on the place the president should hold in the Fifth Republic. What emerges here is certainly a prestigious and powerful figure, but one who seems somewhat remote, intervening to "arbitrate" when great questions of national interest were at stake, but surely not a constant day-to-day source of political decisions. For while he is referred to as the "keystone," Debré sums him up as a man with "no other power but that of appealing to another power." Doubtless Debré knew that de Gaulle would use his powers to the full; possibly this description of the office is how he imagined it after de Gaulle—but no such reservation reaches the reader.

If you will permit me a figure of speech borrowed from architecture, I will say that this new parliamentary system, and this Community which is about to take form, need a keystone. That keystone is the President of the Republic. . . Without a genuine chief of state, the cabinet—given the state of public opinion and our traditional quarrels—lacks the support which is normally essential for it. That means that the President of our Republic cannot be, as in other parliamentary systems, a head of state who names the prime minister and even other ministers, in whose name international negotiations are conducted and treaties signed, under whose authority are set the army and the administration. In our France, where internal divisions have such power on the political scene, he is the higher judge of the national interest. In this capacity, if he believes it useful he may ask for laws to be considered again before the expiration of the time allowed for promulgating them[1] (a provision previously contemplated and which is henceforth an established tradition). He can also—and these new powers are of considerable interest—refer laws to the constitutional council if he has doubts about their constitutionality. He can judge whether a referendum, which must be proposed to him by the prime minister or the president of the assemblies, corresponds to a national need. Finally he has that weapon which is all-important in any parliamentary system, the dissolution.

Is there need to emphasize what the dissolution represents? It is the instrument of governmental stability. It can be a reward for a government which seems to have succeeded, a punishment for a government which seems to have failed. It allows a brief

[1]Two weeks. [Editor's note.]

Editor's translation.

dialogue between the chief of state and the nation, which can settle a conflict or let the voice of the people be heard at a critical hour.

This rapidly sketched picture shows that the President of the Republic has, as is proper, no other power but that of appealing to another power: he appeals to Parliament, he appeals to the constitutional council, he appeals to the electorate. But this right to appeal is fundamental. . .

To these normal powers of the Chief of State, whether as President of the parliamentary Republic or as President of the Community, the draft constitution adds exceptional powers. So much has been said about these that they are no longer talked about, for undoubtedly some people were in a hurry to criticize them before reading them attentively. When circumstances of great gravity, whether internal or external, and clearly defined in precise language, prevent the operation of the organs of government, it is normal in our eventful age to seek to set on a basis of legitimacy. It is also normal, even indispensable, to fix certain basic responsibilities in advance. Concerning this article, much has been said about the past. Less has been said about the future, and yet it was drafted for the future. Can one, in 1958, disregard modern forms of warfare? The answer is clear: we have not the right either in this case or in others to disregard the possibility of serious disorder in our constitutional life. It is in case of such serious disorders that we must officially mark out the scope of responsibilities, that is, the possibilities of action.

His normal responsibility as Chief of State within a parliamentary system, his normal responsibility as Chief of State at the head of the Community, his extraordinary responsibility as Chief of State during the gravest crises: all this demands that special care shall be taken in appointing him.

Can we continue, as has been our tradition since 1875, to let him be chosen by the two chambers of Parliament? We know where such an electoral college leads: the president of the Republic is an arbiter between the parties making up Parliament, and this arbiter—however great his moral stature—would find great difficulty in escaping from the narrow domain in which he is confined less by constitutional provisions than by the means by which he is elected. The Republic and the Community need a personality who is far more than an arbiter between the parties, and it is scarcely probable that an electoral college limited to Parliament alone would produce the required result. Furthermore, in future, Parliament will be the Republic alone—that is, metropolitan France, the overseas departments and a few territories. Now representatives of the Community must be included if we are to underline from the very beginning the double role of the President of the Republic.

Universal suffrage does not produce a normal electoral body in a parliamentary system. A President elected by universal suffrage is a political leader tied to the daily work of government and exercising authority. To resort to universal suffrage is to resort to the presidential constitution which was ruled out for the reasons I gave at the beginning of this statement.

We are led, then, by the nature of things, to a college composed of elected representatives but not members of parliament alone—members of *conseils généraux* and *conseils municipaux*.[2] The only difficulty with this college arises from the great number of small communes and the relatively weak representation of the larger cities. This is a political problem, but we must realise that it arises from a national characteristic which must be accepted unless we are to be engulfed by ideology. France is composed of thousands upon thousands of communes: this is a fact of French life, one of the fundamental facets of our sociology. The drawbacks of this sizeable force of

[2]The department is the administrative subdivision next below the Republic. Each department (metropolitan France is divided into 94) has a *conseil général* with rather limited functions. Similarly every hamlet, village, town and city has its *conseil municipal*. [Editor's note.]

small communes must be corrected, it is true. The draft submitted to you grants fair representation to the big cities by allowing their *conseils municipaux* to elect additional electors in proportion to their population; furthermore, by reducing the representation of the *conseils municipaux* of the *communes* and small towns either to the mayor alone, or to the mayor and his deputies, or to a small number of *conseillers municipaux*, the draft re-establishes a reasonable equilibrium . . .

In order to ensure the legitimacy of the head of the French Republic, the body electing him must take a shape which conforms as closely as possible to that of political France. In order to ensure the legitimacy of the future head of the Community there must be fair representation of the member states in this electoral college. The draft seeks to meet that double objective. As you see, it does not amount to a device invented to ensure the election of General de Gaulle—who has no need of any such device! The draft has as its aim to rest the election of the President of the Republic in foundations which meet the needs of our century.

Michel Debré

THE CONCEPTION OF THE PRESIDENCY, 1962

Why was it that only four years after the constitution had come into force it was revised to provide for election of the president by universal suffrage? Here Michel Debré explains and justifies the change, revealing the way in which his own thinking about the presidency had altered over the four intervening years.

The 1958 constitution created a chief of state, first by providing that he should be chosen by a college of around a hundred thousand electors, drawn like the senatorial electoral college from departmental and municipal councils, then by granting him powers of the highest importance, including the right of dissolution, the referendum and extraordinary emergency powers. Beside the chief of state, and appointed by him in the first place, is the government with power to lay down policy, control the administration and direct the work of parliament. In other words, the 1958 constitution set out to give a fresh face to the power of the Republic. The keystone of the constitutional structure is no longer parliament but the president.

Did the reform go far enough? The presence of General de Gaulle, his authority, and the confidence the people had in him—in a word his legitimacy—both disguised and emphasized the problem. Disguised it because General de Gaulle has invested the office of chief of state with greater significance than the letter of the constitution actually conferred. Emphasised it because it was soon clear that the reform was in danger of being eradicated by a return to the past once General de Gaulle was no longer there.

What could be done to avoid such a mistake? Simple observation gave the answer. The Assembly, as the only organ elected by direct universal suffrage, was the only one issuing from the source of legitimate power. Thereby it was armed with a moral strength which would have inevitably

From Michel Debré, *Au Service de la Nation* (Paris: 1963), pp. 196–198. Reprinted by permission of Editions Stock. Editor's translation.

brought about a decline in the authority of General de Gaulle's successors, while governments would have had the greatest difficulty in maintaining their stability and independence, if account is taken of the constitutional amendments which were already being mooted.

Originally various reasons led to the electing of the chief of state by universal suffrage being ruled out. First, there was a personal reason which General de Gaulle himself has explained: he did not wish to give offense by an election which would have amounted to a personal plebiscite by the entire nation—which would surely have been the case in 1959. Other reasons reinforced the first. The heterogeneous character of the electoral college which included a great number of electors outside metropolitan France whose nationalism and ability to form alliances could have brought about absurd results. There were also memories of the nineteenth century precedent.[1] Finally there was the impossibility of introducing an American type constitution in France, with a separation of powers which, far from remaining theoretical might well have become a reality here, leading to constant opposition (between the president and the assemblies) because of our multiplicity of parties and the Communist Party.

It might perhaps have been possible to preserve the 1958 constitution in its original form. This would have required sincere acceptance of the new régime by the traditional political parties. It became clear very quickly that nothing of the sort had occurred. From the earliest months of the legislature the attitude of parliamentary circles both right and left gave ample ground for apprehension. Everything which amounted to a restraint on parliamentary omnipotence was viewed as a flaw which should be corrected at the first possible moment. Plans were carefully laid so that once the Algerian rebellion was over, the choice of

General de Gaulle's successor would give the signal for a return to a constitutional system founded on the old principles—that is, on the old errors.

Only an audacious measure could halt this offensive, while at the same time preserving the 1958 constitution and with it the possibility of France being governed. Facing the assembly elected by universal suffrage there must be another authority, also elected by universal suffrage, and having in consequence, the same legitimacy but capable of taking decisions and, because of its origins, able to oppose any perversion of the new institutional rules. That is why, with the African colonies independent and the Algerian war ended, General de Gaulle decided that his successor should be elected by the entire people.

The resulting quarrel was lively: a procedural consideration was advanced to justify its violence. There was also talk of the dangers of dictatorship—as if our society, with its strong labor unions and employers' organizations, its mass circulation newspapers and other channels of communication which are quite free of state domination would allow anyone to interfere with impunity with freedom of association and expression! Legalistic pretexts and historical analogies poorly camouflaged the real reason for their hostility. By giving the chief of state the seal of popular legitimacy, the reform raised an almost insuperable obstacle to the campaign for a return to pre-1958 constitutional rules and morality.

The people decided, and decided rightly.

Henceforth, the new features of our republican system of government give it a better chance of being defended against modifications and perversions by ensuring that legitimacy is shared. The Assembly has no longer a monopoly of universal suffrage; the chief of state even has the advantage thanks to his longer term of office and to the preference the mass electorate will rapidly acquire for choosing a man who is a national figure rather than choosing a

[1] i.e. Napoleon III. [Editor's note.]

host of parliamentarians, most of them purely local figures.

The President, henceforth a legitimate authority, has the appropriate powers to act as arbiter of the national interest and, in this capacity, to make the major choices and take the really important decisions. His term of office is not too long. It represents a tradition and, above all, France has such a need for stability that it seems to me vain to try to lop one or two years off his term. I would add that it is right for the president's term to be longer than the Assembly's. This gives the President a sense of higher authority which is essential to the conduct of his office. As for the president's rights: reference to the Constitutional Council, dissolution, referendum and special powers, there must be no curtailment

of these. We must never forget that while the French are a difficult people to govern at the same time they feel a profound need to be governed! The President of the Republic can prevent the undermining of the executive, threaten the Assembly with having to face the voters, submit major policy options to the entire nation and strengthen the authority of the State in the face of grave and immediate danger to it. For these reasons, without necessarily insisting on acting as head of the government in everyday matters, and without claiming to be the effective leader of the parliamentary majority from now on in respect of all major problems, he will be able to represent the highest thought and the supreme will which, in any régime, make up the legitimacy of the sovereign.

DE GAULLE AND THE PRESIDENCY

Any consideration of the presidency in the Fifth Republic must obviously give pride of place to the man who reflected upon the office for so many years, and who became the first to occupy it. The following passages contain some of de Gaulle's most important statements on the presidency, and thus are documents of fundamental importance in understanding the present régime. In particular they show the changing terms in which he describes the presidency, and the increasingly direct assertions of presidential authority; his views on the election of the president by the entire nation, his objections to the adoption of a full-blooded, overtly presidential system, and finally his own comment on the criticisms that France under de Gaulle has become a system resting on "personal power."

Presentation of the constitution, Paris, 4 September 1958.

"It is therefore for a people such as we are, for the century and the world in which we live, that this proposed Constitution has been drafted. The country is guided effectively by those to whom it gives the mandate and grants that confidence which

alone creates legitimacy. *A national arbiter, above the political struggle, elected by citizens who themselves hold elected office, charged with ensuring the normal functioning of institutions, having the right of recourse to the judgment of the sovereign people,*[1] responsible at a time of extreme peril for the independence, the honor and the integrity

[1]Here and subsequently italics are mine. [Editor's note.]

Editor's translation.

of France and for the safety of the Republic. A government made to govern, and which is left the time and the opportunity to do so, which, never straying from its appointed task, thereby merits the support of the country. A Parliament intended to represent the political will of the nation, to vote laws, to keep check on the Executive without venturing to overstep its role. A government and Parliament which work together but retain their separate responsibilities, with no member of one allowed to be, at the same time, a member of the other. Such is the balanced structure that power should assume. The rest will depend on men."

Broadcast to the nation on being elected president, 28 December 1958.

"Above all, men and women of France, I want to tell you that I accept the mandate you have conferred upon me . . .
Guide of France and head of the republican state, I shall exercise the supreme power in all the breadth that it now involves, and according to the new spirit which led to its being awarded to me."

October 1960.

"The State will not allow its duty and its responsibilities to suffer encroachment. It will not allow persons who have acquired a certain position in politics, the unions, the armed forces or the press to claim to have a say in the conduct of France. *The conduct of France belongs to those whose responsibility it is. It therefore belongs first and foremost to myself.* I say so without any circumlocution."

30 December 1961.

"I am not in favor of a presidential system, for here in France conflict between the President and Parliament would be inevitable. This may of course be regrettable, but

only two parties. It is not like in Britain where M. Macmillan is to all intents and purposes elected by universal suffrage. The President of the Republic should not get mixed up in parliamentary quarrels. It is the Prime Minister who is the head of the parliamentary majority. The present system will continue; moreover the country approves the present constitution."

Broadcast address to the nation during the referendum campaign, 20 September 1962.

"If the President of the Republic is to be able to bear and exercise such a burden, he must have the explicit confidence of the Nation. Allow me to say that when I took the head of State again in 1958, I thought that in this respect historical events had already done what was needed for me personally. By virtue of what we have willed and achieved together, through so much trouble, tears and blood, but also so much hope, enthusiasm and success, there is an exceptional bond between you and me, men and women of France, which confers on me both power and obligations. Thus I did not lay particular importance on the details of the procedure by which I was to be selected, since that had been done in advance by the nature of the situation. Furthermore, taking into account political susceptibilities, some of them respectable, I preferred, at that time, that I should not become the subject of a personal plebiscite. In short, I agreed to the initial draft of our Constitution providing for the election of the President by a relatively restricted college of about 80,000 elected representatives.

But although this electoral system, no more than any other, could not settle my responsibilities towards France or by itself alone express the confidence the French people feel in me, the question will be very different for those who, of necessity, not having received the same national mark from events, will come after me in turn to take the post I at present occupy. If they are to be entirely capable of bearing the supreme burden, whatever its weight, and entirely obliged to do so, and if also our Republic is to continue to have a good chance of remaining solid, effective and popular despite the demons of our divisions, they must receive their mission directly from the whole body of citizens. Without there being any need to modify the respective rights or reciprocal relations between the executive, legislative and judicial powers as laid down in the Constitution, but with a view to maintaining and consolidating in the future our institutions in relation to factious enterprises from whatever quarter, or in relation to the manoeuvers of those who, from good motives or bad, want to lead us back to the baleful system of the past, I consider it right to make this proposal to the country: when my term ends, or if death or illness should interrupt before its end, the President of the Republic should from henceforth be elected by universal suffrage."

Broadcast address to the nation during the referendum campaign, 4 October 1962.

"From the beginning I knew that before the end of my term I would have to propose such a decision [to elect the president by universal suffrage] *to the country. But pressing reasons lead me to take this initiative now, as I have the right and duty to do."*

"Press conference". 31 January 1964.

"A Constitution consists of a conception, institutions and their application.

As far as our own is concerned, its conception is derived from the need to ensure that organs of government have the effectiveness, stability, and responsibility which were structurally lacking under the Third and Fourth Republics. . .

A system which left authority at the mercy of the parties, which vegetated amidst compromises, which was obsessed by its own crises, was unfit to conduct our country's affairs. That is why in accordance with the conception of the new Constitu-

tion, *although a Parliament is retained to legislate, it is so ordered that authority shall no longer be a partisan possession, but that it shall emanate directly from the people, which implies that it shall flow from and be held by the Head of State elected by the nation.* This is what was accomplished as everyone could see, when I returned to the direction of affairs and then when I took up the duties of the Presidency. . .

As for the distribution of powers, it has been observed as our Constitution prescribes. Distinct functions are assigned: to the President, guarantor of the destiny of France and of the Republic, charged therefore with momentous responsibilities and disposing of extensive authority; to the Government, appointed by the Head of State, meeting around him to decide and apply policy, and directing the administration; to Parliament, exercising legislative power and supervising the activities of the ministry. The fulfilment of these functions has met the exigencies of the will of the country, the conditions in which we find ourselves, and the obligation to conduct affairs in a vigorous, firm and consequent manner.

It is true that, concurrently with the conception and the text, there has been the application. In part this has naturally depended upon men. As for the Head of State, it is quite obvious that his *personal equation* has been significant and I should be surprised if this had not been expected from the beginning. As for the ministers and above all the Premiers: first M. Michel Debré and then M. Georges Pompidou, they have both acted with evident effectiveness, but in their own—and quite dissimilar—ways. Finally, the first and second Parliaments of the present régime have, each in turn, given a different stamp to the work and outlook of the legislature. It must also be said that for over five years our institutions have had to function in very changeable conditions, including at certain times the threat of serious attempts at subversion. But this test of men and circumstances has indeed shown that the instrument answers to its purpose . . .

[President de Gaulle went on to attack advocates of further constitutional change, including those who] making the best of a bad job, advertise their acceptance of a real Head of State—but only on condition that Parliament, for its part, be built up into an impregnable citadel, in which the parties would regain their safety and their sway. They evince a preference, . . . rather recent on their part, for a so-called "presidential" régime which would be analogous to that of the United States. "Let the President," they say, "be elected by the people at the same time as the National Assembly and himself assume the executive power; but, on the other hand, let Parliament wield exclusive legislative power. Above all let each be strictly confined within its own domain, and have no power over the other: the President unable to dissolve Parliament, Parliament unable to oust him." Thus, these neophytes allege, the government would be concentrated in the hands of a single man, which would avoid the inconvenience of authority divided between a President and a Prime Minister, while Parliament, finding itself absolutely secure, would accept or reject bills and the budget as it saw fit.

It cannot be denied that a Constitution of this sort has managed, up to the present, to muddle along in the United States, that is in a country that, because of its ethnic composition, its economic wealth, and its geographical position has never known an invasion, nor even, for a century, a revolution; in a country with only two political parties which are divided on no essential point in any area, national, social, moral, or international; lastly, in a federal country where the government assumes only general tasks—defense, diplomacy, finance—while it rests with the 50 states of the Union to attend to all the rest. But how could such a system suit the French nation, very strongly centralized by the long struggle of the centuries; for seven generations victim of every internal and external shock and still liable to undergo others; and where the many political parties are, except

for the one which foments disruption, divided and unstable?

First, because France is what she is, the President must not be elected at the same time as the deputies, for that would confuse his selection with the direct struggle of the parties, and would alter the character and reduce the term of his office. Furthermore, it is not normal practice for us to have one and the same man as both President of the Republic and Prime Minister. *Indeed it would be quite unacceptable to have a dyarchy at the top. But that is precisely what we do not have.* In fact the President, who according to our Constitution is the man of the nation, which has put him in that position to answer for its destiny, the President, who chooses the prime minister as well as the other ministers, who is entitled to change him, either because the prime minister has completed the task assigned to him by the President who wishes to keep him in reserve for a future occasion, or because he no longer has the President's approval; the President, who formulates the decisions taken in the cabinet, promulgates laws, negotiates and signs treaties, enacts or rejects the measures which are proposed to him, is commander-in-chief of the armed forces, appoints to public offices; the President who in time of peril must take it upon himself to do all that is necessary; *clearly it is the President alone who holds and delegates the authority of the State.* But the very nature, the extent, the duration of his task imply that he not be absorbed without remission or limit by political, parliamentary, economic and administrative situations of the moment. That, on the contrary, is the lot, as complex and meritorious as it is essential, of the French prime minister.

Certainly there can be no watertight separation between the two planes on which on the one hand the President, and on the other the man who seconds him, daily perform their tasks. Moreover, cabinet meetings and conversations are there to allow the Head of State to define as required the orientation of national policy, and to permit ministers, and the premier first of all, to put their points of view, explain their activities in detail, and report on the execution [of policy]. Sometimes, on a subject so important everything depends on it, the two planes overlap and in this case the President makes whatever distribution of tasks he judges necessary. But as it must of course be understood that the indivisible authority of the State is confided in its entirety to the President by the people, who have elected him, that *no other authority exists, neither ministerial nor civil nor military nor judicial, which is not conferred and sustained by him*, and finally that it is his business to relate the supreme domain which is his own with those areas whose management he assigns to others—so in ordinary times everything bids us preserve the distinction between the functions and fields of action of the Head of State and of the prime minister.

However, those who have not yet freed themselves from the conceptions of former days sometimes object that the government, which is that of the President, is at the same time responsible to Parliament. How can this be reconciled? The answer is that the sovereign people, in electing the President, invest him with their confidence. That is, indeed, the crux of the matter and the essential feature of the changes achieved. In virtue of this, the Government, named by the Head of State and whose members, moreover, may not sit in Parliament, no longer has anything like the same relation with the two houses that it had when it exclusively issued from party cabals. Also, the relations between the ministry and Parliament are so arranged by the Constitution, that a vote of censure is provided for only in conditions which give an extraordinarily grave character to such a rupture. In this extreme case, the President, who has the duty of assuring the continuity of the State, also has the means to do so, since he can appeal to the nation to judge the dispute by way of a new election, or a referendum, or the two together. Thus there is always a democratic solution. On the contrary, if we were to adopt the American system, there would be none. In a country such as ours, the fact that the Head of State was also Prime Minister and would find himself unable to refer back to the voters in case of a legislative or budgetary blockage, while Parliament would be unable to oust him, would lead ineluctably to the chronic opposition of two indestructible powers. The outcome would be either general paralysis, or an imbroglio which could be resolved only by a pronunciamento, or finally the resignation of a feeble president, who on the pretext of avoiding catastrophe might choose to surrender to it by submitting, as in the old days, to partisan pressures. It is possible to suspect that it is this third alternative which the unexpected champions of the "presidential system" most readily cherish.

"Press Conference," 9 September 1965.

Of course the Constitution which the French people, who had been enlightened by so many lessons, gave the Republic in 1958, grants the power to legislate and the right to scrutiny to parliament. For in the conduct of public affairs there must be debate and balance. But the new element of capital importance in our constitution is, on the one hand, the advent of the people collectively as such as the direct source of the power of the Chief of State and one to which he can, if need be, appeal directly, and on the other hand the *granting to the president who is, and who alone is, the representative and agent of the entire nation, of the duty to lay down both its course in essential fields and the means to carry it through.* It is in virtue of this two-fold creation, and because it has been fully operative that the present regime has been armed with the stability, authority and effectiveness which have enabled it to resolve the grave problems with which France was confronted, and to direct affairs in such a way that today her position seems better and more secure in every way than yesterday. . . .

There has been some talk about "personal power." If this means that the President of the Republic has taken personally the decisions it fell to him to take, the term is quite correct. In what post, whether high or low, has the holder the right to evade his responsibilities? And anyway, did anyone ever really believe that once General de Gaulle was called to the helm he would be content with opening flower shows? For example, when the whole of France was preoccupied (which is the least one can say) by the Algerian problem, who but he was, with a single voice, assigned the task of resolving it? But if [by personal power] it is meant that the president has cut himself off from everything and everyone, and that he has listened to himself alone before acting, this is quite contrary to the evidence. What a host of opinions and consultations he has armed himself with! So far, during his term of office, the Chief of State has held 302 cabinet meetings and 420 meetings with groups of ministers; he has received the prime minister in his office 605 times; the presidents of the assemblies 78 times; one or other member of the government almost 2000 times; the presidents or reporters of parliamentary committees or the presidents of parliamentary groups more than a hundred times; senior civil servants, experts, union leaders around 1500 times, not to mention the letters, minutes and reports which people in positions of responsibility have sent him, or the files he has studied. Again, taking external problems, some six hundred hours of conversations with heads of state or heads of foreign governments, and a thousand talks with their ministers or ambassadors have generously supplemented the president's knowledge. In any case, at his level no important measure has been taken except after he has brought together and heard the views of those who knew the problem thoroughly and would see to its execution. Moreover, this was quite natural. For public affairs are today too varied and complicated to be dealt with in any other way. In

such matters the danger is less that fiats will be issued from the top of an ivory tower than that interminable examinations will produce no decision.

However, it is above all the people themselves with whom the man who is their agent and guide keeps in direct contact. For this is the way in which the nation can know personally the man who is at its head, perceive the ties which unite it to him, keep abreast of his ideas, his actions, his plans, his cares and his hopes. And it is at the same time in this way that the Chief of State has the chance to make the French people feel that, whatever their region or condition, they are all by the same token citizens of one and the same country, and to learn what is the state of things and of their hearts and minds by going to see for himself, and, finally, to feel, in the midst of his fellow-countrymen, what obligations their encouragements lay upon him.

I do not believe such contacts have ever been so numerous as during the last seven years. Thirty talks to the whole country on radio and television; 12 press conferences broadcast in full; 36 major speeches at public ceremonies; a series of journeys extending to the 94 departments in France and overseas—quite apart from at least two hundred official appearances in Paris—during which the Chief of State has seen fifteen million Frenchmen with his own eyes, invited all members of parliament, all the *corps constitués*, all departmental councillors, all the mayors of France to confer with him, visited 2500 communes including all the largest ones, replied in town halls to the welcome of almost 400 municipal councils and 100,000 local dignitaries, spoken to the assembled populace in more than 600 places, spoken with more people than can possibly be counted, and shaken innumerable hands.

In sum, the President of the Republic, chosen by the national majority, is now the keystone which covers and welds the structure of our institutions together. How can it be disputed that as a result of this the organs of government are now held in balance? The cohesion of the government — which, moreover, has had only two prime ministers in seven years, both invested, supported and maintained by the confidence of the Chief of State — is a new fact and an example compared with the discordance of the chance collections of individuals which used to go by the name of "ministries." From this comes continuity and an obvious improvement in the effectiveness of the work of government and the administration of the country. . . .

Perfection is not to be found in this world. But compared with what it was before, the French State now appears entirely transformed both as to soundness and capability. Nobody in the universe thinks otherwise.

Georges Vedel

ARGUMENTS FOR A PRESIDENTIAL SYSTEM

Professor of Law at the University of Paris, long prominent in left-wing movements, Georges Vedel has been one of the most ardent campaigners for an avowedly presidential system ever since the later years of the Fourth Republic. After succinctly reiterating his case he rebuts the criticisms of his opponents.

Firstly, there is no democratic alternative to such a system. The present system is more and more a plebiscitary consulate, and however sincere the defenders of "rationalized parliamentarianism" may be, this would in practice restore the political morality and practices of the Fourth Republic, which taught us how much mere "formulae" are worth in keeping a parliamentary system alive in a country which lacks the only firm foundation for such a system: a vigorous, coherent party system. Everyone knows a return to impotence and constant change would open the way to all manner of subversion and desperate measures.

In the second place, a presidential system would allow France to achieve the essential characteristics of a modern democracy which are found in every successful system of government: direct choice of the head of the executive and his team, first by selection within the parties then by election by the voters; the combining in the electoral process of the choice of leaders and the choice (in very general terms) of a policy; the change in the notion of political responsibility, which would no longer mean the sanction in legislative-executive relations, but the sanction resulting from the nation's choice between a political group which has governed and legislated for several years, and an opposition offering an alternative policy. Neither a traditional nor a "rationalized" parliamentary system can bring this about in France because of the nature of our national life, but a presidential framework could. The very nature of the election of the Chief of State would compel a degree of polarization of political life around two great political confederations, which would not be solid enough to support a true parliamentary system dependent on a thoroughly coherent majority, but coherent enough for the sort of collaboration between the arms of government that a presidential system can get by with.

Those who propose such a solution are

From Georges Vedel, "Vers le Système Présidentiel," *Revue Française de Science Politique* (February, 1964), pp. 21–23, 28–31. Reprinted by permission of *Revue Française de Science Politique*. Editor's translation.

fully aware of its risks and dangers—of which more later. But they believe that to a large extent these can be warded off, and that in any case all other solutions seem to them to be clearly more dangerous, less satisfactory and either inherently or in practice non-democratic. So, looking to the lessons American experience can teach us rather than seeing it as a model, they believe that the way to develop French democracy lies through the presidential system. The establishment of such a system without either sham or trickery would lead to the suppression of the prime minister's responsibility to the National Assembly, to guaranteeing the Chief of State and parliament equality in the use of such weapons as dissolution and referendum, and to expunging from the constitution the various provisions which at present allow the President to enjoy both the authority conferred on him by a fixed term and election by universal suffrage with the weapons which in a true parliamentary system are traditionally wielded by the government, but which the Chief of State has appropriated for himself. Of course the length of the presidential term would have to be reduced to four or five years.

How would the establishment of a "genuine" presidential system diminish the likelihood of conflict since it would include, if not the suppression of the office of prime minister—which is defensible on grounds of the efficient division of labor—then at least the elimination of the responsibility of the government to the Assembly? Would it not, rather, aggravate them by leaving a president elected by universal suffrage face-to-face with a parliament which, as François Goguel has rightly observed, will revert instinctively to the tradition of parliamentary sovereignty?

These questions can only be answered by trying to gauge the structural changes the presidency could bring to our public life, responding to changes elsewhere in society, and by trying to show that retention of the presidential-parliamentary amalgam which is the heart of the present constitution would hinder and harm these changes. It is quite true that a presidential system, like any other democratic system, presupposes vigorous and coherent parties. But hopes of seeing this have far less chance of being realized if our political institutions promote the dispersion of political forces.

The election of the president by universal suffrage constitutes the most effective stimulus to regrouping and concentration. It will no doubt not provide France with a two-party system on the English model—if we would achieve that here there would be no objection to a parliamentary system. But it is quite probable that it will produce two or three large confederations of political forces something like the American parties, which show little centralization and unity outside presidential election campaigns. This result would be gravely compromised if we were to make the prime minister and his government an autonomous organ responsible to the National Assembly, as the letter of the present constitution provides. . . .

Whether we like it or not, whether he likes it or not, the President, elected by universal suffrage, will be the motor of the nation's policy. Instead, the intention is to place a shock absorber between the President and the Chambers, to prevent every conflict between the two from automatically turning into a crisis—in sum to allow the Chief of State to join in only the most important battles. . . .

The virtue of the presidential system is to settle the question of who governs for a fixed period—of at least seven years. A Chamber will cooperate more willingly with the executive if it knows that though it can hinder it in many ways it cannot dismiss it or change its makeup. A coherent parliamentary opposition and majority will be formed far more easily if it is known that the only real political battle will be fought before the electors, and will call for a degree of solidarity and unity, than if these possibilities are obscured by almost daily parliamentary skirmishes which will foster the instinct to disperse.

55

Having said that, it is clear that since the presidential system presupposes restoring to parliament its full powers over legislation, finance, and the control of foreign policy, there must be "harmony" between the president and his team on one hand and the Chambers on the other. Believers in the presidential régime, who hold fewer illusions about the operation of American institutions than is usually realised, are well aware that the real difficulties begin with this search for "harmony," and there is a risk of conflict between a president who has need of laws and money if he is to govern and a parliament which can refuse him both.

But there must be an effort of imagination, for the American formula is clearly inadequate in the French context. Undoubtedly, it shows us the usefulness of a genuine jurisdictional control applying equally to the President and the Chambers and which, if it certainly cannot resolve every conflict can at least avoid or unravel legal conflicts, which are not always the least irritating. No doubt a French presidential system would also involve big and little "deals" between the executive and the legislature, between ministers and members of parliament. But we must go beyond this to ensure "harmony" and prevent conflicts.

We must first make the parliamentary term begin with and last the same length of time as the President's term. The elections of the President and the National Assembly should take place at the same time, so that the Assembly should resemble the President as closely as possible. After all, such an initial agreement does offer some guarantees about the future of the legislature. The danger of conflict between the executive and the legislature would not thereby be eliminated, far from it. Accordingly, one would have to provide a means of resolving major conflicts between the President and the National Assembly when all attempts at conciliation had failed. This is where the French and American roads diverge. In the United States there is no way of letting the electorate make the final decision in such a situation. While the renewal of the entire House and a third of the Senate every two years provides arbitration at fixed dates, and maintains the concert between the two arms of government under the almost permanent control of public opinion; for obvious reasons there can be no question of imposing such a rhythm on French elections. We must therefore organize a system allowing the electors to give their decision on vital issues over which the executive and the legislature are in disagreement.

This cannot be achieved by the dissolution in the form in which our constitution prescribes it. It depends on the Chief of State alone, and if he fears the electoral outcome he can evade it and, even if he does employ it, his own term of office is never in danger. Taken together with the possibility of resort to referendum on constitutional and legislative matters, this puts an overwhelming arsenal of weapons at the President's disposal, and goes beyond the desired aim by ensuring, instead of a concert between the two powers, the ascendancy of one over the other.

Pierre Mendès-France

A PRESIDENTIAL SYSTEM FOR FRANCE?

Like President de Gaulle, Mendès-France rejects the argument that France would be better off with a full-fledged overtly presidential system. Though he seems to share with de Gaulle a degree of distaste for the American model (*cf.* p. 51), a comparison of the two critiques of the presidential system shows that they converge from quite differing conceptions of politics and the state.

It is worth trying to imagine how a presidential system would function in a country such as France.

How, under this system, would conflicts between the two elected chambers and the President, and disputes between the chambers themselves, be resolved? When confronted by an Assembly whose very nature prevents it from being monolithic, since it represents the divided opinions of the country, is there not a great temptation for one man, who has been swept into power by the electorate, to use the very real power and considerable political prestige at his disposal against other institutions, and so against the interests of freedom?

Unless the Constitution provides some means of settling such disagreements, unless one of the authorities has the right to impose its will on the others and so prevent a situation arising to which there is no legal solution, there must be a risk of encouraging irresistibly a man who is sure of his popularity and has at his disposal all the modern means of communication to abuse his trump cards in order to overcome opposition. Should he himself hesitate to do this, it is easy to imagine the pressure that would be brought to bear on him by his Party and his advisors who would be continually obsessed by the fear of losing the next election. A statesman, after all, is always sincerely convinced that his policy is the best one. Under these conditions how could he possibly resist the desire to pursue this policy at all costs, even if it meant a few incursions into illegality?

The United States is the only country in the world in which the presidential system has ever worked normally. But, apart from the danger of acting on the inspiration of a single precedent, it must be clearly understood that the United States is a federal state and therefore there is no risk of the President's acquiring too much personal power. For many years the President of the United States possessed only very limited powers: the real authority, financial control and the machinery of administration were in the hands of the different states. This was the framework within which the system was first drafted and began to work. There has certainly been a gradual increase in presidential powers; but the initial context is always very important to the life of any political system, and here it differs profoundly from that of France. Then again, presidential powers in the United States are still limited today. If the President of the United States should wish to overstep his rights he would find the elected governors and assemblies of the majority of the

From *A Modern French Republic* by Pierre Mendès-France, pp. 35–40. © 1962, Editions Gallimard. English translation © 1963 by George Weidenfeld and Nicolson Ltd. Reprinted by permission of Hill and Wang, Inc.

states aligned against him, with their administrative bodies, police forces, radio and television stations, financial resources and so on. There would be a new war of secession, in which the President would be defeated from the outset. For this reason disputes between the White House and the Capitol can only lead, at the worst, to stagnation and immobility and the deferment of decisions and reforms. There are countless examples of this in the history of the United States, and it is really remarkable that the advocates of a presidential régime have never taken any notice of them. But everything goes to show that the American system would take on quite a different and a singularly disturbing appearance if it were transplanted to as strongly centralised a country as France: instead of stagnation and immobility it would lead to an explosion.

The last and most serious objection to this régime is that, beneath the democratic façade of a dual election, there is a very real risk of draining the lifeblood from the country's democratic spirit and activity.

When the people elect an Assembly they are voting for parties whose principles they already know, at least as far as general policy is concerned; they are choosing specific programmes and proposals. When, on the other hand, the electorate places one man at the head of the state they are voting for him personally. Literally they "put their trust in him," they rely on him, and they sometimes do so on the basis of more or less spurious promises. In this respect American presidential campaigns tend towards a mediocrity which one hardly wishes to see imported into France.

An election of this kind cannot provide an authentic element of political control; it even tends to make the electorate lose interest in politics, encourages it to abdicate, to develop the habit of not exercising its rights and of taking little interest in the affairs of state. At a time like the present, nothing could be more dangerous. Encourage the nation in the belief that everything will be decided without its intervention, and you present an unlooked-for chance for

adventurers. You protect them from the only force able to hold them in check: a people which has made its choice between the policies and solutions put to it, and which means to see that its choice is respected.

Certain other conditions of French political life cannot be passed over in silence when the presidential system is under consideration. De Gaulle has created a number of precedents: by reducing the position of the Assemblies; by the use he has made of the Constitution and by the interpretation he has given to it, and imposed on it by his use of the referendum. If a presidential system based on the American pattern were to be established in France tomorrow, it would be very difficult to persuade the next President to move backwards. It is true to say that, by his abuses and exaggerations, de Gaulle has made any attempt at an authentic, balanced presidential system even more difficult.

Moreover, in France today the election of a head of state by means of universal suffrage presents other difficulties which stem from the present division of public opinion. The American system is based on the existence of two huge parties engaged in a struggle for power. Because of this the presidential election can, in fact, be summed up by a ballot. This gives the system an undoubted clarity and avoids many tiresome combinations and intrigues. In France, the bulk of the electorate is split up into numerous parties, and although everyone deplores this fact, it cannot be remedied; or at least not from one day to the next. This proliferation of parties makes it impossible to elect a president after a single ballot and all sorts of arrangements and concessions are inevitable between ballots. Even so, there is nothing to show that the president will obtain an absolute majority, or that a candidate whose initial poll was very small might not scrape in and consequently be unable to face strong oppositions throughout his term of office. This is something which has often been criticised in local elections; in this limited field, it presents only very minor inconveniences after all but it becomes very serious on a national level. This is no way to choose the supreme arbiter of the nation, the symbol of unity and of the will of the people.

If we study these hypotheses still more closely, it is not difficult to predict that candidates in a nation-wide contest will try to mobilise the greatest possible number of votes by resorting to the kind of over-simplified arguments which have already proved their worth in earlier campaigns. For the spokesman or spokesmen of the right, anti-communism is a convenient way of side-stepping more awkward subjects, as well as a way of uniting moderates and extremists and helping to win over doubtful or nervous voters from the center. It is easy and tempting to denounce the red peril — not so much with a view to damaging a Communist candidate who stands no chance of being elected but to dissuade the electors from giving their vote to a socialist or democratic candidate who, it is implied, will receive the floating Communist vote in the second round and is therefore as good as in the pay of Moscow. . . .

There is no possibility of avoiding this trap. The Communist Party represents some twenty to twenty-five per cent of the electorate, so that its candidate will come fairly high up in the poll and will always be in a good position to play a decisive part in the second round of an election. This is another fact which can neither be denied nor ignored. . . .

What would be the final result? The easily aroused fear of Communism would, as is intended, lead to a mass movement from the center towards the right.

The left will soon realise this and half the country will reject a system which gives its views no chance. Also the right will have a permanent advantage and a hold on the executive, and if the National Assembly is left wing, conflict between it and the President will be inevitable from the very first day.

Those who advocate a presidential system are therefore endangering the whole political future of the nation in their anxiety to strengthen the executive without departing from the ways traced — whether they like it or not — by Gaullism, rather than by looking for a solution in some other direction. Without realising it, they are moving backwards to the Bonapartist orbit which has dogged the country persistently for the last century and a half and has led to catastrophic set-backs each time it has come to the fore.

Maurice Duverger

THE FUTURE OF THE PRESIDENCY

We can only speculate about the eventual importance of the presidency in the Fifth Republic, should the régime outlive its creator. Plainly, in the hands of a less exceptionally prestigious figure, redistribution of power seems inherently probable. Some commentators would even see a possibility of the constitution reverting to something approximating to the distribution of power originally conceived by Michel Debré in 1958, and functioning as a fairly conventional parliamentary system. Maurice Duverger, one of the most tireless campaigners for the adoption of a full-blooded presidential system, argues here that such

Le Monde, 30 November 1965. Reprinted by permission. Editor's translation.

thoughts are outdated. After the constitutional amendment introducing universal suffrage for the election of the president, the inherent weight of the office
has changed.

Many legal commentators make the mistake of considering that the 1962 reform
deals solely with the means by which the
President of the Republic is elected and not
with his powers. Appearances are in their
favor. Strictly speaking the 1962 document
changes only the system by which the
Chief of State is elected, not his prerogatives as laid down in 1958. But universal
suffrage is not a procedure or a technique,
it is also the very basis of sovereignty in a
western democracy. Article 3 of the constitution says this quite clearly: "National sovereignty belongs to the people, who exercise it through their representatives and by
way of referendum." The "representatives
of the people" are those the people themselves have elected. Even if article 3 did not
exist, the situation would be exactly the
same. In a democracy, sovereignty—that is,
the power of ultimate decision—belongs to
the people. The more directly a man or institution issues from the people, the greater
its authority.

In a normal parliamentary system the
government is far more powerful than the
Chief of State because it is closer than he is
to national sovereignty, by means of its
responsibility to the people's elected representatives. A parliamentary monarchy in
no way rests on this sovereignty; a parliamentary president only rests on it very tenu-
ously by means of a very indirect election.
Then it is accepted that the Chief of State
cannot even exercise in practice the powers
the constitution nominally grants him, and
that decisions are taken by the responsible
ministers. It must be stressed that this interpretation leads to the letter of the constitution being disregarded, by giving the
general principles of the system it regulates
precedence over it. If one is to break away
from a literal interpretation of the constitution in this manner, the constitution-makers'
determination to establish a traditional

parliamentary system must be quite clear.
Even in its original form the 1958 constitution left some doubt on this point because
it assigned to the President powers he had
not customarily held—notably the referendum and article 16—which moved away
from the traditional parliamentary system
and moved towards an "orleanist"[1] system
in which the Chief of State has real authority and his powers are not nominal.

At all events, once the 1962 reform had
been adopted the traditional parliamentary
interpretation had to be completely set
aside, and the letter of the constitution had
to be better respected. If the President of
the Republic is elected by universal suffrage his position changes. For henceforth
he is closer to national sovereignty than the
government. He issues directly from it,
while ministers emanate from it only indirectly through the confidence extended to
them by the deputies. He, not they, is the
representative of the people. The fact that
he is not responsible to the Assembly in no
way alters the situation. How could he be,
since he is in reality the equal of the Assembly which is, like him, elected by universal suffrage? Since the ministers have
less authority than the President they cannot exercise in his stead the powers that
have been granted to him.

To consider the substitution of universal
suffrage for election by *notables* as a mere
modification in the selection procedure is
to forget that universal suffrage is the very
foundation of democracy. In a democracy
electing someone by universal suffrage is
equivalent to his being crowned at Rheims
under the monarchy. This is not merely a
theoretical mutation but corresponds to
reality—as the present presidential election

---

[1] A reference to the style of government in the later years of Louis-
Philippe (1830–1848), when the King attempted to be accepted
as an impartial constitutional monarch while acting as a partisan
political leader. [Editor's note.]

campaign clearly shows. The voters are forcing the candidates to take up a position on all the major problems confronting the nation. They simply would not understand a refusal to do this. Nor would they understand a president they had directly elected being reduced to a secondary role and not exercising the powers the constitution vests in him.

From now on, the powers the constitution grants to the President of the Republic should be considered real powers which he exercises personally, and not nominal powers which are exercised on his behalf by the government. This interpretation is in conformity with both the letter and the spirit of the constitution since the Chief of State expresses national sovereignty as a representative of the people: the powers of a sovereign body cannot be purely nominal. It remains true that some of the president's decisions require the collaboration of the Prime Minister or another minister because they must be countersigned. This countersignature can be refused and the President's wishes thereby limited. Accordingly, the Prime Minister is not a mere chief of staff. But the President, too, can refuse his signature, and this means that he has to be associated with every important decision by the government.

When article 20 asserts that "the government decides and conducts the policy of the nation," that does does not eliminate the President of the Republic from that "decision" or that "conduct", since these are drawn up by the cabinet—that is, under his direction. The fact that in the cabinet, he is the only representative of the people who issues from universal suffrage, obviously confers considerable authority on him. It is inconceivable that a decision should be taken without his consent. Moreover, he would only need to refuse to sign any decrees applying it for it to remain a dead letter. Article 21 in no way invalidates this interpretation. It clearly states

that "the Prime Minister directs the *work* of the government," not that he "directs *the* government." That means that the Prime Minister directs the application by the government of the policy decided on by the cabinet in the presence of the President of the Republic and with his agreement.

This is the only interpretation of the constitution which can be reconciled with both the 1958 document and the 1962 reform. It maps out an original political system, half presidential, half parliamentary, which corresponds to the juxtaposition of these two contradictory ingredients. Two organs of the state are sovereign because they issue directly from universal suffrage: the National Assembly and the President. The Prime Minister and the ministers need the confidence of both if they are to govern, and they are subordinate to both. However because of the provisions of article 8,[2] he cannot directly dismiss the ministry as the Assembly can; but he can force it to resign by refusing to sign decrees or even by refusing to call meetings of the cabinet. The President is free to dissolve the Assembly even if the ministers are opposed to it. The Assembly cannot force him to resign but if, after a dissolution, a majority is elected which is opposed to the president, he will find it difficult to cling to office. Such a system will not operate easily, and it may be felt a presidential system would be more viable. The government's responsibility to the Assembly tends to make it the Assembly's representative against the President, thus aggravating the rivalry between the two organs which issue from universal suffrage rather than seeking to reconcile them. But that is a matter of the practical working of the system, not of the way it is defined in law. In law this system is in conformity with the present constitution, and as long as the system has not been modified it should be applied.

[2]This article deals with the resignation of the government. [Editor's note.]

THE PEOPLE, THE PRESIDENCY AND DE GAULLE

Beyond the public debate over the nature and future of the presidency there are the views of the people themselves both on the office and President de Gaulle's tenure of it. From the poll findings collated below one can see clearly enough their acceptance of the new system of electing the president by universal suffrage, and their general approval of President de Gaulle's record. But both these broad impressions need qualifying. For despite the enthusiasm for electing the president directly, conceptions of the desirable role and powers of the president seem far less well defined—perhaps even a trifle contradictory. And general support for de Gaulle breaks down into strikingly different reactions to various aspects of his policy.

1. Should the President of the Republic be elected by universal suffrage?

	NOV. 1945 percent	NOV. 1961 percent	OCT. 1962* percent	MAY 1964 percent
Yes	50	52	46.4	74
No	40	17	28.8	10
No reply	10	31	25.0	16
	100	100	—	100

*Result of 1962 referendum on whether the President should be elected by universal suffrage; figure in the No Reply column represents non-voters.

2. Distribution of support for the election of the President by universal suffrage according to party preferences, May 1964.

	COMMUNIST percent	SOCIALIST percent	RADICAL percent	M.R.P. percent	U.N.R. percent	CONSERVATIVE percent	NO PARTY percent
Support	61	70	68	82	91	73	61
Against	24	14	19	3	3	18	7
No reply	15	16	13	15	6	9	32
	100	100	100	100	100	100	100

3. It is sometimes said General de Gaulle has set up a system of personal power in France. In your opinion is this true or not true? (November 1965).

TRUE	60 percent
NOT TRUE	22 percent
NO REPLY	18 percent

4. If "True": is this on the whole a good thing or a bad thing?

GOOD THING	15 percent
BAD THING	36 percent
NO REPLY	9 percent

Material from *Les transformations sociales de la France contemporaine . . . Sondages*, by permission of Institut Français d'Opinion Publique. Editor's translation.

5. In your opinion should the President of the Republic play an important political role or should he have purely formal duties? (March 1946).

IMPORTANT POLITICAL ROLE *48 percent*
FORMAL DUTIES *37 percent*
NO REPLY *15 percent.*

---

6. Do you consider that at the present time a great country can only keep its place in the world if it has a Chief of State who is also its effective political head? (October 1962).

YES *65 percent*
NO *18 percent*
NO REPLY *17 percent*

---

7. In the future should the President of the Republic have a more important role, a less important role, or the same role he has at present?

	FEB. 1962 *percent*	APRIL 1962 *percent*	NOV. 1963 *percent*	OCT. 1965 *percent*	MARCH 1966 *percent*
More important	12	11	7	11	11
Same	33	35	37	54	43
Less important	26	32	33	20	33
No reply	29	22	23	15	13
	100	100	100	100	100

---

8. In your opinion, should the President of the Republic be the head of the largest political party, or a man outside the parties? (November 1965).

HEAD OF THE LARGEST PARTY *23 percent*
OUTSIDE THE PARTIES *56 percent*
NO REPLY *21 percent*

---

9. Do you think that during the last seven years General de Gaulle has acted as head of the largest political party or as a man outside the political parties? (November 1965).

HEAD OF THE LARGEST PARTY *44 percent*
OUTSIDE THE PARTIES *31 percent*
NO REPLY *25 percent*

---

10. In your opinion, during his seven years of office, has General de Gaulle had a good influence, a bad influence, or no influence at all on: the standard of living, the place of France in the world, the way France is governed, social questions? (November 1965).

	PLACE OF FRANCE *percent*	GOVERNMENT OF FRANCE *percent*	STANDARD OF LIVING *percent*	SOCIAL AFFAIRS *percent*
Good influence	76	57	48	33
Bad influence	7	16	16	24
No influence	4	8	22	20
No reply	13	19	14	23
	100	100	100	100

---

11. Judgments on de Gaulle's first term (January 1966).

	GOOD *percent*	BAD *percent*	NEITHER ONE NOR THE OTHER *percent*
Sex			
Men	56	18	21
Women	62	12	19

	GOOD percent	BAD percent	NEITHER ONE NOR THE OTHER percent
Age			
20–34	53	19	22
35–49	56	15	22
50–64	64	11	18
65 and over	70	11	14
Occupation			
Farmers	48	16	27
Businessmen	64	10	20
Managers, professions	54	19	19
White collar workers	61	18	18
Workers	57	16	22
Not employed	65	13	15
Region			
Paris area	57	18	19
North West	61	14	20
North East	68	9	17
South West	54	17	23
South East	50	21	22
Party preferences			
Communist	16	44	28
Socialist	48	23	24
Radical	47	16	33
MRP	63	11	22
UNR-UDT	96	1	3
Gaullist Conservative	76	6	15
Conservative	56	19	21

"DON'T KNOWS" excluded

12. What do you think of General de Gaulle? What do you like about him, and what do you dislike about him?[1]

Among the 75 percent making some favorable judgments on him, the qualities mentioned were:

	*percent
Qualities as a leader and Chief of State (authority, prestige, etc.)	43
Moral character (rectitude, loyalty, honour)	20
Patriotism and contribution to French prestige	20
Replies relating to political issues (Algeria, stability)	9
General replies (very good, great man, etc.)	9
Replies relating to the past	9
Courage	7
Others	7

[1]From *Le Référendum d' Octobre et les Elections de Novembre, 1962*, A. Colin, 1965, pp. 247–8.

Among the 66 percent making adverse judgments, the qualities referred to were:

	*percent
Faults as leader and Chief of State (pride, scorn, machiavellianism, etc.)	36
Favors dominant groups (concerned only with the 'big mass' and not the 'small man', etc.)	20
His way of governing (personal power, arbitrary decisions, etc.)	20
Precise political reasons (abandoning Algeria, anti-communism, idea of Europe)	9
His ideas of greatness (receptions, wasteful expenditure)	6
He's a soldier	5
Other	17

*Total exceeds 100 percent owing to multiple replies.

V.   *President and Prime Minister: Power in the Fifth Republic*

Merry Bromberger

GEORGES POMPIDOU BECOMES PRIME MINISTER

When Georges Pompidou became Prime Minister in April 1962, he was not only not a member of the gaullist UNR party, but he had until then held no elective office whatsoever—though he had served as de Gaulle's *chef de cabinet* and discharged a number of political missions for him. It was not until several years later that he got himself elected first as local councillor and then as deputy in his native department. This recruiting of a non-parliamentarian from the banking world was itself a striking illustration of the changed position of the prime minister in the Fifth Republic. This extract and the following one—taken together with the subsequent articles on the cabinet—shed some light on the prime minister's role and his relationship with the president. They should also be read in conjunction with M. Pompidou's own exposition of the role of the prime minister which is printed above. Both following accounts come from a book which set out to create a highly sympathetic image of M. Pompidou, and which was apparently written with his close cooperation. Within the inherent limitations of the narrative techniques they can probably be considered substantially accurate descriptions.

A steady stream of people came to Georges Pompidou's office in the rue Lafitte to tell him he would be called on to take power. There was Michelet who came to tell him in October (1961) that he could not decline.

"With the heaviest of hearts and the greatest reluctance," he replied.

There was Michel Debré, who wrote to him, having offered his resignation yet again. He protested that he had no intention of returning to public life.

There was Chaban-Delmas who announced at the end of 1961: "You are going to be made Prime Minister."

There was Michel Debré once again who spoke to him personally in January 1962: "You are going to be my successor."

Towards the end of February Georges Pompidou was called to the Elysée. "You

Le Destin Secret de Georges Pompidou, Fayard, 1965, pp. 192–195. Reprinted by permission of the publisher. Editor's translation.

are going to take over the government," General de Gaulle told him. "You have no right to refuse. If you do refuse, you will regret it for the rest of your life. . . ."

The bank director had been expecting this summons for a long time. On many occasions the President of the Republic had given him to understand he regretted not having had him at his side during the three years which had just elapsed. Nevertheless it was a shock. And it was also a cross. The former teacher was horrified at the idea that from now on he would spend his life in the public gaze. He had never wanted a conspicuous position. He had done nothing to obtain it. . . .

"Since you refused to be Finance Minister last August you will keep Giscard d'Estaing."

Pompidou then tried to delay the inevitable. He pointed out that it would be distressing for Michel Debré to be dismissed from office overnight. Why not wait until the forthcoming elections? A change of government would be quite natural then, and would be in keeping with the great change in the political atmosphere, and the relaxation which would follow the ending of the Algerian affair.

"There is no question of linking the two events. The government is one thing. Elections are another. . . ." The Chief of State intended to keep his hands free to change Prime Minister if it seemed necessary to him. The possibility of a parliamentary majority—even one composed of his own supporters—imposing a government or a policy on him was quite unacceptable to him. So, in this spirit, without consulting anyone, and without the Debré ministry having been threatened in the Palais Bourbon, de Gaulle took a new Prime Minister.

At that moment the idea of a dissolution was widely canvassed among the UNR. The Assembly had approved the Evian agreements . . . the referendum on the Evian agreements would be a triumphant success. The UNR and Michel Debré thought that

new elections in the wake of this triumph were bound to be very favorable to the gaullists.

. . . Attempts were made to get the General's agreement. But the General did not reply. He had two good reasons. He did not intend to retain Michel Debré, whose nerves needed relaxation after three terrible years. Michel Debré had ideas of his own which were not always the same as the General's. The General also needed to relax. If the UNR, which was strongly attached to its leader, Michel Debré, returned from the electoral battle under his banner victorious and strengthened, it would appear most surprising if the chief of the gaullist majority were not immediately invited to remain Prime Minister.

Michel Debré was counting on this: during the differences he had had with the General he had announced to Pompidou that he was going to leave his post, which would be offered to Pompidou. But the President of the Republic had asked him to stay so many times that . . .

De Gaulle had another reason not to dissolve the Assembly. The government had a majority at the Palais Bourbon which was threatened but still possible. He preferred to keep the dissolution in reserve in case of real crises. If the elections went badly for him, or if a grave unexpected political difficulty arose during the first year, the constitution would not allow him to dissolve a second time. It would be a very difficult year.

"You will take power immediately after the referendum which is to be held on 8 April," he told Pompidou.

The referendum was the expected triumphal victory. The following Monday Michel Debré went to the Elysée to recommend a dissolution. The General explained to him that the decision would be a matter for his successor, thanked him, embraced him and accepted his resignation. An hour later he received Georges Pompidou and charged him to form a new government.

Merry Bromberger

GEORGES POMPIDOU FORMS HIS CABINET

The new Prime Minister had only 48 hours to make his cabinet, to rally wider political support than his predecessor. He had many friends who sat on parliamentary benches well removed from the UNR's. Since 1958 he had remained on good terms with Guy Mollet who had been Minister of State in de Gaulle's government. He had no hope of winning over the socialists who had declared open war on the Fifth Republic, any more than the extreme right. But between these two groups he hoped to obtain the broadest support for a government of détente and conciliation, and find room for ministers of every political hue.

However, the political atmosphere was scarcely propitious . . . The parties were hardening against de Gaulle's nuclear strike force, his European policy and his severity towards the United States. Their leaders saw the Algerian war as an opportune moment to get rid of the presidential president who was depriving them of their influence in the country and their hold on power. The broad center-based majority Pompidou wanted to form would plainly be difficult to achieve.

Nevertheless, this political beginner entered the political scene with his customary optimism. First he made a friendly telephone call to Guy Mollet. The socialist leader replied in the same vein, "I would be happy to meet you. I am ready to come and see you. But given our positions there is little I can say at the moment which would be of interest to you."

Pompidou next went to see Edgar Faure at his home, his first meeting with the Center-Left . . . The brilliant Faure had recently been summoned to the Elysée. He was talked of as a possible Premier. He was shortly to be the General's unofficial ambassador to the Peking government. He did not hide his admiration for de Gaulle. Pompidou offered him the Ministry of Education with Scientific Research added. "My dear fellow," Edgar Faure replied, "it was quite amusing to be expelled from my party once. But twice would look a little . . . But I will gladly be your personal ambassador in the Senate." The attempt to seduce the Radicals had failed. Later Faure was to regret his refusal. . . .[1]

Pompidou tried a crucial démarche with the MRP. He personally called Pierre Pflimlin who agreed without any enthusiasm to enter the government with four of his friends in the uncertain hope of bringing de Gaulle closer to a United Europe. He insisted on the need to include Robert Buron whose jovial humour he liked and who should win over the left wing of the MRP.

Olivier Guichard, who was helping the head of the government in these démarches reached Maurice Schumann[2] in Strasbourg by telephone. He talked to him of a major ministry which was to be created: the Ministry of Development, the ministry of the future. Such a great ministry (it would have had to include the Plan, and a large part of Education, Construction, and Public Works and two-thirds of all ministerial proposals) that it was never to be created. However, at least Maurice Schumann became Secretary

[1]He in fact accepted the Ministry of Agriculture in 1966. [Editor's note.]
[2]At the time a strongly gaullist/MRP deputy. [Editor's note.]

Le Destin Secret de Georges Pompidou, Fayard, 1965, pp. 202–205. Reprinted by permission of the publisher. Editor's translation.

of State responsible for Development.

The UNR ministers were to remain at their posts, as was Valéry Giscard d'Estaing as foreseen, and Couve de Murville, the flawless interpreter of the general's foreign policy, one of the men who enjoy the almost unqualified confidence of the Chief of State.

Georges Pompidou kept Edgar Pisani, who had just succeeded Rochereau at the Ministry of Agriculture, without knowing much about him, because he needed a senator. . . .

The Ministry of Education, which Edgar Faure had declined, was offered to Sudreau who was responsible for Construction under Michel Debré. "In short, you want me to sell de Gaulle to the younger generation?"

The formation of the government ended in a scramble. In the end Pompidou had only 40 hours. He had to hand the list of ministers to the President of the Republic by noon on Saturday. At 11:30 that morning he still had no Minister of Posts and Telecommunications.

Olivier Guichard telephoned Jacques Marette, a UNR senator, who was just about to take his dog for a walk. "Marette, do you want to be a minister?"

"You're joking."

"No, I couldn't be more serious. Pompidou's about to leave for the Elysée. If you agree his list is complete!"

"So if my dog had been in a bigger hurry there wouldn't have been anyone at Posts and Telecommunications?"

But Guichard had already hung up, and the senator remained incredulous. On returning home with his dog the congratulations of his *concièrge*, "who had heard about it on the radio," confirmed to the new minister that his friend Olivier Guichard does not joke about serious matters.

PRESIDENT AND PRIME MINISTER: TWO CONFLICTING ANALYSES

Since the advent of the Fifth Republic there have been few great parliamentary occasions in France. But one great exception to this was the debate of 24 April 1964, arising from parliamentary questions challenging the way the constitution had been operated. Two outstanding speeches dominated the day. First came the left-wing opposition leader, François Mitterrand, remorselessly contrasting the gaullists' presentation of the constitution in 1958 with its working—and their interpretation of it—six years later. Then later the Prime Minister, Georges Pompidou, in a performance which for the first time established his skill as a parliamentary debater, made a sustained justification of constitutional evolution since 1958 and forcefully asserted that despite the prominence of the president, the prime minister and his cabinet are not the mere ciphers that critics have alleged them to be. Essentially his speech embodies the claim that in practice the constitution of the Fifth Republic is working as the parliamentary system Michel Debré claimed he was establishing in 1958.

M. FRANÇOIS MITTERRAND.

Ladies and gentlemen, on September 28th, 1958 the French people voted for the establishment of a system of parliamentary government. No doubt some of the articles of the constitution were inimical to such a system; no doubt, too, the political context made it highly unlikely that this type of system would establish itself in France; and

---

Journal Officiel, Débats Parlementaires (Assemblée Nationale), 25 April 1964. Editor's translation.

no doubt successive changes for the worse rapidly destroyed its meaning. But both legal minds, attached to the letter of the constitutional documents, and millions of ordinary citizens who trusted the official explanation even though it completely evaded the real issue, had every reason to believe that although some of the reforms did modify the traditional institutional structure of the Third and Fourth Republics, both fundamentally and by its main outlines the Fifth Republic nevertheless remained, like its predecessors, a parliamentary system.

Among the host of assurances supporting my point—assurances given to republicans who were anxious about the circumstances in which the new regime was born—I shall quote only one for the moment. But it is the most weighty and conclusive of all, both because of the place where it was uttered—here at this tribune—and because of the circumstances which led to the investiture of the government which resulted from events in May, but also because of its author: General de Gaulle. Here is what he told the National Assembly on June 1st, 1958: "The government which I am forming will put a proposal for reform before you without delay. . . ." He went on, ". . . the government will lay down three principles which must be the basis of republican government in France and it gives its word that its proposals will conform to them: Universal suffrage is the sole source of power. The executive and legislature must be effectively separated, so that both the government and parliament can exercise their full powers independently and on their own responsibility. The government must be responsible to Parliament. . . ."

Let me quote just one of the many expressions of approval which turned this statement into a binding contract. M. Pierre-Henri Teitgen, speaking for the MRP but unquestionably echoing a very widespread feeling, said: "The MRP will vote for investiture because the constitutional reform envisaged would respect and confirm the basic principle of democracy, that is,

that the executive and legislature are expressions of national sovereignty, and that the government is responsible to an Assembly elected by universal suffrage." I do not believe, ladies and gentlemen, that there can be any dispute on that point. Incidentally, if there was, the opinion of an expert who was Minister of Justice at the time would be conclusive. Speaking to the General Assembly of the Conseil d'Etat, M. Michel Debré declared, "The government has set out to renovate the parliamentary system. I am even tempted to say that it wishes to establish it because, for a number of reasons, the Republic has never succeeded in doing so." Later he said, "This draft constitution which is submitted to you, sets out to create a parliamentary system." And finally, "Not assembly government, not presidential government, the way before you is narrow: it is the way of parliamentary government.". . .

Do not misunderstand me. At the moment I am neither making a case for the parliamentary system nor making a choice between different representative systems. I am simply explaining and commenting on the system of institutions adopted nearly six years ago by 18 million Frenchmen, so that today's debate may be placed as accurately as possible in its context. I am keeping to the terms of a constitution which I did not support because the surrounding circumstances seemed so suspect, but which still, strictly speaking, rules our country today. And I am saying that if anyone should guarantee both its letter and its spirit, before all others, it is the man who put it forward for the approval of the French people and who is now responsible for seeing that it is properly respected.

I am not therefore concerned if the new rulers thought it was clever politics in 1958 to soothe the susceptibilities of the public by submitting to it a proposal which was apparently in keeping with tradition and practice. Nor am I concerned with secret motives or hidden intentions. Since there is a parliamentary system, all I want is for the mutual obligations accepted by the executive and the legislature with the approval of the electorate to be defined exactly and respected scrupulously . . .

In this connection I have consulted a basic document, the collection of papers on the drafting of the constitution which includes the opinions and discussions of the Constitutional Consultative Committee.[1] How reliable is this document? How far can it be considered binding on the people who express themselves in it? I shall let you be the judges of that, ladies and gentlemen. I shall simply note that the various statements I will quote amount to confirmation of the initial assertion on which I based my argument: that on September 28, 1958 the constitution for which the French people voted provided for a parliamentary system.

Thus, on Tuesday, 29th July 1958, General de Gaulle spoke to the CCC in these terms: "I could have mentioned these rules in the first place . . . But they are so self-evident that I shall limit myself to a simple reference to them, for the record as it were: all organs of government must issue from universal suffrage; the government must be responsible to the Assembly which must remain as it is at present; finally, the different powers must be separate." A little later, on Thursday, 31 July 1958, M. Janot, representing the government, spoke in these terms: "The document which is submitted to you sets out to create a purified parliamentary system. A parliamentary system, since the government"—the repetition becomes tedious but it is indispensable—"is responsible to parliament." M. Janot went on, "Executive power belongs to the government. The Prime Minister is in charge of its work. He is appointed by the President of the Republic, proposes the appointment of ministers to him, and holds the powers which are traditionally his . . . among them the preparation and implementing of national defense."

Later on the same day the government representative touched on the heart of the problem which is now going to occupy us.

"M. Barrachin," he said, "is afraid that Title II may set up a two-headed executive or bicephalic government. In reality nothing was further from the minds of the authors of this draft than such a bicephalism. The head of the executive is the Prime Minister. The President of the Republic sees to it that the constitution is respected and ensures the normal operation of the various organs of government. Outside altogether exceptional circumstances he is essentially an arbiter. Of course, he is not a passive arbiter. The President arbitrates by taking decisions. But this does not alter the fact that the Prime Minister is the head of the executive."

A little later during that sitting M. Janot went on: "M. Dejean and M. de Bailliencourt asked how the President could rid himself of a Prime Minister whose policy he disagreed with. The answer is very simple and very clear—he cannot. The executive is not doubly responsible to both the President and parliament. The Prime Minister is appointed by the President, but he is responsible to parliament, not to the President." (*Applause on the* rassemblement démocratique, centre démocratique *and socialist benches.*) . . .

I must ask you not to treat this transcript as a document unearthed from the depths of some library stack; we must go back to such sources if we want to understand what the authors of the regime wished it to be. The CCC was, as usual, presided over by M. Paul Reynaud, and this sitting was particularly important because the Premier of the day, General de Gaulle, came to express his views in person.

I note the following exchange: "M. Paul Reynaud.—The second question concerns the Prime Minister. He is appointed by the President: can he be dismissed by him? The Premier.—No! For in that case he would be unable to govern effectively. The Prime Minister is responsible to parliament, not the President, for the political situation. The role of the Chief of State is essentially to ensure that the various organs of government function normally. Accordingly he

---

[1]Hereafter CCC [Editor's note.]

appoints the Prime Minister, as he did under the constitution of 1875, thus suppressing the investiture procedure without excluding the use of the question of confidence. The Prime Minister then forms his government and the President signs the decrees appointing the ministers. If the Prime Minister wants to dismiss one of his ministers the President signs the decree, but the initiative in taking the decision does not lie with him. If it did the balance would be jeopardised. Let me underline that the President is essentially an arbiter whose task is to make sure that, whatever may happen, the organs of government continue to function."

M. Paul Reynaud's reply to this was: "Your answer is of the highest importance. It will dispel the disquiet of those who have been wondering whether the inspiration of the provisional draft was presidential or parliamentary. In my view this exchange between us amounts to a contract." And so M. Reynaud felt able to write to General de Gaulle on 14 August 1958, summarising the observations and objections of the CCC on the completion of its work: "Your answer to the question I had the honour of putting in the name of the CCC when you appeared before it on August 8th leaves no room for any misunderstanding whatever. The government, you said, is responsible to parliament; it is not responsible to the Chief of State. This declaration confirms and clarifies the terms of the article in the provisional draft. It follows from this that despite the increase in the Chief of State's powers, this is a genuine parliamentary system."

How is this exchange to be interpreted? Merely as casual remarks thrown out by a pair of individuals making polite conversation? Not in the least! It binds those who took part in the eyes of the nation and of history. Thus we can see that at the moment when the constitution was put to the people and lawyers were scrutinizing these documents, it was quite clear on General de Gaulle's own word that the government and the head of the government were in no way responsible to him but to Parliament alone.

. . . In my opinion the pledges made by the man who was to become Chief of State, at the moment when the binding contract linking the state and the nation was being submitted to the French people, are of some importance. If not, that is conclusive proof that the Fifth Republic is a régime without any fundamental law. (*Applause on the* rassemblement démocratique *and socialist benches.*)

For a final reformist interpretation of the constitution concerning relations between the Prime Minister and the President, let me quote the President's own words at his press conference on 31 January last. He asserted, "Of course there is no double responsibility. There cannot be a diarchy at the summit. And there is not one!" Who doubted it! "The President, who belongs to the entire nation, is chosen by it and entrusted with its destiny; he appoints the government and, in particular, the Prime Minister, and can change him when he considers that the task he laid down for him has been completed, or if they no longer agree."

But, ladies and gentleman, . . . changes which alter the balance between the arms of government, changes for which the executive will accept entire responsibility, are a matter for parliament. That is why I now intend to analyze the position of the Prime Minister *vis-à-vis* the President. Mr. Prime Minister, under article 20 of the constitution "the government lays down and conducts the policy of the nation"; and it "is responsible to parliament." If I find that these phrases have in practice become emptied of all meaning, have I not the right to ask you, as Prime Minister and therefore as the man who under article 21 directs the work of the government, not only how and why, by continually transferring your powers to the President (who is not responsible to parliament) you are relinquishing the most important of your prerogatives; but also how and why you thereby take it upon you to deprive parliament progressively of the fundamental right of control and political decision, without which this parliamentary system would be merely a front for the power of a single man? (*Applause on the* rassemblement démocratique *and socialist benches. Interruptions from the UNR/UDT.*)

How can one be surprised that from being a parliamentary regime the Fifth Republic has become a limited monarchy, while evolving to its final goal of personal rule? How can we be surprised after reading the public declaration that "the indivisible authority of the State is completely" —note that word—"delegated to the President by the people who elected him, and no authority"—note that one too—"whether ministerial, civil, military or judicial can be conferred or retained except through him." According to this the President has the right to take it upon himself to modify as he pleases the "supreme domain" in which he can take decisions of his own responsibility—though if and when he pleases he can delegate his powers to others, the government, perhaps parliament, even the judiciary! . . .

We must choose. Either we need an honest, genuine presidential system which will give the head of the executive authority and stability while giving parliament a worthwhile role, or we need to return to the source of a parliamentary system adapted to modern needs. We must return to a system of liberty and balance, and be finished with the present one, which rests on nothing but authoritarianism and irresponsibility. (*Applause on the* rassemblement démocratique, centre démocratique, *socialist and some communist benches. Exclamations from the UNR/UDT.*)

THE PRIME MINISTER. M. GEORGES POMPIDOU.

The question of the powers of the President of the Republic and their relationship to the powers of the Prime Minister and the government is of capital importance. The whole future of our institutions turns on the answer that one gives. Let me first discuss the powers of the President and the way he exercises them. Then I will talk about the Prime Minister, and the way he shoulders and exercises his responsibilities, and finally I shall try to draw some conclusions about relations between the Chief of State and the government and Prime Minister, and about the establishment of a balance between the legislative and executive powers.

The authors of the questions recalled articles 20 and 21 of the constitution. Perhaps first I had better recall too the articles which deal with the powers of the President. First there is article 5 which lays on the President the task of ensuring regular operation of the organs of government and the continuity of the State, and makes him the guarantor of national independence, of our boundaries, and of Community agreements and treaties. (*Applause on the UNR/ UDT benches.*)

M. Paul Coste-Floret. By his arbitration!

The Prime Minister. You talk about arbitration, M. Coste-Floret. As it happens that word is used extremely often with regard to the Prime Minister. The Prime Minister is constantly exercising his arbitration or being asked to do so. Arbitration by the Prime Minister means simply decisions by the Prime Minister. (*Applause from the UNR/UDT benches.*)

Next, article 8 which gives the President the power to appoint the Prime Minister and end his tenure of office when the Prime Minister presents his government's resignation; article 9 under which he presides over cabinet meetings; article 10 under which he promulgates laws, and which gives him the right to ask for a bill to be considered again—which cannot be refused; article 11 dealing with the referendum; article 12 which gives him the right of dissolution after consulting the Prime Minister and the presidents of the two assemblies; article 13 under which he signs ordinances and decrees as well as appointments to all civil and military posts; article 15 under which he is "head of the armed forces and president of the national defense councils;" and article 16 of whose scope I need not remind you. (*Chuckles*).

The question is: do these different articles mean anything, or do they mean nothing? (*'Hear! Hear!' on the UNR/UDT benches*). Let us note, on this point, that constitutions are subject to change in practice. The 1875 constitution granted the President even broader powers than the 1958 constitution—for though there was no article 16 or referendum, neither was there a premier or Prime Minister. Change came rapidly, and you will remember the form it took: the basic right of dissolution vanished and the premier who, as M. Mitterrand would say, had no institutional existence, became the real chief of the executive, the presidency being reduced to a mere figurehead stripped both of its power and effectiveness. This withering away of the office of president was, moreover, confirmed by the 1946 constitution, in which the principal innovation was to create a premier who received the investiture of the National Assembly and drew his power from it, and who was the sole holder of authority or what passed for it.

We know what happened, and how the course of constitutional evolution weakened still more the last weapon at the executive's disposal by seeking to make dissolution impossible through the practice of governments resigning before being defeated by the absolute majority in the Assembly. That is why, ladies and gentlemen, the articles of the 1958 constitution which deal with the powers of the President should be examined both as they stand and in the light of circumstances. For the 1958 constitution, which was presented as a reaction against the 1946 constitution and the practices of the Fourth Republic, solemnly asserts the powers of the Chief of State. The significance of this assertion was all the greater because at the time everyone looked on General de Gaulle as the future president. The articles dealing with his powers can only be interpreted by giving them their full meaning.

Moreover, General de Gaulle has never made any secret of his views. As early as 1946 he laid down the principle at Bayeux: "Executive power should emanate from the Chief of State." And on the eve of the referendum on the constitution he underlined forcefully the President's part in the exercise of power and responsibility. Is there really anyone who can assert in good faith that he did not expect to see General de Gaulle take the helm? This was the period of the Algerian war, to which every Frenchman knew General de Gaulle alone could bring a solution—so much so that some people would have liked to delegate absolute power to him for two or three years with the idea that he would settle the Algerian problem, and then they could return to business as usual. (*Applause on the UNR/UDT benches*).

For them, as Albert Bayet said, "de Gaulle is an unpleasant moment to endure." (*Laughter*) But the point is that by accepting the constitution and making General de Gaulle President the country revealed its determination for a lasting change. Moreover nobody, or almost nobody, raised his voice against the way the Chief of State used his powers as long as the Algerian war and the threat of subversion were so pressing. Yet, in applying the constitution, General de Gaulle clearly asserted the presidential power that the constitution set out to establish. On 4 January 1960 he declared, "The nature of the President's powers has changed profoundly by comparison with the past." Far from concealing his intentions, as early as 11 April 1961 he declared, "It may be thought that the President should be chosen by the entire nation through universal suffrage."

So I come to the referendum of October 1962, which not only established the election of the President by the entire nation, but at the same time confirmed the powers at the President's disposal to lay down the orientation of the country's policy. Guarantor of all that is really essential to the nation, deriving his mandate from its confidence in him, the President has become, beyond all possible question, a keystone in the constitutional structure. The voters who an-

73

swered 'Yes' in October 1962 had had clear warning.

"To work effectively," General de Gaulle said, "our constitution requires a Chief of State who really is one. For the last four years I have played this part. The French people must now say whether I should continue. They must decide whether future presidents, after me, shall in their turn have the means and the obligation to bear this very heavy burden, thanks to their direct investiture by the nation.". . .

Therefore, ladies and gentlemen, no one can claim that these ideas have not been clearly expressed, or that they have not been strikingly endorsed by the electorate. Even if there has been an evolution, this evolution has not been a modification of the internal practices of the world of politics (as was the evolution in the reverse direction of the 1875 constitution), but one which took place in the full light of day and with the approval of the country. (*Applause on the UNR/UDT benches*).

Furthermore, why do we have this feigned amazement today? M. Mitterrand, you talk about the order to commit our strategic forces. There again, the constitution and the country's common sense agree. The provisions making the President guarantor of the nation's independence, its boundaries, and respect for treaties, and also making him head of the armed forces and president of the councils of national defense, lay down with a clarity that every Frenchman considers obvious, that it is for the Chief of State to give the supreme order on which the nation's very life depends. Moreover, is this not the only method by which, in such tragic circumstances, our system of defense could retain its full effectiveness?

Does that mean that the Prime Minister is reduced to a modest adviser, a subordinate carrying out orders, a nonentity? May I say that this is not in the least my view? Firstly, if the President is to take action he requires a government. Apart from the exceptions specifically listed in the constitution, no act of the President's is valid without the Prime Minister's signature. I must ask you to believe that I attach just as much importance to that signature as the President attaches to his. (*Applause on the UNR/UDT and* républicains indépendants *benches*.) That means that every political decision fully commits the government, and particularly the Prime Minister. That means that whoever may have initiated them, decisions are only taken after agreement between the President and the Prime Minister. I consider it the elementary duty of a Prime Minister never to reveal publicly the differences which on this or that question may arise between him and the Chief of State. (*Lively reactions*). In my eyes united leadership and policy comes before all other considerations. (*Applause on the UNR/UDT benches*).

But I can state flatly that there is no reserved domain in any sense of the word; that in all matters, whether taking the initiative, general policy or continuity, I consider the Chief of State to play a vital role; but that I could not continue with my work or carry on my responsibilities except insofar as I am, or will be, in full agreement on all the aspects of a policy which it falls to me to conduct in the face of events, with the government whose work I direct. (*Applause on the UNR/UDT and* républicains indépendants *benches*). That is why I consider I am fully responsible for this policy to the Assembly, which may vote its censure if it sees fit.

Make no mistake. The Prime Minister's role, far from being diminished, is considerably reinforced by such an arrangement. The support he draws from this double expression of confidence which he must have—from the Chief of State, without which he would be paralysed in any event; and from the Assembly on which his existence constantly depends—and the stability provided for him by the balance of the two, allow him to act and achieve the effectiveness that comes with continuity. . . .

People talk of "personal power." But what does this "personal power" mean? It means, firstly, a person claiming by virtue of either force or divine authority, to hold total power for an indeterminate period. But the President is—and will be—elected for a fixed term. Next, personal power means that the man who holds power wields it personally. Do you imagine that this corresponds to reality? It is certainly not my habit to lay bare the discussions and even the disagreements which proceed important decisions by the executive. But I can assure you that none of them are taken without lengthy discussions between, firstly, the Chief of State and the Prime Minister, then with the ministers concerned and finally with the whole government. When these decisions are taken, they are the decisions of the whole executive, and consequently of the government, which accepts full responsibility for them.

Finally, power is personal when the only check or limit on it is the whim of the holder. The power of the President has closely defined limits. First, there is the need, except when article 16 is in force, for him to have the support of the government, and of the Prime Minister in particular, if his acts are to be legally valid. Next there is the fact that the government is responsible to the Assembly, which can at any moment dismiss it by voting a motion of censure. It is here, in the exercise of the government's responsibility to the Assembly that we find conclusively, not only the clear mark of democratic power but also the means of achieving the balance of powers . . . I am well placed to know the importance of the censure motion, since I have the privilege of being its only victim to date—though admittedly a very fleeting one. (*Applause and laughter on the UNR/UDT benches*).

Whatever part the President may play in the preparation of policy, this policy can only be conducted by the government—which can be overthrown at any moment. Thus equilibrium is established between the executive and the National Assembly, the Assembly having the power to overthrow the government, and the Chief of State having the right to dissolve the As-

sembly. The sovereign judge of this equilibrium is the people who arbitrate or will arbitrate fundamental disagreements.

To sum up, and give the results of my own experience during the two years I have been Prime Minister, I would say that if our system of government is to function properly there has to be a close identity of views between the President and the Prime Minister, thus giving homogeneity to the executive and, by the same token, giving full meaning to the government's accountability to the Assembly: by controlling the government the Assembly is fully and genuinely controlling the policy of France. If you wish, M. Mitterrand, you can attempt a demonstration here and now. (*Applause on the UNR/UDT benches*).

That is why this essential cohesion between the government, its head, and the Chief of State makes the problem of whether or not the President has the power to dismiss the government a trifle academic. Personally I cannot imagine how a Prime Minister who had lost the Chief of State's confidence—with the risk that the President would refuse to accept and to countersign governmental decisions—could do anything but hand in his resignation. But that in no way lessens the Assembly's prerogatives. For while the government cannot govern against the Chief of State who presides over its discussions and signs its decrees, the Chief of State cannot dispense with a government which enjoys the support of the National Assembly.

The only departure from our traditions is that, with the authority which election by universal suffrage will henceforth give him, and with the possibility of appealing to the people by referendum or a dissolution, the Chief of State has it in his power to eradicate the malady which in the past gave birth to instability and weakness—that is, the lack of parliamentary majorities or the danger of disparate and divided majorities. Moreover, it is self-evident that the system will function all the better, and with fewer hitches, because the ideas of the majority in the Assembly will conform more closely to those of the executive. This is what—by other means and with the help of the two-party system—creates the stability of the British and American systems, and this is what is creating stability here, thanks to the coherence and unity of the governmental majority.

Whatever may be the conditions in which the political struggles of the future are to be fought, the country cannot, on pain of death, give its confidence to those who fail to pledge themselves unhesitatingly and unequivocally to prevent the dis-appearance of a Chief of State who really is a Chief of State, for on this depends the stability and the independence of France. As M. François Mauriac has so splendidly remarked (*Exclamations on the socialist benches*): the people do not always know what they want, but they know what they do not want, and what they do not want at any price. If there were any danger of their forgetting, you will be there, praise be, to remind them. (*UNR/UDT deputies rise in prlonged applause*).

Michel Debré

THE NEED FOR A PRIME MINISTER

The way in which the president has dominated the political scene during the early years of the Fifth Republic has led many commentators to consider the prime minister as little more than the president's creature. (One article published during the premiership of M. Debré was entitled *Does Michel Debré Exist?*) Other critics have argued that it might be better if the office of prime minister were in fact abolished, paving the way for an uncomplicated, overtly presidential system. We have read already M. Pompidou's insistence that in fact the prime minister exercises appreciable power in his own right. He and Debré appear to agree that if the Fifth Republic is to stay in any sense a parliamentary system the office of prime minister with a government responsible to the Assembly cannot be abandoned. But Debré's argument here diverges notably from M. Pompidou's in its frank acceptance of presidential dominance. For him the prime minister becomes a buffer or screen for the president much more than a political force in his own right.

From the moment the importance of the office of chief of state has become a constitutional certainty, the government's rôle declines. In that case should there, and can there, continue to be a prime minister? Can, and should, the government's responsibility to parliament be preserved? It seems to me the prime minister's functions are in keeping with both the nature of the régime and its efficient functioning. Government involves the carrying out of many routine tasks that should not fall on the head of state even if he exercises the full prerogatives of power in every domain. Political life makes many heavy impositions, chiefly parliamentary, which the chief of state should be spared even if at some time in the future, the constitution is amended to allow him to address the assemblies. Finally, the office is indispensable

From Michel Debré, *Au Service de la Nation* (Paris: 1963), pp. 211–214. Reprinted by permission of Editions Stock. Editor's translation.

to the operation of collective responsibility. If there was no prime minister there could only be the individual responsibility of each minister; such a system is no longer conceivable for it is the negation of the notion of government, in which there is no responsibility at all. It seems to me that governmental responsibility to parliament remains a useful rule in our system. If the government wishes to carry a controversial measure, or if parliament wishes to make clear its position on some major issue, there must be some procedure by which it can accept or reject, declare support or censure. Moreover, collective responsibility is the counterpart of the ways in which the President and the government can act on the Assembly. Since these powers are necessary, particularly in preventing the development of that omnipotence to which every assembly aspires, equilibrium must be established by giving parliament the right not only to exercise a constant public check on executive action, but also react effectively. Thus the office of prime minister is a political necessity of the highest order.

Admittedly, certain arguments against this conclusion are worthy of consideration. What is the meaning of this governmental responsibility when all fundamental political decisions are in the hands of the chief of state, and his steadily increasing authority casts its shadow over that of the government? What will happen if the majority in the National Assembly tries to impose a prime minister and a government on the President against his will? And in either event, will there not be occasions when the Assembly is in effect voting to censure the President? There are measures in the constitution which provide a solution to these difficulties. The President can accept the government's resignation and try, temporarily or permanently, to conform to parliament's wishes. He can bow to its verdict. He can also dissolve the Assembly and, in the light of the results of the ensuing election, either resign or submit if it goes against him. One cannot both want

democracy and not want internal conflicts. The important thing is that these should be rare and that they should be settled.

Moreover, other possibilities are worth considering. In accepting the government's resignation when he himself is the real object of the Assembly's attack, would not the president be shrinking from the truth? In dissolving the Assembly at a moment when the national interest would preclude it, would it not be running an excessive and intolerable risk? It seems to me that if the system is to operate in the national interest, it must provide for such conflicts to be solved in other ways. It should be possible to give the president the right to delay acceptance of the government's resignation or to call for reconsideration of the censure motion at the end of a period of reflection of, say, ten days. At all events, the president should have the right to submit the question which gave rise to the censure motion to referendum, which would amount to giving the assembly the right to bring about a referendum instead of the resignation of the government. But the president—and this is indispensable in the national interest—should never be obliged to hold a referendum; a referendum should never be an obligation, a purely automatic procedure.

A second debate and possible resort to referendum are the two conditions on which it seems possible to maintain the provisions on censure motions, and consequently governmental responsibility to the Assembly. Thus parliament retains control over policy and a means of censuring the government, a procedure which is also most useful to the government in ensuring its bills are carried. At the same time, the solution of the conflict is not necessarily at the president's expense.

"The balance of powers" is once again fashionable. It is in fact an ambiguous expression. If it means a sort of impotence arising from two or more equal partners watching each other's every move to the point where action becomes impossible, no political system can survive on such a basis. Effective power must lie somewhere. There must be limits, to prevent this power being abused in unjustifiable arbitrary ways. But this must be real power, that is able both to look forward and to decide, to reflect and to command. These conditions are not fulfilled when power is granted to an assembly, and such a power destroys itself where there is an omnipotent assembly with no coherent durable majority. Let the citizen beware: too many sanctimonious hypocrites are at present using the slogan "balance of powers" as a means of removing authority from those who can usefully wield it, in order to hand it over to those who are incapable of exercising it.

With modern institutions our Republic can take a new lease of life. The essential thing is to see to it that once authority is established in the right place and in appropriate conditions, thereafter it is maintained. Any additions can only result in increasing the number of occasions when the President has a right of reference to the electorate, which is the source of all power, either at his own initiative or in order to bring to an end a conflict arising, naturally enough, from the normal operation of the processes of democracy.

Pierre Mendès-France

TWO FALSE DEMOCRACIES: THE FOURTH AND FIFTH REPUBLICS

To many commentators the Fourth and Fifth Republics are quite dissimilar, but to Mendès-France they stand equally condemned as unbalanced political systems with a common failure to provide France with genuine parliamentary government based on firm and decisive leadership yet fully responsible to the people. His views are shaped by a long political experience; first elected to the prewar Chamber of Deputies in 1936, he opposed the authoritarian Vichy regime from its birth; later he resigned from de Gaulle's government after the Liberation when he judged the General to have chosen expediency rather than the tough economic reforms he believed necessary. Frequently a lonely critic in the Fourth Republic Assembly, when called on to liquidate the Indochina *impasse* in 1954 he stamped his seven months of office with a determination to decide and lead in marked contrast with both those who preceded him in office and those who followed. An opponent of the present régime from the first hour, he paid the price of parliamentary defeat in 1958 and years in the wilderness, finally reentering the Assembly only in 1967. The conception of democracy he advances here may be tinged with the *naïveté* of nineteenth-century humanitarian rationalism—but there is little doubting Mendès-France's personal commitment to it or the influence he has had on a whole political generation.

In any system of government an efficient division of labour and responsibility can be achieved by organised relations between the various authorities, each with its own particular sphere of influence. Both the Fourth and Fifth Republics were characterised equally by a total lack of equilibrium between the principal state organisations: the Assemblies and the executive powers.

Under the Fourth Republic all power was effectively concentrated in the hands of the National Assembly. Besides exercising the power of legislation the Assembly was able to paralyse government action by various legal and other devices. The executive existed under the constant threat of having its decisions countermanded; it was deprived of any prospect of continuity and was thus incapable of displaying a will of its own. It was trying to reconcile incompatible interests and at the same time giving way to the pressures that harried it. The price of these attempts was total immobility. For all practical purposes no government worthy of the name existed. A dozen men calling themselves ministers sat in the seats of power, but they did not constitute a government. They enjoyed no margin of freedom or time in their everyday work and in the end they could make no decisions, start no new undertakings and finish none of the tasks they were supposed to do.

Public opinion was shocked by the frequent ministerial crises, but, even between

From *A Modern French Republic* by Pierre Mendèsè-France, pp. 47–52. © 1962, Editions Gallimard. English translation © 1963 by George Weidenfeld and Nicolson Ltd. Reprinted by permission of Hill and Wang, Inc.

crises, the debilitated state of the government prevented it from taking any real action.

The Fifth Republic contains the same flaw, but in reverse. This time it is the head of state who, not content with hampering the executive, is arrogating a part of the legislation to himself by manipulating, or actually infringing the Constitution, and reducing Parliament to a subsidiary rôle.

The 1958 Constitution completely reversed the republican tradition in which Parliament is the statutory legislative body, the government intervening only as a secondary measure—either when Parliament has taken no decision or acting on authority delegated by it. The realm of parliamentary legislation is now defined by means of limiting clauses: article 34 of the Constitution contains a list of matters on which the assemblies are considered fit to lay down "rules" or "basic principles." By virtue of article 37 all other matters come within the jurisdiction of the government alone. Thus the government exercises wide statutory powers in complete independence of Parliament, even to the extent of modifying or amending laws which were formerly subject to act of Parliament. Consequently, as Professor Rivero has observed, it is the government which becomes the normal and common legislator, the principal legislative body; while Parliament is able to legislate only in so far as the power is explicitly delegated to it. . . .

Furthermore, when Parliament cannot legislate officially on matters which henceforth come within the government's jurisdiction, then government legislation may well encroach on parliamentary matters: all that is needed is an enabling clause, such as that provided for in article 38 of the Constitution, which can suspend parliamentary powers of legislation for an indefinite period. Moreover, these rules are applied in a particularly extensive spirit. Many students have commented on the timid interpretation given to the text of the Constitution as a whole by the president of the National Assembly. One of them, Léon Hamon, draws attention to his "caution" and points out that he always preferred "to keep well within the limits of his legislative powers (rather) than risk another clash with the Constitutional Council." There has never been any doubt of this Council's conciliatory attitude towards the executive and on more than one occasion it has ruled that one of the assemblies has overstepped its authority in legislating on some subject which it declared to be within the government's province. The executive is also within its rights in ratifying a budget if this has not been finally passed by both chambers within seventy days of its presentation—clearly a considerable increase in the government's legislative powers.

Is there, in fact, any longer any real point in talking about "the government" and its prerogatives? A government, properly speaking, with a personality of its own, no longer exists, thanks to the application of principles already built into the Constitution, or to the repeated extension of them in daily practice. During the Fourth Republic the government may have been to all intents and purposes absorbed in the Assembly: today it is absorbed in the person of the head of state. Policy is conceived, adopted and carried out by one man only. If he lacks the time or inclination to deal with a particular problem he will delegate it to a minister or to one of his close advisors: their job is to interpret the president's wishes in much the same way as their predecessors tried to follow the views of certain political parties or lobbies.

But Parliament cannot lightly be dispensed with. An active Parliament serves as a check on the government, forcing it to explain its policies to the public, to publish the facts for discussion and give an account of its progress. In other words parliamentary questions are the basis of a free flow of information. The history of France, like that of other countries, teaches us that every kind of freedom is equally bound up with the existence of a respected Parliament.

"Unlimited power is madness. . . . A

people is free to the precise extent that it exercises its own sovereignty and declines to leave it in the hands of one Assembly, one Party or one man . . ." This dictum of the philosopher Alain, quoted by Professor Vedel, applies equally to the Fourth and Fifth Republics. Both of them have overlooked the necessity for a balanced division of duties and prerogatives and, as a result, we can see that both of them have progressed with increasing speed towards a monopoly of power: yesterday by the National Assembly, today by the head of state. Yesterday we were moving towards anarchy; today we are heading for despotism. What is lacking in both cases has been balanced co-operation, a counterweight, which other nations have been able to supply. In both cases power has been almost entirely onesided, and as a result the entire administration is unbalanced. In both cases, however dissimilar they may appear, the effect has been the same: a weak, wavering system which the country does not understand, and which it puts up with but does not believe in.

Public opinion was admittedly able to make itself felt during the Fourth Republic by the way people voted. From time to time it has also been satisfied under the Fifth (the peace in Algeria is one example of this). But it has never been able to control events and obtain satisfaction at the same time. It has never been able to initiate and watch over its own chosen policy from the beginning, to see its own view expressed in action and feel pride in its sovereignty, first in the decision taken and then in the way it is carried out. Under the Fourth Republic the people felt cheated; under the Fifth they feel they are being treated like children. What is certain is that they may allow themselves to be treated like children today, out of disgust at the frauds practised on them yesterday, but they will not allow it for ever.

If we hope to provide the France of tomorrow with a system of government which on the one hand guarantees the electorate's effective participation in determining policy, and on the other ensures efficiency and continuity in carrying it out, it is essential that a correct balance of power should be achieved. Montesquieu, two centuries ago, put the matter in a nutshell. *"Give any man"* (and I would add, any organised body of men)" *power and he is naturally tempted to abuse it; he will carry it as far as he can. . . . If the abuse of power is to be prevented, things must be arranged so that power checks power."*

Democracy lies in the correct balance of power. In itself such a balance is democracy.

VI. *The Cabinet*

Robert Buron

CABINET MEETINGS

While there is no lack of analytical comment on the place of the president, the prime minister and the cabinet in the Fifth Republic, our stock of descriptions of them actually in operation is as yet rather sparsely furnished. But one man who has been fortunately more ready than most of his contemporaries to sketch than to engage in abstract commentary is Robert Buron. Buron is a leftish member of the MRP who came into politics at the Liberation and has followed his profession with notable zest—politics to him is *le plus beau des métiers*, the finest job there is. He was a minister under the Fourth Republic before serving in the Debré government of 1959–62, and more briefly in the Pompidou government from April-May 1962, leaving it with his MRP colleagues in protest at de Gaulle's contemptuous references to European integration. His description of the cabinet which follows is therefore that of a participant who can draw on experience of both the Fourth and Fifth Republics. While in some respects he puts in perspective allegations of personal rule by the president, he also implies fairly clearly the limitations on ministers' ability to sway decisions in matters where the president is directly interested.

Since 1959 the Cabinet has met every Wednesday, in the morning when parliament is in session, in the afternoon when it is not. Everyone arrives between 9:20 and 9:25, for strict punctuality is the rule. Around the table there is an exchange of handshakes—and of memoranda which it seems useful to hand direct to one's colleagues to underline the importance one attaches to a question, so that they will instruct their advisers personally on the matter.

The hubbub dies down and an usher announces the President of the Republic who enters, accompanied by the Prime Minister, while ministers hastily take the places appointed for them according to long-established protocol. The Prime Minister sits opposite the Chief of State; on the President's right and then his left, and next on the right then left of the Prime Minister, and subsequently on the President's right and so on, sit the Vice-Premiers and Ministers of State if there are any; the Ministers of Justice, Foreign Affairs and the Interior; then the Ministers of Defense, Finance, Education, Public Works, Industry, Agri-

From Robert Buron, *Le Plus Beau des Métiers* (Paris: 1963), pp. 218–223. Reprinted by permission of Librairie Plon. Editor's translation.

culture, Labor, Health, Veterans' Affairs, Posts and Telecommunications, Construction, and so on.

Sometimes the arrival formalities are delayed because the President and the Prime Minister have extended their preparatory discussion. This often happens at moments of tension. However, as a general rule the meeting starts more or less on time. The first part of the agenda is devoted to decrees and bills which have already been agreed to in principle by the ministers directly concerned, but which require the approval of the whole cabinet. The minister chiefly responsible for them gives a brief explanation, and if nobody has any comment the measure is adopted.

The Chief of State or the Prime Minister often asks for further information. A colleague who has not been dealing with the matter sometimes raises an objection. But if a full-scale debate is building up, the dossier is held over until the next meeting and those involved are instructed to reach agreement with the minister concerned either directly or through the Prime Minister.

Next comes discussion of matters which are, or should be, important, firstly the weekly examination of the international situation. Nothing surprises the uninitiated more than those long monologues, delivered in as low a tone as possible by the Minister of Foreign Affairs. The tradition continues unaltered despite all constitutional changes; it is still as difficult for the average minister to follow his colleague's exposition. But when, by listening carefully, he can tell what his colleague is saying, it will seem to him that it is less informative than what he has been reading during the previous week in his daily paper. He therefore wonders what interest such a communication can hold for the President and the Prime Minister, who are the only two people present who have spoken with the Foreign Minister before the meeting. And yet, Vincent Auriol, René Coty and General de Gaulle have successively been extraordinarily attentive to what was said. This reminds me of the remark the Chief of State

addressed to Maurice Couve de Murville at a cabinet meeting in 1959, when the ministers who had only just returned to Paris after overnight train journeys were a trifle drowsy after twenty minutes of an exposition delivered in a low monotone: "Minister, I don't want you to bellow, but I would be grateful if you would raise your voice a little; the subject merits it." The speaker's tone rose for only a few brief moments, but the attention of his listeners was permanently reawakened.

In fact, the Minister of Foreign Affairs has a triple aim, in agreement of course with the head or heads of the executive:
— to inform his colleagues of the official French position on every issue; naturally what he says therefore differs very little from what has already appeared in the serious press;
— where necessary to prepare the minds of his colleagues for some shift in our original position, by nuancing his remarks with the extreme caution appropriate to such delicate matters.
— to mark out a position on certain events so that he can declare two months later, "As I told you on 25 February, China is attempting to . . ."; the allusion to 25 February was far less clear than the reference to it in April would lead one to believe, but in this way our policy gains the appearance of being more thoroughly thought through.

Discussions of the international situation are generally very brief — if the ratification of any treaties is under consideration this comes later in the agenda, as will any proposal for a new move in European affairs. During the last fifteen years the most lively discussions have dealt with "the birth of Europe": the European Parliament, the Coal and Steel Community, the European Defense Community, the Treaty of Rome, and so forth; also on Indochina and North Africa. (It is incorrect to say that in the Fifth Republic the Chief of State rarely consults his ministers; on the contrary under General de Gaulle's chairmanship there have been highly dramatic debates on Algeria, which were even more moving than the announcement of the Cao Bang disaster by René Pleven and Jean Letourneau in 1950, and even more poignant than the discussion of the Carthage declaration which almost led to the break-up of Pierre Mendès-France's government in 1954.

The other problems touched on in this second part of the agenda can be summarized as statements by the Minister of Finance on the budgetary situation, with repeated appeals to the spending ministers to make necessary economies, or on the monetary situation during periods of crisis; or communications from the Minister of Labour, often followed by his colleagues at Industry, Public Works, and State Employees on social conditions, the need to raise family allowances and old age pensions; on strikes which are threatened or have broken out; on long discussions between the Ministers of Agriculture and Finance on the prices of various commodities — wheat in July and August, then milk and sugar-beets before the winter; finally the departmental ministers make statements on the policy they intend to pursue in their particular field.

The third section of the agenda includes proposed bills or decrees which must be discussed in the presence of the Chief of State. This is a diminishing category. If questions are at the exploratory stage and require initial agreement on their general direction they are usually dealt with in the second section of the agenda. Subsequently the drafting is completed by interministerial committees called by the Prime Minister for the purpose and then, finally, unless there is some special difficulty the matter will go direct to the first section of the Cabinet's agenda.

On matters of general policy the discussion is often lively, as it is on any problem which has a direct impact on an important section of the nation — agricultural orientation law; the struggle against multiple farm-holding; the attitude to adopt on a strike; the setting of a price . . . There is much less discussion of strictly technical matters. This is where understandings between ministers of the same party or between ministers in charge of neighboring sectors have their greatest effect — the basis being "support me today on the farm rents bill, and I'll back you next week on reorganization of the Petroleum Bureau."

In the eyes of his permanent officials an efficient minister is one who secures the necessary support from his main colleagues before the matter is put on the Cabinet agenda. Politically the same holds true, and the weekly visit to the Hôtel Matignon, and in recent years requests to be received by the Chief of State, generally weigh more heavily in practice than speeches in Cabinet. Yet these remain indispensable in really important questions, the ones where a man shows himself worthy of the political career he has chosen, by making his position known, by showing that he stands for something.

In this respect, despite the legend which has grown up, Cabinet meetings are no less interesting under the Fifth Republic than they were during the Fourth. It is up to the ministers to bring them to life by the firm expression of their views. I know of no instance when General de Gaulle prevented their doing so. I have even seen him show greater patience than some of his predecessors, notably Vincent Auriol, whose urge to get things done at times prevailed over his complete courtesy.

The reason why ministers express themselves less frankly today than in the past is that many of them are former civil servants, who are not used to giving overtly political advice, and also because others are overwhelmed by the towering personality of the Chief of State and lose heart, afraid they will be given a black mark. I believe that in both cases they are wrong. The Cabinet should be a place where every minister can speak his mind.

Robert Buron

THE CABINET DISCUSSES ALGERIA (I)

In the first of two contrasting accounts of cabinet meetings on the Algerian problem, Buron, who was one of the French negotiating team, describes how the cabinet discussed the talks with the nationalist leaders early in 1962 which shortly afterwards led to the Evian agreements which ended the war.

The Council of Ministers devoted to the preliminary talks at Les Rousses begins, curiously, with a long debate on the role of a State financial body and the need to replace the present president by a man who had been proved incompetent but who happened to be in favour.

I intervene vigorously: "I was in charge of this company at the Liberation, and I know what can be done with it; moreover the victim is a friend of mine."

The Chief of State is not over-fond of long incursions by his ministers into fields which are not strictly speaking theirs. However, he lets me talk, agrees with the force of several of my points but . . . maintains the decision made before the meeting even began.

He then asks Louis Joxe to speak, and Joxe gives a long, complete and detailed outline of the discussions we have had and the bases on which it has become possible to begin the procedure of "cease-fire, appointment by France of the members of the provisional executive, preparation of the referendum on self-determination and finally proclamation of independence, tempered by close cooperation."[1]

Like me talking to the MRP last night, he emphasizes the guarantees obtained for the European minorities on the one hand, and

for France on the other hand in military affairs and the Sahara.

I am asked to speak next. Firstly I rapidly describe the atmosphere, mentioning particularly the state of mind of the men with whom we were negotiating. When I amplify what Louis Joxe said about cooperation . . . Then I insist on two matters which seem essential to me: (1) From their point of view the price that Ben Khedda and his friends have agreed to pay is very heavy and several times our partners showed fears about the National Council of the Algerian Revolution . . . The military clauses are in contradiction with the policy of neutralism advocated by the GPRA . . . The political clauses . . are as many hindrances to the implementation of the socialist programme drawn up by the FLN. There is a danger the Algerian Left might outflank them. (2) The agreement . . is not necessarily a recognition that two quite different thought systems have converged at a single point . . . Rather it serves to set down on paper the moment they passed through the same point . . . The evolution goes on and not only among the friends of Ben Khedda or in France. In my view we must act quickly and speed up the timetable. "I have confidence in the men we are talking to—but will they still be there tomorrow?" "Public opinion wants peace but, if the delay be-

[1]Joxe headed the French negotiating team. [Editor's note.]

From Robert Buron, *Carnets Politiques de la Guerre d' Algérie* (Paris: 1965), 241–245. Reprinted by permission of Librairie Plon. Editor's translation.

tween the cease-fire and self-determination is too long, is it not to be feared that various influences will do their best to change it . . .?"

Jean de Broglie speaks next. He analyzes the clauses relating to the common exploitation of the riches of the Sahara, then stresses the "tough points" of the discussion. He too hopes the transitional period will not be too long.

The discussion then opens, following the well-established protocol for important cabinet debates, General de Gaulle goes round the table, beginning on the Prime Minister's left (omitting himself, so that he can make his point of view known last) and ending with Michel Debré.

Most of my colleagues approve of the outline given by the negotiators and are delighted that the conflict will soon be over. They add a few remarks or make reservations on points where they are directly affected. P. Guillaumat on tests in the Sahara; M. Messmer (Defense) on the tenure of the Mers-el-Kebir base; B. Chenot (Justice) on the amnesty provisions; P. Bacon (Labor) on the employment of North African workers in France; and naturally V. Giscard d'Estaing (Finance) on the burdens we agreed in advance to shoulder.

The most moving statement is by Nafissa Sid Cara, our Moslem secretary of State . . . She focusses all her questions on the likely fate of Moslems who are not attracted to the FLN. Her eyes are filled with tears when at the end the Chief of State interrupts her to say: "Do you really believe, Mademoiselle, that, apart from the exceptions with which we shall have to concern ourselves tomorrow, the great majority of Moslems are not in favor of independence, and that it does not appear to them to be inevitable . . .?"

Raymond Triboulet (Veterans) who has seemed very tense since the beginning of the discussion attacks, with considerable courage, the machinery which comes out from our discussions with the FLN. He goes to the heart of the matter. He speaks with the honesty I would have expected from him.

André Malraux (Minister of State for Cultural Affairs) has been inspired and, while many present do not appreciate his commentary, I fully agree with its underlying theme, "Agreements are not important, the problem is to know whether we are changing battles; the new one may perhaps be harder but in the end it will mark in its way a certain 'liberation of France'."

Maurice Couve de Murville (Foreign Affairs) is chiefly worried at the middle and long term prospect. He refers, not without anxiety, to a revolutionary totalitarian Algeria with which cooperation may prove difficult.

Michel Debré (Prime Minister) is very moved and makes an impression on all of us. Deeply unhappy, he presents a juridically remarkable and honest exegesis of the agreements. He then expresses his anxiety, his fear of the reaction of the French in the short term, his fears for the fate of the Moslems who have compromised with us, his reservations about the practical operation of the agreements in the future. He ends with his voice full of emotion, "Algeria has existed by France. Can she really exist without France? This is the end of a painful trial. The victory is, alas, one to be won over ourselves."

The Chief of State, noting the almost unanimous agreement of the Council of Ministers, thanks the Minister of State and his two colleagues. "This is the way we must continue if, as I believe, the other side really wants peace. For us this is an ending . . . but an ending is always a beginning . . . What will happen tomorrow? We cannot know. We will be fair with Algeria, to which we are giving her chance. Later, we will see. . . . As for France, she must speak. These results which we are now reaching will be submitted to referendum and only after that can we put them into force . . .

Thank you, gentlemen."

Jacques Soustelle

THE CABINET DISCUSSES ALGERIA (II)

Jacques Soustelle is one ex-minister of the Fifth Republic who quite emphatically rejects Robert Buron's conclusions about the role of the cabinet. A gaullist since wartime days and a parliamentarian during the Fourth Republic—whose downfall he assiduously plotted—he was one of the key figures of the May 1958 revolt which brought de Gaulle back to power. A firm believer that Algeria must be kept French, he became a minister in the de Gaulle and Debré governments, his period of office partially coinciding with Buron's, and finally left it in disagreement on Algerian policy in 1960. Thereafter his extreme opposition to de Gaulle led to his going into exile to avoid arrest. In the following passages, his conclusions clash strikingly with Buron's and he claims that far less came before the cabinet than Buron suggests. Yet his description of an Algerian discussion, in 1959, and Buron's in 1962, seem not wholly dissimilar both in form and in the power relationship between ministers and president they imply.

As for me, although I was a member of the government, I had no precise information. An iron curtain had come down between Algeria and me. Not once, during the year and a half that I was in the government, including a year as vice-prime minister, was I consulted about Algeria by either de Gaulle or Debré; my opinion was not sought either on the general line to take or even on a point of detail, nor was there any attempt to use the knowledge I had of the problem. It seemed, on the contrary, to be a *sine qua non* for anyone having to deal with Algeria never to have been there and to speak of it as I would speak of the hidden face of the moon.

* * *

Naturally the foreign policy of France was never discussed in cabinet. Every week we heard a colorless outline by Couve de Murville (Foreign Minister), conceived and delivered like a civil servant's report and

the observations and proposals of a minister—and even then this outline often ignored some of the most important matters.

The same held true of military policy. Guillaumat (Defense) regaled us with proposals for postings or other trivia of that sort, but as for getting ministers to give their views on the basic problems on which the future of our armed forces depended —there was no question of that.

African affairs were no less troubling . . . members of the government were held in ignorance of developments and learned only by reading the newspapers or confidential newsletters what was secretly brewing in our former overseas territories . . . .

Of all the subjects "reserved" for the president, on which the members of the government were often the last to be informed, Algeria was nearer my heart than any other. General de Gaulle on no occa-

L'Espérance Trahie, Editions de l'Alma, 1962, pp. 75, 97–98 and 112–114. Reprinted by permission of the publisher. Editor's translation.

sion put the problem to the cabinet clearly; no clear and unequivocal policy was ever formulated.

* * *

I can still see the long table around which the cabinet sat. I was on Michel Debré's right; Robert Lecourt (Minister of State) was on his left. Opposite him was the President of the Republic flanked by André Malraux (Minister of State) and Louis Jacquinot (Minister of State). Beside me sat Couve de Murville and further along Pierre Sudreau (Building). At the end of the table sat the youngest member, Giscard d'Estaing (Junior Minister, Finance).

The prime minister spoke first, outlining the main points of the problem; there was no Algerian state and there never had been one; one could not expect Algeria and the mainland to be treated as completely identical; finally France had strategic, economic and political positions and interests in Algeria and the Mediterranean which she must maintain . . . How was this to be achieved? "By ensuring a democratic solution in Algeria," replied Debré. On this last point, he continued, two ways lay open. . . . One had no need to be a scholar to realize at once that the views Debré outlined that day, clearly after heavy briefing by the General, were far removed from those he had been professing only a few weeks earlier . . . .

Everyone spoke in turn. Some, like André Boulloche (Education) and Sudreau considered some "innovation" or "initiative" before the opening of the next UN session essential. Bernard Cornut-Gentille (Posts and Telecommunications) on the other hand considered that we should go no further with the FLN than the cease-fire already suggested, otherwise "Arab ambitions would be rampant" through the Maghreb . . . . Paul Bacon (Labor) wanted the recognition that Algeria had a distinct personality of her own. Jacquinot thought we should not attend the UN unless we were sure the US would vote with us. Michelet (Justice) suggested a fresh call for peace and called on the lawyers to find a form of words linking an Algerian state with France . . . . Antoine Pinay (Finance) arguing from the principle that Algeria must be held on to, wanted to know whether the right method was being used . . . . Frey (Interior), while not committing himself, stressed that a choice had to be made between Algerian policy and international policy.

Guillaumat opposed any new measures, which surprised me. "Algeria has no distinctive personality," he said. According to him any relaxation of French authority in Algeria would lead to chaos and massacres, and he felt no blind confidence in democratic and electoral processes.

All in all the cabinet seemed about equally divided between supporters and opponents of an "initiative," the supporters, moreover, interpreting that in rather different ways. A minority leaned towards making Algeria an autonomous entity, a sort of State, a minority opposed this, and another group followed the prime minister along the way he had mapped out at the beginning. Each spoke only once. There was no discussion but a series of statements, which produced a confused impression. It was at the same time obvious that most ministers knew nothing whatever about the matter.

Finally, before bringing the meeting to a close, the President of the Republic said, in substance, "Gentlemen, than you. . . . In matters like this one must march forward or die. I have chosen to march—but this does not rule out dying too." Thus enlightened the ministers returned to their respective occupations.

VII. *Parliament*

François Goguel

FACTORS IN THE WEAKENING OF PARLIAMENT (I)

The Fifth Republic, said M. Debré, was to break with the former practise of parliamentary omnipotence, yet nevertheless establish a clearly parliamentary system, in which parliament would retain a major role and would actively scrutinize government policy. And indeed even now everything turns on there being a majority in the national Assembly for the government which the President of the Republic has selected. Yet clearly parliament has failed so far to play the role that Debré seemed to hold out for it. Why? This paper advances one explanation of the decline. It is followed by a somewhat different interpretation.

Undoubtedly M. Michel Debré, who had been one of the principal drafters of the 1958 constitution and who, as Prime Minister, had a major part in putting it into force, intended to establish a parliamentary system in France, though naturally in a renovated form in which the one-time sovereignty of the National Assembly would be ended, and the government would no longer be subordinated to parliament—but nevertheless a system in which parliament would have a major role to play and would be active in scrutinizing government policy. Why have his intentions not been translated into reality, and what is the explanation of the rapid shift towards a system in which parliament seems purely secondary.

It is not easy to answer because the evolution has been produced by a variety of factors whose importance varies. One of the first and most important is undoubtedly the character and actions of General de Gaulle, the product not only of his personality but of circumstances in which he exercised political power for the first time after 18 June 1940. Since his return to the leadership in June 1958 was approved by parliament in June and the electorate at the September referendum, it was obvious he could not consider his elevation to the presidency, which resulted from the vote of a college of departmental and communal notabilities set up by the 1958 constitution, would result in any diminution of his personality or his rights. It was therefore inconceivable that, once President of the Republic, he could limit himself to being the symbol of the state, and arbitrating very occasionally between the government and parliament. As early as 8 January 1959, the official communique in which the Presi-

From François Goguel, *The Evolution of the Legislative Power in France* (1966), pp. 18–23. Reprinted by permission of the author.

dent's office made it known that M. Debré had been appointed Prime Minister after having "submitted for the approval" of General de Gaulle "the membership and programme" of the cabinet he proposed to set up, showed in the clearest possible way the changed role of the Chief of State. Since it "proceeded" from him and could meet only under his chairmanship, the government was obviously going to find itself so closely associated with the President of the Republic that any criticism of the government would appear to be directed at him. One of the essential ingredients of the traditional parliamentary system — a Chief of State who was not politically responsible, and therefore was in the political background — was therefore lacking right from the very beginning of the Fifth Republic.

But there is doubtless another reason why, right from the beginning of 1959, parliament did not fully exercise the powers which seemed due to it under certain sections of the constitution; it did not want to exercise them in the most onerous area of all — the Algerian problem. Knowing how difficult this problem was, and that the previous regime had foundered on it, and also aware of the confidence the public in both France and Algeria had in General de Gaulle to find a solution — often for quite contradictory reasons, the great majority of members of parliament decided more or less consciously to give the President a free hand in Algerian policy. During the debate of October 1959, after the speech of 16 September on self-determination, spokesmen for the left-wing opposition group openly declared they intended to do nothing which might "hinder the execution of the Algerian policy outlined by the President of the Republic," which amounted to recognizing his right not only to lay down the nation's policy in this key area, but also to put it into force. In February 1960, following the "barricades revolt" in Algiers, when the government asked parliament to delegate legislative power to it so that it could take by ordinance the measures required to remedy the situation revealed by this insurrection, it was on the initiative of an MRP deputy that the Assembly specified that these ordinances would be signed by "General de Gaulle, President of the Republic": yet his signature would have been needed in any case under article 13 of the constitution. This amendment therefore had only one meaning politically: that the Assembly was more ready to trust the President, who was not constitutionally responsible to it, than the government which was responsible, for everything relating to the policy to be carried out in Algeria. By the same token the Assembly renounced control, in the strict sense of the word, on what was at that time the key element in national policy.

By concentrating its activity, or rather its attempted activity, on such problems as veterans' pensions, aid to church schools, the "indexing" of farm prices and the road building programme, that is on questions which were thought to be electorally profitable, while renouncing active participation in the Algerian problem, the parliament of the early years of the Fifth Republic contributed to lessening its own prestige and circumscribing its own role. When in June 1962 the majority of deputies signed a semiofficial statement in which they condemned the foreign policy of General de Gaulle, while during the same month and the following one, on two occasions this majority could not be brought together again to vote a censure motion, this was a further aggravation of the self-renunciation by which the Assembly eluded the responsibilities which the parliamentary principles of the regime assigned to it.

The reason for this attitude is no doubt the fact that at first the majority of deputies who belonged to the old political parties considered the Fifth Republic as a passing phase. They thought that the alterations General de Gaulle made in the system of institutions were purely a result of the predominance of the Algerian problem, and that once this was settled things would settle down to normal. Many of them had realized the only possible outcome would be more or less complete recognition of Algerian independence, but they feared that once the initial relief at the ending of hostilities had passed there would be a public reaction to the loss of the Algerian departments, the value to the national economy of which had been exaggerated by supporters of French Algeria. They believed that this reaction would contribute to a restoration of the former habits and political structure because it would break General de Gaulle's hold on public opinion. This led to what has been called the "submarine tactic," followed more or less deliberately by a number of politicians. This consisted of lying as low as possible in parliament so as to be able to come to the surface again after the Algerian war ended without the risk of suffering personally from any public reaction.

Beginning with the first legislature it was also clear that the procedures laid down in the constitution to permit members of parliament to force the government to explain and justify its policy publicly were not achieving the importance that M. Michel Debré hoped to give them. It is true that, at least in formal terms, the system by which the Assembly must set aside one sitting each week during ordinary sessions for oral questions, with or without debate, has worked correctly. But after the Constitutional Council's refusal to ratify the clauses of parliament's Standing Orders, which would in certain cases at least have allowed debates on oral questions to end in the voting of resolutions or "guidance motions," thus letting the chambers pass a verdict on the government's policy without threatening its survival, deputies seemed to lose much of their interest. Most of the sittings given over to questions are very thinly attended, and the main opposition leaders rarely speak. It seems that the old French parliamentary habit of considering that the most important debates in the Assembly are those in which an attack on the government is either prepared or launched, have remained so strong that the members of the Assembly have found it impossible to adapt to a system which eliminates such debates — those of censure motions apart.

Yet up to October 1962 it was reasonable to feel that some incident occurring during a debate might reveal a crack in the majority, and thus give the debate some significance in terms of the government's solidity. Since the 1962 elections the existence of an almost wholly homogeneous majority in the Assembly has completely removed this possibility and interest in debates on oral questions has fallen still lower, except on one occasion when, exceptionally, an opposition leader, M. Mitterrand, put a question to the Prime Minister on his views about the country's political institutions.

Members of parliament, particularly if they belong to the opposition, but even government supporters at times, often complain that the government uses its prerogative of settling the agenda to prevent discussion of private members' bills. It is true the proportion of laws of governmental origin is very high — over 90 percent since 1959. But during the last three years the proportion of laws originating in private members' bills has risen slightly. It was almost 16 percent in 1963, 11 percent in 1964 (a year when the number of government bills was artificially inflated by some 25 laws ratifying customs decrees), and 15 percent in 1965.

Furthermore, a closer scrutiny shows that very few private members' bills which are reported out of committee are not put on the agenda. And it should be noted that if the assemblies really wanted to discuss private members' bills they could easily draw up a supplementary agenda and add it to the end of the agenda prepared by the government, and sit on Monday or Saturday in addition to their regular Tuesday to Friday sittings.

In addition, they could scrutinize governmental activity by deciding, as they have every right to do, to set up temporary commissions to examine the administrative, financial and technical operations of the public services. But since 1959 only two commissions of this type have been set up, the Senate having employed this procedure in 1961 to look at the management of state theatres and opera houses, and the assembly in 1962 to consider State aid to the cinema industry.

All in all one has the impression that parliament has made almost no effort to adapt itself to the new modes of activity which were the consequence for it of the 1958 constitution. The loss of its old ways of exerting pressure on governments has quite demoralized its members. Convinced that the new system offers them no means of bringing any influence to bear on government policy they remain passive. The result is the absenteeism which is so evident at sittings of both assemblies — and the lists of members present at committee meetings, as published in the Official Journal, shows that they have also been affected.

In this way a kind of vicious circle has become established: convinced that they can no longer influence the general character of government policy to any great extent, owing to the provisions of the constitution and the existence of a disciplined majority, members of parliament fail to use fully what powers they have. The result is that year by year the government's autonomy in relation to parliament increases.

The opposition seems to consider it cannot act effectively within the present system and puts all its hopes in a problematical future where, thanks to an electoral victory, it will be able to create a new one. Meanwhile the withering away of parliament, far from abating, seems to progress from one session to the next.

Philip Williams

THE WEAKENING OF PARLIAMENT (II)

Why is the role of parliament so much less substantial than Michel Debré had hoped it would be? Philip Williams takes issue here with the author of the previous contribution. While the former points to the influence of the political context of the Fifth Republic's earlier years, and the failure of the opposition parties to play a responsible role, Williams emphasises the responsibility of the leaders of the régime. In fairness to both it should be emphasized that the passages printed here are chosen to reveal their divergencies — the common ground between them is considerable. In particular both agree that the place of parliament has been weakened in recent years. One might well conclude that one of the underlying problems of creating a healthy parliamentary regime in France is the weakness of the genuine spirit of parliamentarianism among both the rulers of the system and their opponents.

The gaullist leaders, in their natural desire to restrain the deputies by procedural means from harassing the government, have gone far to restrain them also from exercising those parliamentary functions which the House of Commons still per-

From Philip M. Williams, "The Weakening of Parliamentary Power," pp. 8–13. An unpublished article excerpted here with the permission of the author.

forms: first, the function of persuading the government to change its mind, either by argument or by an appeal to public opinion outside; secondly, the function of persuading the electorate to return a new government at the next election. These restraints were understandable in the crisis years of the first National Assembly, when the government had no reliable majority and an assertive Parliament might merely have produced an insoluble crisis by obstructing de Gaulle over Algeria without being able to provide an alternative. But in the new Parliament elected in 1962, with a loyal gaullist majority and no external crisis, the government has used its immense powers no differently. I agree, therefore, with Goguel that the new situation of a Parliament with a dominant executive and a disciplined majority has disconcerted both sides. But he would put the main stress on the responsibility of the victims for their own misfortune, point out (rightly) that the opposition has contributed to the weakening of Parliament by its failure to adapt. It seems to me that the beneficiaries of the new situation have at least as great a responsibility, and considerably less excuse. For first the government took for itself a formidable arsenal of powers to serve as a *substitute* for a majority. Then they acquired a majority also, which should have allowed them—assuming they really wanted an effective Parliament—to use their arsenal of powers with prudence and moderation. Not a bit of it. They have taken full advantage of both their political and procedural strength so as to ensure that the all-out opposition has few opportunities to appeal to the country, and the moderate opposition exercises no influence on policy.

For the losers from the new regime, however justified the reproach that they might have adapted better, are not the sole authors of their own misfortunes. The government, which gains from it, has exploited its advantages at every point to the great detriment of the prospects of an effective parliamentary system. Let me give three examples of this proposition. First, the way

the government uses its control over the parliamentary timetable. Secondly, the failure of oral question day. Third and principally, the procedure for amending legislation through parliamentary discussion.

First the parliamentary timetable. In the Fourth Republic this was managed with extreme inefficiency; the house always insisted on keeping control of its business and frequently made last-minute changes, postponing essential but disagreeable government business in order to discuss some popular private member's proposal. In the Fifth Republic the government enjoys complete priority, except on oral question day, for the business it puts down. Many people, including me, thought at the time that this was clearly an improvement since Parliament had plainly proved incapable of organising its own timetable effectively; it has been disappointing to see the old faults survive in a different form. Rightly relieved of the danger of opposition obstruction, the government has not bothered about parliamentary opinion. All too frequently it has shown no consideration whatever for the convenience of members or the efficient working of Parliament. The parliamentary analysts of the *Revue du Droit Public*, one of whom is a member of the UNR Central Committee, record similar complaints year after year. In 1963 MM. Hamon and Emeri wrote of periods of "almost complete idleness" followed by "days of working at a frenzied pace; the discussion of bills, which is almost non-existent at the beginning of the session, becomes so heavy as the end approaches that its quality suffers." They showed that the Senate sat for one day (and less than 90 minutes) in the second week of the previous session, for five days averaging six hours each in the eighth week, and for all seven days of the thirteenth week. The budgetary debates, they wrote later, "seem, since 1959, to have been dominated by the sole aim of speed."

Secondly, oral question day. Michel Debré described it as the opposition's time, in which the government's critics could freely debate questions on which they wished to attack the ministers. I fully agree . . . that the opposition have failed, and failed badly, to use the opportunities that question day could provide—though the senators have made much better use of it than the deputies. But the government has not given them much encouragement, and a rather timid attempt to improve matters has been blocked by the Constitutional Council, taking once again an attitude even more Gaullist than the government. The government soon developed a bad practice of sending along a single minister to answer all the questions down for debate on a given day. Clearly there can be no useful debate when the minister's statement is simply a departmental brief read by a man with no knowledge of, responsibility for or interest in the subject.

It is not . . . my impression that oral question day is as badly used as it was. But in the National Assembly, as distinct from the Senate, it is certainly not an occasion when the opposition can dispose of the house's time to discuss whatever topic will, at that particular moment, most thoroughly embarrass the government—for after all what is the purpose of an opposition except to draw public attention to the weaknesses and misdeeds of the government and the grievances which its policies arouse? But oral question day cannot be such an opportunity for opposition time since it is, in the last resort, controlled by the majority! The President's Conference decides which questions to call, in which category and in what order, and when it votes—which it does very rarely—the parties are mandated according to their numbers in the Assembly (as they have been since 1954). The government's critics can therefore get their way only by persuading their political opponents, and it is hardly surprising that while their innocuous criticisms are debated frequently, a really awkward and controversial question rarely finds its way to the order paper at a moment when it might embarrass the government . . . On the other hand the prime minister took the

first opportunity to debate an opposition question on his own role in the government because he thought, rightly, that he could turn it to his own advantage. Responsibility for the failure of question day cannot rest exclusively with the ineptitude of opposition deputies unable to adapt to a new situation; for the majority has both the power and the will to block any attempt by the opposition to use its opportunity to criticise the government in a damaging way. The majority can accept debate at times convenient to itself but can stifle criticism when the opposition might benefit. Surely it must bear some of the blame for members' disillusionment.

My third example is the way in which legislation can be amended. As in the old days, bills still go first to committee for consideration, though it is the government's draft which is debated on the floor. The committee, however, still puts its point of view in the floor debate. As in previous Republics, speaking time on the floor is allocated roughly equally between the four interested groups: the government, the Committee, the majority and the opposition. But this arrangement has quite different results today from those it had in the past. Then the committee was expected to represent the views of those members of the house who specialised in the subject discussed, and it spoke through a rapporteur who might well belong to an opposition party. Now the existence of a majority has changed everything. All committee chairmanships go to members of the majority, who also report all bills. The four-sided arrangement of debating time therefore means that the majority enjoys three shares of it, speaking through gaullist ministers, gaullist rapporteurs and UNR spokesmen, while the fourth share has to be divided between all the opposition parties. It is true that this has no importance on non-political bills, and that the house can play a real part in shaping a measure like the reform of the adoption law which the Assembly amended and then adopted unanimously in 1965. It is also true that the opposition may not find itself short of time, that when it does the majority sometimes concedes some, and that UNR rapporteurs are often very critical of the government and produce very vigorous debates. M. Poirier's report on the education budget in 1964 has since been quoted frequently by opposition leaders, and perhaps offers them some consolation for the fact that in the debate in which he spoke the opposition had 2 hours 10 minutes in all, UNR deputies had 7 hours and André Malraux 45 minutes to reply. The contrast is marked with the House of Commons, where the Speaker will always ensure that minority points of view are heard by giving them quite disproportionate time; if one wants a lively Parliament it seems a better arrangement. Once again, traditional arrangements that worked well enough in other circumstances have been carried over into a new Republic and a Parliament with a real majority. They have been retained precisely because they hampered the opposition and gave an advantage to the majority. Who then has failed to adapt his habits to a new situation?

Robert Buron

THE IMPORTANCE OF DEPUTIES

The traditional role of the member of parliament as an intermediary between his constituents and the central authorities has been increasingly challenged in recent years. On the one hand it is urged that the development of national interest groups has provided alternative and often more efficient channels of access. On the other, the lofty insistence of men like Michel Debré and General de Gaulle on the paramount importance of unity and the national interest has brought the humbler tasks of constituency representation into a degree of official disrepute. Against this twofold attack Robert Buron draws on his own experience as a deputy to assert the continuing need for the traditional mediation of the parliamentarian.

A member of parliament has certain specific functions to perform; these are laid down in the constitution. The main part of his work consists of carrying out these functions. But for this he needs to be elected. If he wants to play a significant role in politics his first duty to himself is therefore to get himself elected, and, once elected, to be constantly preparing for his re-election by winning the good opinion of his constituents both by the way in which he defends their interests, and by his work in the National Assembly or Senate.

Within parliament his function is twofold. He *legislates;* that is, he takes his full part in discussing and amending bills, either voting for them or opposing them. But also he must *control* the actions of the government, which he can dismiss by withdrawing his support or by voting a motion of censure. But *above all else* the member of parliament is the elected representative and advocate with the central government machine for the general interests of his constituency and the private interests of the families living there.

From Robert Buron, *Le Plus Beau des Métiers* (Paris: 1963), pp. 22–34. Reprinted by permission of Librairie Plon. Editor's translation.

This is a very absorbing role. I can remember a Premier who, nearly ten years ago, carried a crushing load of responsibility, but who nevertheless devoted two hours every day to the affairs of his department, even during the worst crises. And another premier who was held in the highest esteem and affection who for years sat at a table in the reading room of the National Assembly, writing his sixty letters a day by hand.

Many highly important men have no hesitation in camping in the waiting rooms of senior civil servants — or even relatively junior ones — in order to defend, not sectional interests, but the rather special collective interests of their constituents or of a commune, a company or even an elector in a constituency. There has been widespread criticism of these obligations, but they cannot be explained in electoral terms alone. The need they meet is so important that if parliament were abolished tomorrow, we would soon have to bring representatives of the departments to Paris to take the deputies' places, at least as far as defense of local interests is concerned, in order to mitigate the effects of excessive centralization. For France is so centralized and the Administration is so complex that there must be a double link between the ministries in Paris and those they deal with in the distant departments.

Admittedly the government delegates civil servants to work in the provinces, but despite the ability of some prefects and senior administrators in the departments, these local representatives of the government are too often unable to gain their minister's ear and they have little standing with the central ministries. When local notabilities come to see them to talk about some new measure or to explain a special case, their reply only too often boils down to: "You are no doubt quite right, but I must follow my instructions, and I have no power to make exceptions, though I will mention this to Paris." There must therefore be a second link between the citizen and the central authorities. Often the member of parliament is the best intermediary.

Any industrial company, however important, knows that if its headquarters are in the provinces it cannot compete equally with a competitor based in Paris. The various permits which are needed to build or extend premises; import licences; foreign exchange certificates; investment bonuses, are all decided by the central administration, and without in the least casting aspersions on the honesty of the civil servants involved, the plain fact is that unless one is on the spot one's interests are likely to suffer. Similarly, banks will only advance large sums after a thorough investigation at the company's headquarters; contacts with buyers and suppliers are easier in Paris than elsewhere. In short, the entire economic life of the country turns on the capital, and companies which have no Paris office feel they are outsiders. . . .

It is true that the steadily increasing number of economic development committees and local economic organizations are relieving the work of members of parliament in this sphere. But even today the administration is more willing to talk to a member of parliament, particularly one with some reputation, than to the president of a regional association. Prefects and senior officials in the departments are even more ready to enlist the help of members of parliament in getting action on matters which have had to be referred to Paris. There can be few conscientious deputies who have not visited the gloomy offices of the rural engineers in the rue de Varenne to persuade the ministry to move more quickly in giving the necessary approval for a water supply project. At the Ministry of the Interior he must get the state to pay its share of the communes' expenses — the balancing of their budget depends on it. He must persuade the Ministry of Health to include a country hospital or home for the aged in the next five year plan. At the Ministry of Finance he takes his place on the delegations which are the customary way of obtaining more generous contributions to the fund for relieving electrification costs, or the publication of a circular required to put a tax relief measure into force.

Unfortunately the Paris bureaucracy is more interested in devising schemes and producing plans than in dealing with the minutiae of everyday administration, and they quite readily let decisions on proposals advanced by the local authorities drag on indefinitely. Accordingly the deputy must be constantly spurring on the central machine, which is too complicated and too bureaucratized. One may regret that a department owes so much to the drive and personal standing of its representatives rather than to any objective evaluation of its legitimate rights—for many years the larger cities, and the seaports in particular, have either chosen a successful politician as their mayor or, if they have chosen a purely local figure, they have insisted that he must go into parliament too. But without the work of the member of parliament, the provinces, taken as a whole, would be even less well treated by Paris than they are at present.

Like the doctors in Molière, professors of law, lawyers and senior civil servants who prepare legislation are accustomed to employing a stilted language which is difficult to use—which bars those unable to use it from ever reaching the higher posts. To become a civil servant in France one must speak "the language"—which only an "elite" knows in all its subtlety . . . And so a screen comes down between the worker in the fields, the factory and the workshops and those who control his fate. I can still recall a high Vichy official who declared, "I've no time to waste. I will not see anyone who has not at least a Bachelor of Laws degree."

The best interpreters of French legal language, in fact the only ones who are prepared to translate it into plain language without charging a fee, are beyond any question the deputies and senators:

— For explaining to a taxpayer the meaning of a bill drafted in these terms:

Article 1: Article 5 of the law of 13 March 1957 is hereby repealed.

Article 2: The following words are to be added to the end of article 8 of the said law: "This declaration must be drafted in conformity with the provisions of article 6 of the document known as the law of 11 February 1943, and sent to the appropriate authority before April 15."

— For making a young couple understand that it is natural for the Mutualité Agricole to make them pay Social Security contributions in respect of the 7½ acres of field surrounding their house, and that they are not exempt from contributing because the husband already pays social security as a clerical worker in a small local factory, while his wife is paying as a lessee of a cafe which serves a few glasses of white wine and a few beers to the local peasants on a Sunday morning, while on the other hand participation in the Mutualité Postale is also proper because the only telephone in the hamlet is the one in the cafe. . . .

— For instilling patience in a farmer who bought a piece of farm machinery eight months ago and wants to know how much longer he must wait to receive the 15 percent rebate the agricultural press has been talking about for the past year.

— For helping the elderly who have qualified for a pension; the village haberdashers who are eligible for tax relief; the farmers who are waiting for the rural engineers to pay the bonus promised for various improvements they have carried out on their farms, to draw up their requests in the sacred language, then to ask the secretary at the *mairie* to fill up the necessary forms, then to attach the necessary accompanying documents—failing which they will receive a form-letter ending in the fatal phrase, "Your request could not be considered in the absence of the necessary documentary evidence. . . ."

These are the essential tasks of the French member of parliament, or at least those to which he devotes most of his time. But the fault does not lie entirely with the civil servants. The ordinary citizen can often be muddle-headed or fail to express himself precisely. Moreover, he is often guilty of bad faith. He hopes that the very complexity of the laws and regulations, which so alarm him, will also be of use to him, and he will rarely hesitate to twist the truth and even to resort to extensive lying by omission in the hope of obtaining a larger pension or the payment of a subsidy.

So the member of parliament must use his discrimination. When his constituents consult him he must discourage unjustified requests, detect obvious lies, and, after informing the citizen of his real rights, help him to present his request, in the interests of good administration as well as of the rights of the citizen.

In recent years employees of the Social Security system or the Mutualité Agricole, local government officials or members of a variety of organizations have increasingly undertaken this kind of work. This is a matter for rejoicing. Nevertheless, when a difficult case arises, these people still ask the member of parliament to intervene. He can be particularly useful in matters which are referred up to higher authority, for in such cases the human aspect of the matter can be submerged by the awe of existing precedents and the fear of creating new ones. The great strength of the administration, when it disagrees with those it administers, is its "negative patience." Which is why the practically non-existent standing of the small pensioner, the prisoner-of-war, and the ordinary citizen must be supplemented by the pressure that can be brought to bear by the member of parliament, who is not only capable of turning the government out (particularly in former times) but who may himself be a minister one day.

In short, the chief preoccupation of the member of parliament has only a distant relationship with policy in the strict sense of the word. The elected representative is first and foremost an advocate, interpreter and go-between. He is also a "social worker"—often the hardest worked and most effective in the department.

Many politicians deplore this state of affairs. Many deputies dream of the day when they can escape from their mailbag, from the continual interceding, the endless appointments, the mundane requests which shower on them after meetings at which they have tried to talk about higher policy. This is understandable. But if the member of parliament did not undertake this work, who would in this country with its complex legislation, and centralized administration? The job must be done, and though in principle it is apolitical, it is inevitably linked with politics.

For there must be an intermediary between citizens and the central government; there must be a permanent check on the administration in the name of those who are administered. This is needed in every country in the twentieth century . . . Modern life demands a system of shock-absorbers and brakes against the inevitable omnipotence of the administration. In a parliamentary system, the member of parliament is the man who keeps the machinery oiled . . . In an excessively centralized system like ours the defense of local interests is of capital importance. For the flaw in our political system does not lie in the relationship between the representative and his constituency. Despite some tenacious myths and a few genuine abuses, the fault lies with the nature of men rather than with the institution itself.

Jacques Isorni

SPEAKING IN THE ASSEMBLY

Probably every parliamentary assembly puts its own distinctive perils and pitfalls in the way of those who speak there. Here Jacques Isorni outlines some of the problems of speaking effectively in the Palais Bourbon, with its half circle of red plush benches. He does so from several years' experience as a conservative deputy—with some reputation for his parliamentary performances during the Fourth Republic. What he says remains as true of the Assembly today.

There is nowhere more difficult to speak than the Palais Bourbon. The criminal or civil bar, the speaker's table and glass of water, the platform at public meetings, from the school hall to huge rallies, the lecture to students, do not involve as many perils. Why is this rostrum, which unmakes reputations faster than it makes them and judges those who confront it without appeal, so greatly feared? . . . . Firstly its physical position. It is set in the middle of a huge chamber in such a way that the speaker finds himself at mid-height with the uncomfortable sensation of being in a suspended gondola completely unattached to the ground. The audience, rising before his eyes like a great concave wall, is at the same time below him (the benches for ministers and committees and the first rows of seats) at the same height, and above him in the most distant benches and the public and press galleries. The speaker dominates and is dominated. Further, he is separated from those listening to him by a terrible void in the shape of a vast basin, which breaks in advance the almost physical contact which should usually be established between the speaker and his audience.

And this is the most demanding audience possible. Members of parliament are sick of listening. Almost all of them have wearied of the charm of speaking, which can be as real and profound as the pleasure of a conquest. They know all the secrets. Having paraded them at meetings of every kind, election meetings, unveilings of statues and openings of squares, distributions of prizes and awards of medals, banquets, golden wedding celebrations or centenaries, agricultural shows and party committees, they have used and abused them and are wearied of them to a degree that they dare scarcely confess. They come in or out of the chamber, move about, gossip, sit at their benches, go through their mail and answer it, read the paper, and an indefinable murmur which has no origin and no meaning, rises towards the speaker, which scarcely makes his task easier. To the right and left of the President, secretaries carry out their administrative duties and, however discreet they may be, with the continual comings and goings they are obliged to make, a similar murmur reaches his ears from behind. He is hemmed in on every side by an anonymous buzz.

Then, apart from the obscure figures who people all assemblies, there are some who are known, and are celebrated, who have played an important rôle in the nation's life. They have seen much, heard much,

From Jacques Isorni, *Le Silence est d'Or* (Paris, 1957), pp. 40–43, 44–47. Reprinted by permission of Flammorion et Cie. Editor's translation.

and occasionally taken note, and they listen with a distant and distracted ear. It requires very exceptional circumstances and very great speeches for a complete silence such as one finds only in church, to fall for even a moment.

Yes, this is a demanding audience which wants quality, accurate information and thorough knowledge of the problem . . . but it is as ready to admire real talent, without always saying so, as to rejoice at failure . . .

This permanent danger of the rostrum includes the unexpected interruption which may spring from any bench at any moment, harsh, flippant or ironical; and can sometimes disrupt the entire order of a long-prepared speech, ruin the most sought-for effects—the speaker fears it but cannot prevent it.

One of the best interruptions I have heard, because despite its brevity it contained both observation, true political insight and humour, came from Michel Raingeard, deputy for Loire Atlantique. In April 1957 there was a debate on the abolition of by-elections, which would have resulted in the person known in electoral jargon the "next on the list"[1] taking the seat, if one fell vacant between general elections. A complicated set of circumstances was outlined:

[1] In the days of proportional representation with lists of candidates [Editor's note.]

how would the "next" be decided then, asked the speaker? The reply followed instantly from a bench on the right: Michel Raingeard rapped out "The government will appoint a socialist by decree! (Hilarity)." (This was the time when M. Guy Mollet was all-powerful and for every job going appointed a member or creature of his party.) Such an interruption had morally judged the debate and brought it to an end.

That is to say that an interruption is one of the imponderables which make the rostrum so perilous. It is prevented when a speech is so good that an interruption would seem more of an inconvenience than a distraction to the listeners.

But it can take a less lively and less electric form, when the interrupter asks the speaker for permission to interrupt him. Custom requires that the latter replies "willingly"—as the *Journal Officiel* shows—even if he has no wish whatever. Then, having gained permission the interrupter puts a question, contributes a detail or a correction, recalls a fact or a promise, which is not without dangers.

Yes, all this which can be analyzed while writing at one's desk but which is felt in a confused imprecise way at the moment of speaking, makes the rostrum of the Palais Bourbon the most dangerous and the most fearsome of all.

Jacques Isorni

COMMITTEES AT WORK

Much of the work of the National Assembly, as with any modern parliament, is done within its committees. But the Assembly's committees, unlike those of Congress, invariably meet behind closed doors. Their characteristic life is therefore something that only the parliamentarian knows. Jacques Isorni is writing here of the committees he knew as a deputy under the Fourth Republic. Since his time the number of committees has been reduced from twenty to six,

From Jacques Isorni, *Le Silence est d'Or* (Paris, 1957), pp. 131–138, 147–150. Reprinted by permission of Flammarion et Cie. Editor's translation.

the membership of which has been sharply increased, doubtless to the detriment of some of the intimacy and camaraderie Isorni describes. Nevertheless, the bulk of what he says remains substantially as under the present regime as under its predecessor.

The committees are the laboratories of parliament. They meet in huge rooms, mostly on the first floor. In the middle is the traditional horseshoe table covered with the traditional cloth of green baize or some strange plastic material in the same colour, except for the Finance Committee where the cloth is pink, the most solemn and luxurious of all, with its heavy pigeon-holes of polished oak. . . .[1] Not a bill or a motion can be discussed in parliament without having previously been reported on by a committee. The committee appoints a reporter with responsibility for preparing a report which will be discussed and voted on by the members. But relatively few reports are in fact discussed in public session. Apart from those which are adopted without any discussion the parliamentary calendar does not allow it. They have been piling up for years in cardboard boxes in the committees' secretariat . . . The public has little conception of the amount of work, knowledge and experience expended — often in vain. Everyone makes his contribution, irrespective of his party. It is in fact surprising to see the way in which some communists assimilate techniques which their original training did not prepare them for at all . . . I was struck, during the long discussion in the Justice Committee on the reform of the Code of Criminal Procedure by what was said by a deputy for Seine-et-Marne, M. André Gautier, a building worker lacking even elementary legal knowledge, and who showed great understanding of the subject, and technical skill in trying to make his party's viewpoint prevail.

The commission secretaries are recruited after a most difficult entry competition. Their role is essential. For many years, at the Justice Committee, I have seen what a secretary can do. M. George, a small, dark, slender, discreet man, with a high-pitched laugh, keeps up to date with everything, and nothing relating to the law escapes him. Having prepared the work of the committee, sitting on the President's left during meetings, he keeps his eye on debates without looking as if he is doing so, corrects mistakes with a word whispered in the President's ear, suggests a solution, the drafting of a complicated clause, illuminating the discussion with an aside, warns against an error, proposes the appropriate expression. In drafting reports nobody would dream of depriving himself of his advice. He looks them over, corrects them, spots things that have been forgotten, proposes drafting changes, giving you to understand with the utmost courtesy that you have found them yourself. While he has no influence over the principles of the decisions taken when these are political, one can nevertheless say that M. George makes the law in France . . .

Speaking in committee is quite different from speaking from the rostrum. The tone is rather like that of a board of directors . . . sometimes familiar, almost always devoid of the passionate character of public debates. Flowery oratory is not acceptable. Human relationships are different. This attachment to a precise task creates a spirit of camaraderie and cordiality between the most determined adversaries.

Vincent de Moro-Giafferri was president of the Justice Committee for several years. He created such a disorder that when the amnesty bill was being discussed in 1953, the feeling grew that it would be better for the committee to be presided over by an

[1] In 1956 the *questeur*, M. Joubert, considering his colleagues to be like school boys who make blots on the desks, rightly no doubt, withdrew the pens and inkwells from the committee rooms. The deputies now had only the right to obtain a ballpoint pen from the secretary at the beginning of the meeting — and dutifully return it at the end.

all-out opponent of the bill such as Jean Minjoz, who was fair and well-organized, rather than by such an astonishing supporter who so bogged down the chariot as he climbed aboard that he completely immobilized it. And the vote went in his favor. And by one of those phenomena peculiar to parliamentary life, it was thanks to Jean Minjoz that the commission was able finally to finish its work. I do not know how many hours Moro-Giafferri made us lose in a torrent of words, striking gestures, expressions and fine phrases. But he had another art—that of lightening the atmosphere, which can become tense even in committee.

One day, in the middle of a discussion, the telephone rang. De Moro-Giafferri picked up the receiver and immediately it was evident that he was showing an unusual deference to the person at the other end of the line. The reporter fell silent. There was no conversation and every glance was directed towards our President, whose verbal bowing and scraping steadily intensified. When he put down the receiver there was something so pressing in the mute interrogation of every eye turning towards him that de Moro-Giafferri felt himself obliged to give an explanation and, leaning back with his eyes half closed, savouring it as if tasting an exquisite praline, he let fall these two words, "A woman." It was the President of the Republic.

There is also a special way of speaking in committee, limits which must be observed. One is particularly aware of this when one exceeds them. Shortly after the suicide of Maître Boumendjel at Algiers in conditions which have still not been elucidated, an unexpected debate began at the National Assembly. M. François de Menthon, and M. Reille-Soult had spoken on the administration of justice in Algeria. Arriving belatedly in the chamber as the debate was ending, I was unable to say my piece; I did not consider M. François de Menthon qualified to make a protest of that kind . . .[2] The

next day the Justice Committee had to deal with the same subject, or at least the procedure for hearing the minister responsible. . . . I literally exploded and made an all-out attack on M. François de Menthon in an irate and oratorical manner. My colleagues, even my political friends sitting beside me, looked at me in consternation. MM. Wasmer and Lacaze, members of the MRP like M. de Menthon, reproached me sadly as one speaks to a child one loves who has misbehaved himself in the living room. I was deeply mortified.

. . . One of the most revealing oratorical "exercises" in committee is hearing a minister and the manner in which he replies to the question addressed to him by the committee members after his initial remarks. Here it is not possible to deceive people into believing you are other than you are; there is no escape. No verbal pyrotechnics nor incidents such as those from which one can profit in sittings of the full Assembly can hide gaps or weaknesses. The introductory remarks are often read, mostly prepared by the minister's staff, and the personal accent of the minister is perhaps not always as evident as when he is caught in the crossfire of questions. That is the moment when the real man appears, with his knowledge, his resources, his qualities at grips with a political matter.

When I belonged to the Foreign Affairs Committee we heard the charming Guérin de Beaumont, who had just been promoted junior minister for Foreign Affairs. He had scarcely recovered from the surprise, and neither had the commission. We heard him on the Franco-German negotiations over the Saar . . . The hearing was a disaster but a smiling, winsome disaster, involving a complete man of the world. . . . He did not hide the fact that he knew nothing about the matter, but he could of course get himself briefed, and all this was said with smiles, a disarming niceness, as in a conversation among friends, with a friendly gesture towards everyone present, so that one finally forgot that this was a minister "informing" the Foreign Affairs Committee

[2]An allusion to Maître Isorni's views on de Menthon's behaviour during the purges at the Liberation. [Editor's note.]

of the National Assembly of the French Republic. Robert Schuman (President of the Committee) was horrified and his nose dropped even further. Since there had been talk of Guérin de Beaumont going to Bonn . . . and the committee had given some consideration to the date, Robert Schuman whispered in my ear: "Well, then, it's lucky he'll never get to Bonn. I know the Germans. They'd eat him alive."

As for René Mayer, speaking to me as a new deputy, he told me, after hearing this charming but unprepared diplomat, "Only one thing counts here, work, work and still more work." Yes, to succeed and be useful in Parliament, even more than elsewhere, it is even more necessary than eloquence. For knowledge and precise information are indispensable. Parliament, and particularly its committees, are less prepared than anyone to be satisfied with mere words.

Pierre Viansson-Ponté

EMPTY BENCHES

One of the things which most distressed Michel Debré about the Fourth Republic was the chronic absenteeism in both houses of parliament combined with the widespread resort to proxy voting by which deputies handed over their voting papers to a friend or the party whip, so that hundreds of votes might be cast by the handful of people who actually attended the sitting. At Debré's behest the constitution contains provisions designed to "moralize" parliamentary life, by punishing persistent absentees and all but eliminating proxy voting. Pierre Viansson-Ponté shows here how among both older opposition deputies and young gaullist loyalists old habits have proved too strong and continue to flourish despite the constitution.

The National Assembly is, as they say, "examining" in all its majesty a section of the budget: a mere bagatelle of a few hundred millions which will go to carry out the industrial, Algerian or foreign policy of France. The discussion is brief: most of the time there are only twenty or so deputies on the benches, rising occasionally to fifty, fewer than the ushers, secretaries and shorthand writers, far fewer than the number of millions involved. A vote is called for. Three long rings balefully resound through the empty corridors and deserted rooms of the palace. They summon any deputies who might be sleeping in the library or lingering in the bar to cast their votes. But nobody comes.

However, in the chamber itself a most curious spectacle meets the eyes. Immediately the division is announced a few deputies rise. They roam up and down the gangways with long strides, rapidly circling the red plush benches, some almost running. They lightly touch each desk as they pass, as if they were playing a piano with a vast keyboard. "This isn't the Palais Bourbon, it's the Salle Pleyel," a humorist would say.[1] These bizarre gymnastics, in which even the ushers join at times, are not some sort of tribal rite; they are just deputies who are present, agile and willing, voting for their absent colleagues.

[1]The Salle Pleyel is a concert hall. [Editor's note.]

Le Monde, 27 November 1963, by permission. Editor's translation.

Yet again the "job" prevails over "ideas": one sees socialists manipulating the buttons marked "C" (*contre*)[2] on the gaullist benches, to reject an amendment which has just been submitted by the socialist group. Tomorrow the gaullists will do the same favor for the opposition by casting votes against the government. The electronic calculator gives the result. The president announces "The National Assembly has adopted the measure by 267 votes to 210." What he really should have said was "By twelve votes to eight with 457 not voting."

Let us re-read the constitution. "The voting rights of members of parliament are personal. The organic law may authorize proxy voting in exceptional circumstances. In this case no person can hold more than one proxy" (article 27). Let us see what the organic law says. It agrees, lists the complicated formalities for assigning a proxy, mentions just six cases where absences are excusable, and refers in turn to the Standing Orders of the National Assembly. Let us leaf through that. Everything is complicated. Stringent penalties are laid down. Any deputy who has not taken part in at least two thirds of the votes cast in full sittings during a session will suffer a cut of one third in his parliamentary stipend. If he has voted in less than half the divisions the cut is doubled, reducing his salary by two-thirds (Standing Order 159). Apart from cases provided for and listed — illness attested by a medical certificate, a parliamentary or governmental mission, military service, participation in the work of international assemblies, cases of *force majeure* — absence is allowed and excused on more than three days during the session. That is clear enough.

Parliamentary absenteeism is not a new phenomenon, and it did not make its appearance with the Fifth Republic. One cannot seriously contend, as *La Nation* did recently,[3] that deputies no longer come to the Palais Bourbon because they are no longer able to overthrow governments at any moment. Neither is there any validity to the argument, often used by members of the opposition that the powers of parliament have been so limited that it is not worth attending. After all, nobody is forced to be elected deputy.

However, on one particular the deputies certainly have a case. When the Assembly debates agricultural estimates for fifteen hours on end until five in the morning, as happened on November 4, then starts on the Ministry of Labor's estimates at 9:30, and when it works at this sort of rate for three weeks at a stretch, it is physically impossible for a deputy to attend every sitting. One can indict the very organization of this "marathon", one can suggest that public holidays and days the Assembly does not sit should be deducted from the strict time-limit laid down by the constitution for parliament to discuss and adopt the budget. One must also agree that the debates are so specialized that there is no need for every deputy to sit through every debate; the existence of large well-organized party groups makes it possible for only those deputies with specialist knowledge of a subject to take part in a discussion which interests them on behalf of their group. Even so, there must be enough of them at the sitting.

Let us admit that there were two noteworthy exceptions in the budget degate; the discussion of the Education and Defence estimates was fairly well attended by day if not by night. But on the other hand there was that scandalous sitting last Friday when the Minister Responsible for Cultural Affairs found he had an audience of eight deputies, which soon dropped to five and finally — one can scarcely credit it — to three.

Having made this qualification, it must be stated that the chamber is more consistently empty now than it was during the Fourth Republic. One can also note, that while it affects every group, absenteeism is most rampant in the ranks of the gaullists.

---

[2] i.e. "against". The Assembly has a push-button system of "electronic" voting [Editor's note.]
[3] The Gaullist newspaper. [Editor's note.]

Allowing for relative party strengths, the communists are the most assiduous, then the members of the Democratic Rally and the Independent Republicans. While they have only 40, 39 and 35 members respectively there are usually more of them in the chamber than of the UNR-UDT which has 232 deputies, including all 31 deputies from Paris itself. Moreover, the hard core always contains the same studious or resigned men, while on the other hand a number of deputies scarcely ever come to the Palais Bourbon.

In the committees things are even worse. Standing orders lay down without any beating about the bush that "the attendance of committee members at meetings is compulsory." They stipulate that absence from more than a third of the sittings entails exclusion from all committees for the rest of the year and a cut of one third in the deputy's stipend. (Standing Order 42). Whatever the reason for this cut it has not been enforced for a long time—to be precise, not since the second month after the Standing Orders came into force in 1959. A timid attempt to apply it the first month led to such a storm that penalties were immediately and finally abandoned. Occasionally a deputy who falls gravely ill and is absent for months and fails to inform the Assembly's administration finds his salary has been cut. This happened to a former minister, though admittedly he is a member of the opposition and not affiliated with any party group, otherwise his group would have taken the necessary action on his behalf. The error was righted.

The penalties and prohibitions on proxy voting are certainly not the only sections of standing orders to fall rapidly into disuse. It is and remains forbidden to read a speech at the rostrum—a measure taken in the naive hope of preventing a speaker from uttering phrases written by someone else. This prohibition on delegating one's thoughts and style is of course not observd by anyone, and here again the violation is committed by all parties, including ministers and *rapporteurs*. The latter know that their reports have been printed and distributed and therefore do not require oral introductions, but many have no hesitation about imposing tedious repetition of them on empty benches. One could give more examples.

But one returns again to that major vice, absenteeism. If one denounces it one is immediately open to the accusation of feeding anti-parliamentary feeling and playing into the hands of the régime, almost of discrediting democracy itself. This type of argument has proved very useful. Everyone knows it is the press and not generals who lose wars, the papers and not ministers who are responsible for the government's failures, and that the demoralization of public opinion is caused by those who denounce excesses rather than those who commit them. Cutting across party lines, *esprit de corps* is just as strong in parliament as in other professions. But in this case, if anyone is assassinating democracy, one feels the wish to reply to the accusers by twisting the celebrated saying, "*Que MM. les députés commencent*" or do another job.

Marie-Thérèse Lancelot

A DEPUTY'S MAILBAG

Writing to one's parliamentary representative is one of the classic channels of political communication in every western democracy. But just who writes and why? In recent years political scientists in several countries have been peering behind the mythology to ask such questions. Marie-Thérèse Lancelot's article is the pioneering effort in France. She has analyzed the correspondence received by an un-named member of parliament over a three-year period. She bases her comments here on file records relating to 1,261 letters from individuals—a further 15 requests from pressure groups and 108 from mayors on matters relating to the needs of their communes were not analyzed. In comparing the nature and volume of French constituents' letters to their deputy with the position in other countries, one must of course remember that the French deputy is in his constituency almost every weekend throughout the year.

WHO WRITES TO A MEMBER OF PARLIAMENT?

Seventy percent of the correspondents wrote on their own behalf. The cards mention correspondent's occupation too infrequently for anything more than a rough estimate to be possible. However, it seems that contrary to general belief these correspondents for the most part occupy modest positions on the social scale: farmers, small shopkeepers, school teachers, railway or postal employees . . . How can we interpret the rarity of letters written by heads of businesses or other leading figures of other kinds? It seems likely that such people use other means of communication; the telephone, conversations at political or nonpolitical meetings etc.

Three hundred eighty one letters, 30 percent, were presented by a third party acting as an intercessor. This "indirect circuit" is more "institutional" than is generally believed. Departmental councillors and mayors are the most frequently asked, less because they are known to be personal or political friends of the minister than because they are the administrative links between central government and the citizen. A table below illustrates this.

The number of letters each departmental councillor wrote varied widely. One wrote no fewer than 81 times, another 35 times, while the remaining letters were divided among 7 councillors: 9, 4, 3, 2, 1, 1, 1. Was the output of letters by the first two due to their own drive or personality, or to their political or personal relationship with the deputy? There was also a striking correlation between the individual councillor and the nature of his requests: one wrote particularly about commutation of fiscal or penal penalties, while the other was more concerned with awards of the Legion of Honor.

Among the figures in the department who sent the most letters were:

a printer (15 letters)

a hotel-keeper (10 letters)

From Marie-Thérèse Lancelot, "Le Courrier Parlementaire," *Revue Française de Science Politique* (June, 1962). Reprinted by permission of the *Revue Française de Science Politique*. Editor's translation.

	ABSOLUTE NUMBERS		PERCENTAGE
ORDER OF IMPORTANCE	Institutional Circuit	Political & Personal Circuit	
1. Departmental Councillor	127		33.33
2. Influential people in the department		92.	24.35
3. The deputy's *suppléant*[a]	63		16.53
4. Mayors	61		16.01
5. State employees (including teachers)	23		6.04
6. Priests, etc.		8	2.10
7. Personal friends		4	1.05
8. Members of parliament from other departments		3	0.08
	274	107	

a director of an insurance company (7 letters)

By and large mayors write less than departmental councillors, and their requests are more often more modest: they ask for educational scholarships, pensions and allowances, and such decorations as the *Mérite commercial* or the *Mérite sportif.*

WHERE DOES THE MAIL COME FROM?

950 of the 1231 cards indicate the name of the correspondent's commune. Classifying these letters according to geographical origin we find:

769 letters	- 80.94% -	come from	the members's constituency		
89	"	9.36%	"	"	immediately surrounding areas
47	"	4.94%	"	"	the Paris area
23	"	2.42%	"	"	foreign countries
22	"	2.31%	"	"	other parts of France.

WHAT DO CORRESPONDENTS ASK FOR?

Twenty-two types of request have been distinguished and classified in order of importance in the table:

[a]A *suppléant* is elected at the same time as the deputy to replace him should he enter the government or die. [Editor's note.]

REQUESTS FOR	Number	Percent
Administrative posts or employment in public or private industry	180	14.27
Pensions of various kinds	138	10.94
Change of post (state employees wanting transfer)	124	9.81
Scholarships (university, secondary and technical education)	76	6.02
Decorations and other honors	62	4.91
Deputy's intervention in disputes with the administration	58	4.59
Promotion of state employees	47	3.72
Suppression or reduction of penalties (taxes, traffic fines etc.)	47	3.72
Housing	46	3.64
Information and documents	39	3.09
Deputy's intervention in a legal case	22	1.74
Tax reductions	22	1.74
War damage claims	22	1.74
Naturalization	18	1.42
Granting of established status to state employees	16	1.26
Administrative reclassification	14	1.11

VII. Parliament

Requests for	Number	Percent
Bureaux de tabac[a]	13	1.03
Decentralization of a firm in the deputy's constituency	9	0.78
Labor permits	8	0.63
Various favors requested by members of the armed forces, including:	122	9.67
posting to metropolitan France rather than Algeria	(42)	
leave or extension of leave	(31)	
Miscellaneous favors, including:	103	
priority in entering school or hospital	(8)	
deputy's intervention over school exams	(7)	

Favors

Although it is not easy to make a clear distinction between what is a favor and what is not, it is clear from the table that these are far from making up a majority of the requests. If we consider as favors:

1. Favors requested by members of the armed forces   122
2. Miscellaneous favors   103
3. Decorations and other honors   62
4. Reductions of various penalties   47
5. Reductions in taxes   22
6. Allocation of *bureaux de tabac*   13
         369

we have a total of 369 interventions, or only 27 percent of the total. *Bureaux de tabac*, which are customarily cited as the most common favor, form only a tiny percentage.

The member of parliament as intermediary

A close examination of these requests suggests that electors expect their member to protect them and help them in their relations with the administration. At times the citizen finds it simpler to get in touch with his deputy than to try to cope himself with administrative procedures whose complexity disconcerts him (this is particularly frequent in claims arising from war damages); because he is not sufficiently well informed, at times he requests as a favor something to which he was already fully entitled (as with most of the requests for educational grants). Often the elector expects the deputy to intervene so that certain administrative rules may be relaxed in his favor: it is in this spirit that postal and railway employees and teachers address their requests for promotion, reclassification or transfer to him;[1] finally, it seems that at times the citizen asks the deputy's help to re-establish the balance — this happens particularly when the administration resorts to such action as requisitions or compulsory purchase.

HOW DOES THE DEPUTY REPLY?

The deputy acknowledges receipt of all letters within ten days at the most. He gets in touch with the relevant government department as soon as possible. Depending on the difficulties encountered the reply is sent on to the person concerned with a delay varying from a month to a year. Of the 627 replies analysed:

  —279 (44 percent) were favorable
  —296 (47 percent) were negative
  — 52 (8 percent) reported a delay, but 32 anticipated a satisfactory outcome.

There is not sufficient data to allow firm conclusions. However, it seems possible to distinguish three types of request according to the reply given them:

1. Requests in which the deputy refused to intervene — to alter the result of an examination, intervention in legal questions.
2. Those the administration readily

---

[a]A permit is required to open a *bureau de tabac* selling tobacco, stamps, official licenses, etc. [Editor's note.]

[1]This is because French railways are nationalized, and French teachers are civil servants employed by the central government. [Editor's note.]

grants—settlement of war damage claims, award of educational grants, payment of pensions.

3. Those for whom the deputy very rarely intervenes, but usually is successful when he does so—posting back to France from Algeria, requests for promotion or transfer.

Christian Pineau

A DEPUTY AND HIS CONSTITUENTS

Christian Pineau, a former Socialist deputy and Foreign Minister in 1956–7, is one of the few French practising politicians to have written a political novel. This brief extract is an amusing reminder of the contradictory expectations constituents may have of their deputy.

"My dear Victor", the *café* proprietor wrote, "everyone here is asking what you are up to at the Palais Bourbon. That is not the place for a deputy when there are so many local problems to be settled, nor for a mayor when marriages must be performed. The Ribiers were very annoyed that you left it to an assistant-mayor to marry their daughter. They were hoping that you would be there and give a proper speech. I'm afraid that they are going to hold your absence against you. What's more, the engineer from the Rural Engineering Department came about water supplies for Saint-Michel-des-Gâtines, and seemed rather surprised not to find the departmental councillor for the canton there. Since he is a supporter of Dolivon he is going to exploit the situation.

"There are a lot more things I would like to tell you about, chiefly about the bandmaster who is rubbing everyone up the wrong way. Finally, I should add that everyone was shocked to read in the papers that there were only fifty deputies in the chamber on the day of the abortive investiture. What a way to carry on!
Yours, Jules"

Robert Buron

LE WEEKEND POLITIQUE

Following M. Buron's argument in more general terms about the continuing need for the ordinary back-bench member of parliament, in more anecdotal vein he describes one of the central features of French political life, the political weekend. While M. Buron is very much describing the kind of relationship he himself had with his constituents in a rural department under the Fourth and

From Christian Pineau, *Mon Cher Député* (Paris, 1959), p. 41. Reprinted by permission of René Julliard. Editor's translation.

From Robert Buron, *Le Plus Beau des Métiers* (Paris, 1963), pp. 83–89. Reprinted by permission of Librairie Plon. Editor's translation.

Fifth Republics, what he says would hold true for deputies for all but the most urbanized seats at any time since the war, virtually irrespective of party. Robert Buron's deputy is perhaps slightly more conscientious and traditional than most; however most deputies are also members of local councils and a fair proportion would sit on departmental councils too, many being mayors of their home *commune* — entailing still more meetings in the course of the weekend. The French deputy also emerges here as a man whose contact with the constituency is primarily personal — the equivalent of congressional assistants does not exist in France — and he is physically present in his constituency for a much greater proportion of the time than either his British or American counterpart.

Eighty-five percent of members leave Paris on Friday evening at the latest, and return on Tuesday. The most unfortunate are the representatives of the more distant departments, who spend two nights in the train every week but are only allowed a limited number of free sleeping car journeys. On average forty to forty-five times per year members spend Saturday, Sunday and Monday in their constituencies. But family life draws little profit from this. The "surgery" in the main town, visits, and sometimes party meetings take first place.

A conscientious deputy or senator maintains the same sort of relationships with the prefect and the ministries' branch offices as he does with ministers and the central ministries in Paris. If he has made any personal reputation, has become a known political figure, and has been a member of several governments, the prefect and his assistants quite legitimately take this into account and help him resolve on the spot many problems which are not important enough to be taken up in Paris. And if he wants to deal really effectively with ministries, the member will find it useful to get himself briefed by the *préfecture*, the Highways Department engineer, or the inspector of schools. In this way he will know which branch is dealing with the question, the objections which have been made already and which must be overcome, and what arguments the relevant section of the ministry might be receptive to.

When it is well-knit and experienced the prefect-deputy or prefect-senator team can be particularly effective in improving a department's roads, schools, water supplies or other facilities. If, by good fortune, the prefect has the skill to foster relations between two influential members belonging to different parties, in such a way that each is given an important role without injuring the other's interests, the trios or quartets formed in this way can bring both political peace and economic development to the region.

Saturday afternoon or evening is a favorite time for holding meetings in the principal town in the department. The departmental agricultural competition; the exhibition and fair; the congress of ex-prisoners of war; the general meeting of a veterans' organization; the congress of the parents of large families; the annual meeting of the agricultural organizations, of the *Mutualité Agricole* or various cooperatives. Then there are the traditional get-togethers of the stock-breeders, grain merchants, bakers, farriers, hoteliers, service station, and restaurant proprietors, and bar keepers.

One problem which arises at these meetings is solved differently in different regions. The local members of parliament feel it their duty to be there and hear those present express their wishes. For their part, they feel prepared to explain to this section of the electorate which is clearly interested since it has taken the trouble to come, what they have already done for the cause in Paris, what they pledge themselves to do, and what they would be able to do if only the country's policy was differently conducted, either at the rostrum during the meetings or after the official banquets.

But it is no small thing for half a dozen politicians to speak after the chairman, and before the prefect who sums up in the name of the government and the Republic, particularly if the banquet has already lasted a considerable time. In the Midi this is usually what happens. The participants have a tradition of courtesy and patience and they are tolerant in the face of eloquence. In the East, where the spirit of discipline reigns at every level, the number of speakers is often limited by formally negotiated agreements, which may even be umpired by the prefect. In the West, victory goes to the strong. The chairman of the gathering warns his friends in advance and asks them to speak at the moment he chooses, carefully ignoring the others. It is not unknown for someone who has been "overlooked" in this way, and who is either tougher-minded or more vexed at not being given the chance to speak to take it without being asked. Before summing up the prefect too may come to the help of a member who faithfully supports the government but has just been deliberately passed over by saying, "Thank you, Mr. Chairman, but I see Senator Martin who knows this question very well, and who can undoubtedly enlighten us on the present state of the controversy before I express the gratitude of the government for this splendid gathering."

Apart from the speeches, the reports in the newspapers and particularly the photographs (some regional newspapers which have little sympathy for the party to which a member belongs in parliament, systematically cut and retouch photographs so as to exclude him), what counts are the informal conversations after a meeting or the apéritif before the banquet which is a lengthy affair just because it provides an opportunity for making useful contacts.

On Sunday and even during the week the member of parliament is a voracious consumer of gasoline, and a spender of money. Local fêtes, village fairs, agricultural shows, official openings follow one another at a frightening rate. Returning home at midnight the representative takes stock. He attended the mass in memory of the victims of the resistance at Criteau, and the annual meeting of paralytics at Lusignan. He arrived at Sicol as lunch was ending, just as the chairman of the veterans was receiving the Legion of Honor and he gave his speech. From there he went to the moto-cross meeting at Nouvilliers and spent a few minutes at the horse-racing at Crix, then on to the fair in aid of the church schools at Trossec, but he did not reach Chanton-Saunier until 8 o'clock and the fair had been over for half an hour; however the mayor invited him to stay for an apéritif. Finally he was able to return to the county town where he arrived pardonably late at a farewell dinner for a local magistrate who was being transferred to another department.

He is tired out. His pockets are filled with scraps of paper on which he has noted the cases brought to him during the day: only two at Criteau, three at Lusignan, six at Sicol—two from people he sat next to at lunch—one each at Nouvilliers and Crix but five at Trossec where he lingered rather a long time, and one again at Chanton-Saunier (but on it he has noted no fewer than four requests from the mayor who conscientiously did his duty while plying him with glasses of Saint-Raphael). Three of these requests are urgent. One concerns a summons brought against a farmer by the gendarmerie ten days ago. Too late to talk to the captain. He will have to have a word with the sub-prefect who plays bridge with the prosecutor every Monday evening. The second is a request for leave for the son of the secretary-general of the Caisse de Crédit Agricole at Trossec. He is doing his military service in Algeria and his sister is getting married next week. Can he have special leave? (The member recalls that last year he had failed to get the boy transferred near Paris. "I'm extremely sorry, but everyone wants the same thing," he had been told by the Army minister's *chef de cabinet*.) He will have to call Paris in the morning. The third matter is one in which the mayor of Chanton-Saunier has taken an interest —an obscure matter concerning a minor road. The mayor supported the Radicals at the last election. He must be shown that they no longer have the political skill that brought them success after the Liberation. Tomorrow he will pay another call on the highways engineer.

His accounts are quickly made up. Ten litres of gasoline three times makes thirty francs.[1] (It is better to buy in small quantities and stop more often at country service stations, where the owners are always ready to talk to their deputy. Ten francs for the collection at Criteau; 50 francs for the paralytics at Lusignan; 15 francs for the lunch at Sicol, for which he insisted on paying despite the chairman's polite refusal. A consolation prize of 20 francs at Nouvilliers, of 10 francs at Crix, and 50 francs at Trossec—including the highly embarrassing purchase of a live duck which he handed on to the presbytery. All told, 185 francs. It could have been worse.

But, more annoying, at several places he got a distinctly cool reception. Although the paralytics applauded Senator Goutal—was it because he is a member of the Senate's social welfare committee?—the deputy had

[1] i.e. 3 × 2½ U.S. gallons = $6.00. $1.00 = 4.9 francs.

only a *succès d'estime*. At Nouvilliers in the afternoon the public was clearly more interested in the prowess of the service station owner's son who came eighth out of eleven than in any important people who might be present. True, everyone had been very kind at the lunch at Sicol, and although the mayor was out when he called at Crix, he had some very useful conversations at the Trossec fair about who should succeed Dr. Bienvenu who, it was decided, would not stand again for the departmental council. Then there was the imbecile he outbid for that duck who declared, "though the deputy's bought it, we pay for it in the end." Plainly he had a nasty mind.

All in all a hard day! He could not have done more, but as his friends say, "he must not fall asleep on the job." But that is precisely what he must do, for in a few hours he has a "surgery" at the other end of the department, and on the way he must stop and see the teacher at Ganiers who is being talked of as the socialist candidate to succeed Dr. Bienvenu. This would only complicate a situation which is already difficult enough. Finally, he must try to settle the urgent problems he has looked at before the 17:45 train takes him back to Paris in time to attend the funeral of Jacquin, one of the Vice-Presidents of the Assembly on Tuesday morning. He always got on well with Jacquin. . . .

François Goguel

THE ROLE OF THE SENATE

When first the 1958 constitution was published commentators noted the substantial number of minor changes which seemed to raise the status of the Senate, which only twelve years earlier had been threatened with extinction. One gaullist commentator even referred to the "senatorial Republic." Yet within a few years gaullists were talking of abolishing or drastically modifying the Senate. The author who is both an eminent political scientist and a long-standing servant of the Senate as its Secretary-General here discusses the changed role of

From François Goguel, *The Evolution of the Legislative Power in France*, (Paris, 1966), pp. 16–18. Reprinted by permission of the author.

the Senate and its quarrel with the régime at the moment when relations were at their worst; since then the extremes of antagonism have been attenuated — without, however, really resolving the problem of the second chamber.

During the last three years the main problem of government-parliament relations has risen in the Senate, since it was resolved in advance in the Assembly. This was aggravated by the personal conflict which broke out between the President of the Senate on the one hand, and the President of the Republic and the Prime Minister on the other, arising from the fact that during the Radical Party congress of September 1962 the former accused those responsible for the constitutional referendum which was to be held on 28 September of committing an abuse of power — that is an offence laid down and punished in the criminal code. At least this is the generally accepted explanation of the fact that usually in 1963 and 1964, and always in 1965, the government was represented only by a junior minister and not by the ministers who would normally be responsible for defending government proposals.

Because of its political makeup the Senate, where the UNR have only thirty members, and where only a dozen Conservatives are affiliated to the Independent Republicans, is not *a priori* well-disposed towards the government. The habitual absence of ministers from its sittings provoked a wholly understandable annoyance which was exacerbated by the government's practice of demanding package votes as soon as a debate opened every time that it had used the procedure for a rather delicate matter in the Assembly, having reached agreement there on the amendments it would accept with the groups supporting it. Finally, the way the Senate is elected makes it particularly sensitive to recriminations from the farmers, and it tends to think the farmers are more likely to obtain parity with other sections of the population, which has been the main declared aim of the state's farm policy since the adoption of the orientation law in 1960, by way of higher prices rather than structural reforms.

Thus everything combines to lead the Senate to adopt an attitude of critical vigilance towards the government. But the government feels no need to pay attention to the views of the majority in the Senate because it has a disciplined majority in the Assembly to which it can always give the last word when the Senate does not accept its proposals. Despite the conscientious work of the junior ministers responsible for relations with the Senate it has made almost no attempt to win over the second chamber. On one exceptional occasion it took a different approach, over the Bill to reorganize the departments of the Paris region in the spring of 1964, when the Minister of the Interior attended in person to defend his Bill, showing that is was possible for the government to convince a majority of Senators to adopt one of its measures. But during 1965 ministers did not once attend full meetings of the Senate, though they attended a number of committee meetings. Also the proportion of Bills adopted against the Senate's wishes has increased markedly since the end of 1962: there were three out of 301 in the four years 1959, 1960, 1961, 1962; and 18 out of 262 during the three years 1963–5, including 3 out of 18 in the autumn session of 1965, which shows how the situation has deteriorated.

The role of the Senate has therefore become caught up in a vicious circle: the non-attendance of ministers makes senators bad tempered and they show this by voting against the government, while the apparently increasingly systematic character of the Senate's opposition encourages the government to discount its views completely, considering them to be dictated by purely partisan considerations. A second chamber whose legislative powers are not equal to those of the lower house can only win for itself a degree of authority by considering every measure brought before it from the same view as its authors—by trying to improve it rather than to change its whole character; it should certainly not succumb to the temptation to take up attitudes towards them intended to serve the electoral propaganda of certain parties by letting its attitude be dictated by mere vote-catching. Between 1947 and 1954 the Council of the Republic won a degree of authority which went well beyond the few powers it formally possessed because it never succumbed to the temptation of engaging in purely negative opposition, and its opinions tended invariably to improve the measures voted in the Assembly, and not to take the opposite tack systematically. Since 1959 and particularly since 1962, circumstances have been such that the Senate has taken up exactly the opposite attitude, and this has robbed it—at least in the short run—of almost all influence not only on the general direction of policy but even on the drafting of the most important Bills in eco-nomic and financial affairs and on administrative reform. The only Bills where the Senate has left any real mark on the final draft have dealt with strictly legal matters such as reform of the marriage system, guardianship and adoption.

All in all it seems that the existence of a coherent and disciplined majority in the National Assembly—an almost unprecedented situation in French political history—has disconcerted all the actors in the parliamentary game. It has led the opposition not to play its full role because its leaders felt there was no purpose in expressing their views fully from the rostrum of the Assembly once they knew there was no chance of winning over a wavering fraction of the majority, and thus some prospect of putting the government into serious difficulties or actually defeating it. It has led the government to think of relations with parliament purely in terms of reaching compromises with the views of the groups constituting its majority in the Assembly and to neglect completely what is said and done in the Senate.

Michel Debré

THE FUTURE OF THE SENATE

The Senate is yet another institution in the Fifth Republic which has failed to play the role that the constitutional architects laid down for it. Michel Debré's views on the present and future role of the Senate, and what should be done with it therefore assume a particular interest. After recalling how under the Third Republic the authority of the Senate rested less and less on the personal character of the senators, and more and more on party considerations, he notes the consequences of the imbalance arising from the failure of the senatorial electorate to reflect demographic change, then continues. . . .

This imbalance, which had become markedly worse in recent years was fatal to the Senate's hope of real political power. It mattered little that in 1946 by changing its name and limiting the term of its members and their functions that an attempt was made to suppress this political rôle; or that during the Fourth Republic various modi-

From Michel Debré, *Au Service de la Nation* (Paris, 1963), pp. 211–214. Reprinted by permission of Editions Stock. Editor's translation.

fications to the electoral system and its powers brought a partial reestablishment; or that in 1958 by restoring its name and increasing the term of its members and granting it greater powers the attempt was made to reestablish it fully. Since the Senate is merely the expression of local government units, it is condemned by the excessive inequality in the representation of the departments and to a lesser degree by the inadequate representation of the towns, never to have the legitimacy which is essential for the exercise of the powers granted to it. It has been calculated that the majority of senatorial electors come from areas with under 2,500 inhabitants—a little more than a third of the population. It has also been pointed out that the majority of senators come from the 60 departments with the smallest population—some 40 percent of the population. These characteristics explain the attitude of the Senate during the last few years: an opposition which extends beyond the government itself and in a way strikes at the policy of a State which is evolving more rapidly and more profoundly than those parts of France that elect the majority of the senators.

This situation has been aggravated by the mistaken calculations and partisan passions of the old parties. In seeking, since the return of General de Gaulle, to turn the Senate into a refuge for the spirit which had already destroyed the legitimacy of the National Assembly, in a few months they accelerated a process that the 1958 constitution sought to halt. In striving to achieve "all-party unity" from the right to the left, in refusing to accept important bills, in opposing taxes, and in seeking to set the local *notables* against both the Chief of State and the electorate, the Senate reached the extraordinary position in 1962 of upholding almost unanimously a position which the Nation was going to condemn by a large majority during the following weeks. The reform of the Senate is therefore essential in order that the Republic may again have a legitimate second chamber.

One other major proposal is worth consideration. These days the Nation has another political reflection, formed by those organisations which consider themselves "representative"—the organisations of workers and employers. The Economic and Social Council which was renewed and revitalised in 1958 is an institution whose qualities and whose limits have become evident over the years. It is no longer possible to conceive of a governmental system which does not find a place for men whose personal records, occupations, and representative character are such that the government naturally consults them—for many of them have a significant influence over important sections of the electorate. Should a third chamber be retained? Should we not, on the contrary, look to representatives of this kind making up, at least in party, the second chamber. The composition and means of appointing members of the Economic and Social Council should be noted. These are not elected representatives as the term is normally employed in democratic politics: these are spokesmen, delegated by groups, and their authority arises from their identification with that group. Furthermore, some come from producer industries, that is they bring to the collectivity the result of their labour, their methods, and their capital. Others come from bodies which qualify because of their importance in our society. Finally there are the "persons with special qualifications" whose appointment by the government recalls —keeping a proper sense of proportion —the creation of peers at the end of the monarchy. From all this one can conclude for or against the transformation of the Senate as one wishes. Before making a final decision we must carry the study further.

First, it must be agreed that the new Senate could not be a single chamber. It is not possible to make men who are chosen in such radically different ways join regularly in common consideration of measures. This Senate would be composed of two, or preferably three, sections. The first section would be "political," and would include senators from the villages, towns and provinces of France. A second section would be "economic," including representatives of the various kinds of producers, leaders of industry, managers, technicians, white and blue collar workers, peasants, shopkeepers and bankers. A third section would include representatives of bodies and institutions of all kinds that are concerned with the division of the national income: this would be the "social" section. In the second and third sections, the senators would for the most part be chosen according to the various systems of selection laid down by their union or professional organization, but a small number might be appointed by the Chief of State. This would be a way of reverting in a form appropriate to the twentieth century, to the practice of having within a parliamentary assembly men whose personal authority could be employed to the benefit of the régime.

Next one should point out that the rôle of a Senate constituted in this way would be very different from the rôle bequeathed to us by nineteenth-century tradition. Its intervention in the consideration of legislation can no longer be subsequent to that of the first chamber. For one thing, one of the reasons for changing the composition of the second chamber is so that it can give a knowledgeable opinion before the decision of the elected chamber. Moreover, this Senate should not be conceived as a watchdog over the first Chamber. Except in urgent cases governmental and even private members' bills should normally be debated first in the Senate. They would normally be considered by each section separately, with plenary meetings of all three in exceptional cases. Then the National Assembly would consider them and one might, possibly, provide for a second consideration by the Senate, perhaps in plenary session, where there was serious disagreement. After this the National Assembly would take the final decision. The Senate would in other words cease to be a second chamber with parliamentary powers and become an assembly

with wide competence but which was essentially deliberative and consultative.

This complete reform of the Senate involves revision of the constitution. A simpler reform, which could be a first stage, lies within the competence of the legislator alone—that is, once the procedure of *navettes*[1] has operated, it depends on agreement between the government and the National Assembly. For, without altering the Senate's character as an assembly issuing from local government units, an ordinary law can change the way in which senators are chosen.

First, it is entirely logical to increase the representation of the urban population. So as not to cause too violent a change in the bases of the traditional electoral system, a beginning could be made by deciding that the mayors of the largest cities would be senators as of right—though they would lose this right if they stood for the Assembly. Above all, there is a real need to increase the proportion of senatorial electors representing towns with more than 10,000 inhabitants.

Next there should be a redistribution of seats. This second reform is fundamental because, even more than the previous one, it can restore the Senate's representative character by obliging the second chamber to embrace the demographic development of the country. The representation of each department should correspond to its population—and since the present size of the Senate should be maintained, many departments should be joined for the purposes of forming a single electoral college. Thus we would return to one of the ideas of the founders of the Senate: the candidates would be some distance removed from the electors and would require a stronger personality in order to attract their votes. A new electoral law for the Senate seems to me a necessity. The maintaining of the Senate in its present state would be fatal to it. The transformation I have proposed,

[1]This refers to the procedure, laid down in article 45 of the constitution providing for cases where the upper and lower house are not in complete agreement on bills. [Editor's note.]

which springs from the very nature of the situation, would bring a welcome rejuvenation of our institutions. It does not close the door to a more complete reform, involving constitutional revision, if this reform appeared necessary to ensure the legitimacy of parliament in the future.

THE PEOPLE'S VIEW OF THE FIFTH REPUBLIC

In the heat of the dispute over the nature and working of the organs of government, it would be easy to overlook the ordinary Frenchman's point of view. Some light on his changing attitudes is shed by this poll data prepared by the Institut Français d'Opinion Publique. While by and large it is self-explanatory, and should be read in conjunction with similar data on pages 62–64 and 124–125, two points merit further emphasis. Firstly the significant revival of confidence in France's ability to govern herself properly between 1958 and 1965, as revealed in the answers to Question Four. Secondly the fact that, despite the period of gaullist rule, the Frenchman remains remarkably attached to the traditional organs of government and channels of political activity. As with his attitudes towards the presidency, one may suspect a degree of ambivalence in his views on how the balance of power should lie.

THE FOURTH REPUBLIC

1. Do you think things would be better or worse if there were no Parliament? (April 1947).

BETTER	21 percent
SAME	27 percent
WORSE	33 percent
NO REPLY	19 percent

2. On the whole are you satisfied or dissatisfied with the work of Parliament over the last four years? (November 1955).

percent

Very satisfied	–	}12
Fairly satisfied	12	
Fairly dissatisfied	38	}66
Very dissatisfied	28	
Indifferent	11	
No reply	11	
	100	

3. Some people advance the following reasons to explain the bad working of the last political régime. Can you say in respect of each of these reasons whether you agree or disagree with them? (August 1958).

	AGREE percent	DISAGREE percent	NO REPLY percent	TOTAL percent
Governments changed too often	95	1	4	100
Too many parties in parliament	88	5	7	100
Bad parliamentary habits	75	5	20	100
Excessive powers of parliament	44	23	33	100
Government had insufficient power	58	17	25	100

From *Les transformations sociales de la France contemporaine*, by permission of the Institut Français d'Opinion Publique. Editor's translation.

4. Do you agree or disagree that one of the weaknesses of the Fourth Republic was that parliament had too much power?

POLITICAL SYMPATHIES

	COM. percent	SOC. percent	RAD. percent	M.R.P. percent	CONS. percent	GAULLIST percent	ALL percent
Agree	25	36	38	56	67	50	44
Disagree	58	31	23	24	7	19	23
No opinion, no reply	17	33	39	20	26	31	33

THE FIFTH REPUBLIC

5. In your opinion, does the political system in (name of country) function better than in France, as well as in France, or not so well?

	BRITAIN percent	ITALY percent	U.S.A. percent	W.GERMANY percent	U.S.S.R. percent
(a) January 1958					
Better	39	10	58	52	31
As well	33	36	17	16	8
Not so well	7	23	5	6	24
No reply	21	31	20	26	37
	100	100	100	100	100
(b) January 1965					
Better	14	3	30	21	15
As well	25	15	26	26	8
Not so well	25	50	11	13	31
No reply	36	32	33	40	46
	100	100	100	100	100

6. In the future should Parliament have a more important role or a less important role than at present, or should its role remain unchanged?

	FEBRUARY 62 percent	APRIL 62 percent	NOVEMBER 63 percent	APRIL 64 percent
More important role	38	41	40	36
Same role	23	26	28	31
Less important role	5	4	4	3
No reply	34	29	28	28
	100	100	100	100

And the President of the Republic?

	FEBRUARY 62 percent	APRIL 62 percent	NOVEMBER 63 percent	APRIL 64 percent
More important role	12	11	4	7
Same role	33	35	42	37
Less important role	26	32	33	33
No reply	29	22	11	23
	100	100	100	100

And the parties?

	FEBRUARY 62 percent	APRIL 62 percent	NOVEMBER 63 percent	APRIL 64 percent
More important role	19	19	32	21
Same role	23	27	28	32
Less important role	22	19	18	18
No reply	36	35	22	29
	100	100	100	100

7. Do you feel that in the future the prime minister should have a more important or less important role than he has at present, or should his role remain the same? (May 1964).

	WHOLE SAMPLE	VIEWS ON DE GAULLE AS PRESIDENT	
		SATISFIED	DISSATISFIED
	percent	percent	percent
More important role	21	15	35
Same	44	56	30
Less important	9	6	16
No reply	26	23	19
	100	100	100

8. Do you consider France is governed better, just as well, or less well now under the Fifth Republic than under the Fourth Republic? (September 1962).

BETTER	44 percent
AS WELL	25 percent
LESS WELL	12 percent
NO REPLY	19 percent

9. Some people say that the present regime is less democratic than its predecessor. Do you personally feel more free or less free than under the previous regime? (November 1961).

MORE FREE	3 percent
LESS FREE	28 percent
NO CHANGE	65 percent
NO REPLY	4 percent

10. When problems of national interest arise, is it better in your opinion for the country's view to be expressed by a vote in parliament or by means of a referendum? (September 1962).

REFERENDUM	28 percent
PARLIAMENTARY VOTE	48 percent
NO REPLY	24 percent

11. Do you think that the interests of people like yourself are best defended by interest groups, the work of political parties or by the activities of deputies and senators? (September-October 1962).

INTEREST GROUPS	54 percent
PARTIES	8 percent
DEPUTIES AND SENATORS	10 percent
NO REPLY	28 percent

12. Where your own interests need defending have you confidence in . . . ? (September-October 1962).

	GREAT CONFIDENCE percent	SOME CONFIDENCE percent	LITTLE CONFIDENCE percent	NO CONFIDENCE percent	NO REPLY percent
(a) Activities of pressure groups	26	34	8	12	20
(b) Local elected representatives	19	38	12	15	16
(c) Your political party	20	29	12	16	23
(d) Your deputy or senator	13	33	15	20	19

VIII. *Political Parties*

PARTY PROGRAMS AND POLICIES

There can be a world of difference between the picture that the political parties present of themselves to the world, and the ordinary voters' perception of those same parties — while the way the parties actually behave may be something different again. Here we see the parties presenting what they believe they stand for — or what they wish the public to believe they stand for. The statements which follow are those submitted by the main party groups in the Assembly following the 1967 elections. Behind the graceless prose, the jargon and the clichés they are drafted with minute care — and require an equally careful reading. Comparing the four statements one can see which subjects are put in the shop-window, and which are dismissed in a hasty phrase or omitted altogether; one can see the points on which some parties are precise, and others retreat into misty rhetoric. The Union Démocratique pour la Cinquième République statement is characteristically governmental, deftly reiterating the key words of gaullist foreign policy, studiously vague in its generalities in keeping with its self-assigned aim of loyalty to the General. The PDM statement is not surprisingly most imprecise of all, reflecting the heterogeneous nature of the group's membership, making its criticism of Gaullist foreign and constitutional policies chiefly by implication. While the Federation is also an amalgam of the left and center-left, and its statement is clearly couched with an eye to cooperation with the communists, it is much the most precise — though relying heavily on constitutional issues and safely traditional left-wing themes. Finally the "opportunism" of the Communist declaration reflects the party's desire for joint action, retreating into striking imprecision in international affairs where in some respects it stands closer to the gaullists than to the rest of the opposition.

DEMOCRATIC UNION FOR THE FIFTH REPUBLIC
[GAULLISTS]

"This group, conscious of the responsibilities which fall on the majority party, and respectful of the sovereign will of the French people, sets itself the task of pursu-ing the work of national renovation undertaken in the political, economic, social and international field, and in particular of watching over the operation of the republican institutions France has given herself;

— making the Fifth Republic live in the

spirit of liberty and progress which guides the actions of General de Gaulle, who the nation has elected;

— promoting true social democracy both by structural reforms and by the introduction of a policy which will provide security of employment, a better division of incomes, and housing for the people of France;

— pursuing, on the basis of the Plan of modernization and investment, the progress of industry, agriculture, the crafts and trade which determines a regional equilibrium advantageous to local authorities;

— providing through economic expansion, a policy favoring the family, improved opportunities for workers and a better lot for the elderly;

— giving young people, thanks to a democratic system of instruction, and to the nation, thanks to permanent educational work, the scientific, technical and sporting facilities they need to prepare themselves for the tasks ahead, and thus make France a strong country with a taste for action and enterprise.

— watching over the development of a fruitful and confident cooperation which respects the freedom of all involved between France and the developing countries, particularly those which have obtained their independence from her;

— defending national independence in all circumstances and on every level;

— developing the power of France, keeping her commitments within her alliances, and within these obtaining from her partners observation of full solidarity, participating in the building of a united Europe respecting the specific responsibilities of every State;

— developing relations between East and West with a view to ensuring lasting peace."

PROGRESS AND MODERN DEMOCRACY

Respecting the Constitution, this group aims to establish a real balance between organs of government, to ensure that Parliament fully exercises its right to legislate and control granted by the Constitution to guarantee basic freedoms, particularly political objectivity by the broadcasting authorities, to promote a great expansion of regional and local liberties.

This group is open, with complete autonomy, to republicans who will not accept the division of the country into two blocks, the permanent confrontation between which would be contrary to the national interest.

Convinced that changes in population structure and technical developments put the time problems of a modern society on a new scale: education and training of young people, housing of families, guaranteed employment, payment for work, farm incomes, market organization, local authority finance, solidarity between citizens above all in relation to the old and the most underprivileged, reconciliation of all Frenchmen through a complete amnesty,[1] the deputies of the Progress and Democracy group intend by their objectivity and the organization of their work, to conduct their activities in a new style.

This activity is armed, notably through a revision of the Fifth Plan, at ensuring a more rapid rate of national progress, at stimulating productive investments, at guaranteeing employment and eradicating unemployment, at narrowing the constantly broadening disparities between citizens and regions by a better division of the national income. The unity and health of the nation demand a dynamic policy of regional development, by means of decentralized industrialization, stimulation of rural activity and modernization of communications systems.

On the international level, the members of the Progress and Democracy group want the process of organizing European unity to be speeded up. They also want France, faithful to the alliances she had entered into, to take active measures to achieve general controlled disarmament, particularly in relation to nuclear weapons, and international organization of aid to devel-

[1] i.e. an amnesty for all who committed crimes in the cause of keeping Algeria French. [Editor's note.]

oping countries, particularly those fighting hunger.

The deputies belonging to the group have faith in democracy which would be more noble if freedom were more fully respected everywhere and in every field, more just if economic expansion were deliberately orientated towards social progress and more humane if it became increasingly more aware of man's responsibilities to man.

Completely free in casting their votes, with a team spirit they will seek the most effective way of achieving these objectives.

DEMOCRATIC AND SOCIALIST FEDERATION OF THE LEFT

The deputies of the Democratic and Socialist Federation of the Left pledge themselves to defend a charter which reiterates the main points of this body's programme.

Personal Liberty and Political Institutions

The federated organizations are resolved to conduct a merciless struggle against personal power.[2]

They pledge themselves:

— to introduce a political democracy effectively reconciling continuity of governmental action with the need for control of the executive by parliament, and, the separation and balance of powers, and to put forward the constitutional alterations required to achieve this;

— to guarantee the independence of the judiciary;

— to reform the Constitutional Council;

— to guarantee the full independence of the Conseil d'Etat;

— to abolish special courts;[3]

— to insist on the neutrality of the State towards all religious beliefs by a return to respect for the principles of *laïcite*[4];

[2] i.e. President de Gaulle's political power and practices. [Editor's note.]
[3] A reference to the much criticized special courts established during and after the Algerian war to handle sedition and treason charges. [Editor's note.]
[4] i.e. the principles of strict separation of Church and State. [Editor's note.]

— to introduce legislation to provide a free and objective system of broadcasting.

Economic and Social Policy.

The federated organisations grant "topmost priority to education, scientific research and vocational training and the extension of facilities for further education.

Socialist democrats are resolved to seek a just solution for the school problem in keeping with the spirit of the law separating Church and State, beginning with the granting of public funds to the public schools and the progressive integration of teachers and schools in the private sector currently receiving public funds only into the national educational system."

The federated organizations also consider housing policy must have priority. They advocate municipalization of land and extension of low-cost housing. The Federation calls for the concentration and strengthening of resources for putting the Plan into effect, the achievement of full employment, the massive development of investment and the introduction of selective credit policies. They foresee the creation of publicly owned undertakings taking the place of private business where necessary, particularly in the field of business banking. The federated organizations declare their support for a tax reform cutting taxes on consumption for a reform of the distributive system and of the machinery for consumer credit and for the liberation of women, in particular by birth control.

Foreign Policy.

The federated organizations will work for:
— "the development of peaceful coexistence;
— general controlled disarmament;
— collective security respecting our defensive alliances, and the abolition of national nuclear strike forces;
— the prevention and solution of conflicts by resort to international arbitration and the reinforcement of the authority and

powers of the United Nations;
—aid to the 'third world' by substituting a part of international solidarity against world underdevelopment for the present competition between rich countries and aid policies motivated by prestige considerations;
—the organization of world trade;
—the political and economic integration of Europe and the resumption of the dialogue with Great Britain. They declare their support for the establishment of a European body with supranational power and the extension of the powers of legislation and control of the European parliament and its election by universal suffrage. The federated organizations desire the achievement of a democratic and socialist Europe and add:

'The Atlantic Alliance which has proved its effectiveness and its exclusively defensive nature must take account of the growing strength of Europe and become more of an association between equal partners.

The policy of Europe, like that of the alliance, should be oriented towards the development of peaceful coexistence between East and West and, in particular, towards cooperation with the countries of Eastern Europe.'

The socialist democrats call on all peoples to be aware of their responsibilities to one another and to take their part in the struggle of universal democracy. They ask the French people 'to reject the false and outdated conceptions of greatness which are currently suggested to them, and to place their ambitions against a vast prospect of democratic development and human progress.'

The Communist Party

The French Communist Party is organizing its efforts so that the mass of workers and all opponents of the capitalist régime in France will be won over to the real fight for socialism—the party's fundamental objective—and so that the conditions for building, safeguarding and achieving it may be realised.

The Communist Party proclaims that the essential objective today is to put to an end the power of the monopolies and to replace it by a genuine democracy.

In this struggle the party is striving for united action by the working class and all non-monopolist elements harmed by the present policy. It is engaged in bringing about a broad majoritarian rally of all the forces of progress.

The most propitious constitution for this rally is agreement between all the left-wing parties and democratic organizations on the basis of a common programme.

In the National Assembly the French communist party will defend the programme adopted by its Congress.

This programme corresponds to the nature of the present stage of development of our country. It rules out any patching up of the gaullist régime and any return to a past of instability and impotence which paved the way for this régime. It is an advanced democratic social welfare programme, striking at the omnipotence of the monopolies in the interest of the people and of the nation.

In the political field this programme bases the stability of the government, responsible to a genuine National Assembly, on agreement between democratic parties and the active support of the popular masses.

In the economic field, this programme bases expansion on the nationalization of the great monopolies, on the democratic management of nationally owned industries, on disarmament, on a democratic reform of taxation and on the development of the resources of the country by means of a democratic development plan.

In the social field this programme lays emphasis on increases in salaries and reduction of the working week, on just reward of the peasant's labour, on the democratic reform of education respecting the *laïcité* of the school, on the problems of housing and public health.

In the international field this programme recommends a coherent policy of peace,

123

solidarity with oppressed or recently liberated peoples, international cooperation, collective security and disarmament.

The French Communist Party will do its utmost to defend this policy of social progress, economic expansion, national independence, liberty and peace in the National Assembly. It will do so bearing constantly in mind the need to strengthen common action, and bring about greater unity of working-class and democratic forces, so as to prepare for the introduction of a new democracy and beyond that the coming of a Socialist France.

THE PEOPLE AND THE PARTY SYSTEM

Hostility to parties and politicians is a venerable strand in the French political tradition which President de Gaulle has done his best to nurture in recent years with attacks such as those quoted above. Yet the health of any democratic political system requires the existence of a number of political parties whose relevance and utility command widespread acceptance among the electorate. Though the survey data is somewhat scattered on this subject, this material from the Institut Français d'Opinion Publique suggests that the ordinary Frenchman, while critical of the political parties, still believes they have a useful role to play within the political system.

1. Do you think political parties are essential for the sound working of a democratic political system?

	OCTOBER 1962 *percent*	APRIL 1965 *percent*
Yes	53	59
No	26	20
No reply	21	21
	100	100

2. In your opinion have the political parties a very important role, a moderately important role, a role of little importance, or no role at all to play (a) in controlling the actions of the government, (b) representing the people? (October, 1962).

	VERY IMPORTANT *percent*	FAIRLY IMPORTANT *percent*	LITTLE IMPORTANCE *percent*	NO ROLE *percent*	NO REPLY *percent*
(a) Controlling government	43	21	13	8	15
(b) Representing citizens	41	29	12	5	13

3. (a) In your opinion, is it better to vote for a man or a party platform? (November 1944).

(b) Would you rather vote for a man or for a party? (January 1958).

	FOR A MAN *percent*	FOR A PARTY *percent*	NO REPLY *percent*
1944	16	72	12
1958	52	27	21

4. Do you think the political parties would return to a regime like the Fourth Republic if they had the chance? (October 1962).

YES	47 percent;
No	21 percent;
NO REPLY	32 percent.

5. In your judgment, are the political parties opposing the proposal submitted to referendum by General de Gaulle [to elect the president by universal suffrage] be-

By permission of the Institut Français d'Opinion Publique. Editor's translation.

cause they want to defend their own interests, or because they are concerned about the proper functioning of the political system? (October 1962).

	percent
- Defend their own interests	54
- Concern about political system	25
- No reply	21
	100

6. In the future should the parties have a more important, less important or equally important role as at present?

	FEB. 62 percent	APR. 62 percent	NOV. 63 percent	APR. 64 percent
More important	19	19	32	21
As important	23	27	28	32
Less important	22	19	18	18
No reply	36	35	22	29
	100	100	100	100

DE GAULLE, POLITICS AND THE PARTIES

One of the most striking characteristics of political controversy in the Fifth Republic has been the repeated clashes, above all at referendums and elections, between de Gaulle and the political parties. Here in these briefer passages are a number of characteristic expressions of his views on the nature of politics and the failings of the parties, which spring naturally from the views on authority and the state already quoted. For beyond the attack on the particular men forming the political class of his day, de Gaulle's attack questions the very conception of party politics as they have come to be understood in democratic states.

Remarks to the Vice-President of the National Assembly, June 1963.

What counts is not the parties. They are impotent, as you know even better than I. Men count for little more: they are mortal. No, what counts in reality, are institutions: if they are mediocre they weaken the country and prevent it getting out of the rut. If they are good they ensure its glory. That is why I want to establish the institutional framework of the régime which will ensure the country's greatness after I have gone.

Speech at Vitry-le-François, April 1963.

It is essential that we do not resume those absurd political disputes which were our practice for far too long and which have brought nothing but woe: the invasion of dissidence, attempts at subversion and, finally, national weakness and mediocrity. On the contrary, we must be united, whatever our calling, our class as they say, our origins, our training, our opinion; we must

be united where the national interest is involved.

Cabinet meeting, 21 November 1963.

"We are now set for several years. For the moment things are peaceful. I wanted to break the parties. I was the only one who could do it and the only one who believed it was possible at the moment I chose. I proved right against everyone.

"I have declared war on the parties. I am very careful not to declare war on the party leaders. The parties are beyond redemption. But the party leaders want nothing more than to be redeemed.

"All that is needed for that is to give them a portfolio."

Television address, presidential election, 30 November 1965.

The President of the Republic cannot be identified with any faction. He must be the man of the entire Nation, express and serve

---

Editor's translation.

the national interest alone. It is on this ground and for this reason that I ask for your confidence.

Five oppositions offer you five candidates. You have heard them all. You have recognized them all. Their words of denigration on every subject, their promises distributed to every group, their appeals for the disappearance of France from the international scene, are the voices, promises and appeals of the old parties attempting, whatever they may claim, to bring back the régime of the past. Thus the only point on which their passions agree is my departure! But this is not enough. For, whatever illusions these varied spokesmen may seek to spread, their mutual contradictions, their irreconcilable followings, their divergent combinations show, for all the world to see, that the accession of any one of them to the supreme post would inescapably mark a return to the odious confusion in which the State once languished, to the woe of France.

Stanley Hoffman

THE CRISIS OF THE PARTY SYSTEM

One could argue that what has kept the style of French politics so alarmingly traditional is precisely the isolation and the personal character of France's present leadership. However, there is another residue we must take into account: France's parties. Although the death of the old ideologies around which they were built and the devastating impact of postwar issues have left the parties in a state of chaos and coma, they are still alive. They have been pushed aside—first by events, then by a man too great for them—but they are watching in the wings. They have had no incentive to reform, being sandwiched between the haughty contempt of a régime which distrusts them on principle and the sarcastic contempt of a public which remembers their antics and observes their present disgrace. The appearance of new parties has only added new sources of confusion and entailed neither a burial nor a *regroupement* of the old ones. The legislative elections of 1958 and subsequent by-elections have shown that the electorate preferred those candidates who stood for de Gaulle's policies. But the downgrading of Parliament has caused the parties to treat the régime as an interlude which requires them to have staying power but not to make any effort at reform. As a result there has been no consolidation, at the level of France's representatives, of a consensus matching the one whose existence in the electorate had been shown by the people's votes. Consequently the duality of a merely latent "general will" among the people and of a fragmented will among the people's representatives has survived. Whatever the well-known faults of France's parties, it is hard to imagine a stable and democratic political system which could dispense with them. Their weaknesses brought their disgrace. Their elimination brought no solution. A system which would try to perpetuate their present "internal exile" would erect them into permanent instruments of irresponsible discontent, and provoke at some stage a "return of the parties" comparable in its effects to the Visit of Durrenmatt's Old Lady and to their own previous return of 1945–46. Indeed, such effects may well be felt again as soon as the Guide who chooses to lean only on the general will and

Reprinted by permission of the publishers from Stanley Hoffman et al. *In Search of France*, pp. 100–105. Cambridge, Mass.: Harvard University Press, Copyright, 1963, by the President and Fellows of Harvard College.

to discard the divided will is removed — unless the parties are reformed in the meantime.

But we find here the second obstacle to reform: the present vacuum. Political life under de Gaulle has been a kind of limbo. De Gaulle either keeps the public at arm's length or seeks it out *en masse* for presidential tours and for plebiscitary referendums in which the substance of the measures proposed disappears under the personal appeal for confidence. Angry citizens express themselves against the state in one of the striking ways that I mentioned. Prosperous citizens prefer the joys of home to the excitement of rallies, and become the spectators of their collective fate. The complacency of a prosperous electorate, the temptation of violence and nihilism among the fanatics, milder forms of irresponsibility and frustration on the left, students divided between those groups but not attracted to parties and party reform — this is what can be observed at the grass roots. Many people have remarked that the new generation of Frenchmen is quite indifferent to its elders' battles — Algeria included — and looks at politics with a healthy mixture of pragmatism and coolness, as one area of problems to be solved, among others, not as a field for clashing conceptions of *le sacré*. But the effect of such an attitude is to divert young men from the political system, since there are no ready-made channels and transmission belts.

As for the "new notables", leaders of the big private interest groups, of civil servants' unions, youth movements, civic associations, it is they who more and more play the rôle of intermediaries, but they do so from outside the political system, and very often with the peculiarly ferocious brand of irresponsibility that such a situation traditionally breeds in France. They no longer address themselves to the old political intermediaries, since such a detour would be a waste of time. Thus the silencing of the old political class has led to the appearance of new political voices, but since they are voices without political experience or *en-*

cadrement their intrusion has resulted mainly in cacophony. Higher up, one constitutional provision which might have been used to fill the vacuum has been a failure — the provision according to which cabinet ministers must resign their seats in Parliament. This measure might have preserved cabinet stability without eliminating parliamentarians from the government, or it might have encouraged a resort to men coming from all sorts of milieux and thus prepared the entry of the "new notables" into the political system. Instead, the result has been the gradual extinction of parliamentarians and their replacement with civil servants.

The worst aspect of the present vacuum is that France is left without any legitimate (i.e., generally accepted) set of institutions. De Gaulle's cavalier violation of his own constitution in both of the referendums he called in 1962 has made this startlingly obvious. Consequently, more than ever the nature of the political system is one of the major stakes in political contests. France remains a bizarre patient whose stomach is too weak to digest political crises, but who throws out his stomach each time he throws up. Nothing has pointed up this gap of legitimacy more dramatically than the army *putsch* of April 1961 and the trials that followed — not least that of Raoul Salan — for they revealed how much the army's allegiance had been divorced from the state. The leaders of the rising — either seasoned officers who had fought on de Gaulle's side during World War Two or young men whose first experience of battle had been in Indochina — claimed that they had sworn an oath of fidelity to the population of Algeria or to the dead comrades of Indochina and Algeria, or followed their sense of national interest and honor. They seemed to have forgotten completely about the régime and about the endorsement it had received from the nation in the referendums. It cannot be said that their military judges have always repudiated them.

Even if the present vacuum could somehow be filled, there would remain a third obstacle to the establishment of a stable political system—the weight of the problems with which it will have to deal. True, one can argue that the worst is over, that the long and tragic thirty-year tunnel is behind France, that with the end of the Algerian War the ordeal of decolonization is overcome, and that on the economic and social front few issues seem capable of testing to the limit the strength of the French state. However, notes of caution must be made. Politics is events, the world of the twentieth century is notoriously tough, and we should not forget that it was primarily the impact of the outside world that upset one French régime after another in the last twenty years. Furthermore, nothing guarantees that even a problem of minor intrinsic significance will not be inflated beyond recognition. The way in which a nation reacts to an issue depends on its political habits and institutions; England and France would perceive and handle quite differently the same kind of problem. What has made French issues so explosive has been the amplification of their impact through domestic dissension.

Such are the obstacles to the creation of a stable political system. They are huge enough to make one understand why changes in society and in France's rôle in the world are not enough to provoke a corresponding reform in politics. The residues of yesterday and the vacuum of today help one realize (with little pleasure) that the present alternatives are the familiar extremes of the pendulum.

At one extreme there is General de Gaulle's change in the mode of election of the President of the Republic, so that he will be chosen by universal suffrage. This development only confirms the *reductio ad absurdum* of Parliament, and it implies that a strong state is possible only if the executive is given an overwhelming preponderance and kept high above the representative factions. Such an imbalance being unacceptable to the parties, the presidential reform is not likely to reach its goals—to increase direct popular participa-

tion, to shock the parties out of their rut, or to make government possible without them. It is not likely to prove definitive.

Precisely because the political pendulum has swung so far already and the "new notables" are still outside the door, the risk is great that parties and parliamentarians, now lying low and unreconstructed, will try to get their revenge by carrying matters back to the other extreme. They may challenge General de Gaulle as in 1945—smoke him out, so to speak, by denying him a majority in Parliament. Or they may wait until after his disappearance and then build a régime which may be to the Fourth Republic what the Fourth was to the Third, that is, a new parliamentary game with a few provisions for executive strength, provisions no more likely to be effective than were those of the constitution of 1946. De Gaulle may not be wrong in fearing that after he has gone France may be the victim not of a vacuum but of an overflow. Once again, French politicians, especially on the left, having noticed that constitutional reforms are not the complete answer, may fall back on the equally old illusion that the only thing needed to make the political system work is a "contract," an alliance between the major parties on a program of action, as in 1936, and in 1946 . . . .

Let us then go back to Harry Eckstein's conditions of democratic stability: *primo*, a government capable of action; *secundo*, decisions made by the representatives of the people, not by other forces; *tertio*, an electorate provided with genuine alternatives. Whether those conditions can be met depends on the problems, the institutions, the parties, and the electorate. We have seen that the problems may not cooperate. France's institutions will be ultimately shaped by her parties; but the only political forces to which the French electorate will be able to turn after de Gaulle are France's unreformed parties, and they are not likely to tolerate institutions capable of reforming the parties.

The lesson is only too clear. In a nation with no tradition of political consensus and legitimacy, "spontaneous democracy" leads to the peculiar kind of politics which consists of the parliamentarians' confiscation of power for themselves, and "corrected democracy" leads to confiscation by the correcting Guide. As we saw earlier, both types of political systems, resting on the same Procrustean bed of bureaucratic centralization, are in accordance with the national style of authority. Both maintain the traditional distance between the leader and the led which protects them all from "l'horreur du face à face." Both excuse the leaders from having to mobilize the led for action and preserve the happy irresponsibility of the led. Both avoid the blend of leadership and participation which mixed government aims at. But both types would have to operate in the context of a new economy which fosters participation, and of a state whose scope has considerably increased. Modern France has become a society in which the problems to be dealt with by the state embrace such a wide range of social activities—and in which the number and scale of social organizations whose functions affect the public welfare have increased so much—that the very simple patterns of plebiscitary or parliamentary rule no longer suffice. Inevitably, those patterns result in arbitrariness, and then provoke protest and revolt. Complaints about *le peuple absent* in French political life did not begin until the thirties; the theme was used then by Tardieu, today by Duverger and René Capitant. The people were just as "absent" before, but in those days the range of public affairs was much narrower. It is therefore not surprising that recent discussion center on the question: how can the nation be reintegrated into its political system?

IX. *Political Attitudes*

J. Meynaud and A. Lancelot

POLITICAL PARTICIPATION

The venerable stereotype of the Frenchman endlessly debating the political issues of the day at his table in the Café de Commerce has in recent years given way to the fresh picture of the "depoliticized" figure, caring only about *bifteck*, and the family Renault, who "couldn't care less" about politics. Yet as Meynaud and Lancelot show, the ordinary Frenchman seems about as interested — and uninterested — in politics as his counterpart in other western European countries, while the breakdown of interest by age, sex and social criteria are already broadly familiar to anyone who has read comparable British and American studies. The Frenchman is rather less likely than the Briton to join a political party — but the 85 percent turnout at the 1965 presidential election and the 81 percent who voted at the parliamentary elections of 1967 are ahead of the turnouts achieved in Britain since 1950, and far ahead of anything the United States has ever known.

One thing must be said immediately. The French have generally a very modest interest in politics, and the extent and accuracy of knowledge of politics reflects this. This general indifference is confirmed by every public opinion poll that has been taken on the subject. Here is how people replied to the question "Are you interested in political questions?" in June 1951:

Very much	10 *percent*
A little	39 *percent*
Not at all	51 *percent*

The replies to a slightly differently worded question, "Are you interested in politics . . . ?" in December 1962 show little variation:

Very much	8 *percent*
Moderately	24 *percent*
A little	37 *percent*
Not at all	30 *percent*
No reply	1 *percent*

This is not a peculiarly French phenomena. Substantially the same is true in all the surrounding countries, as was shown by a comparative enquiry in the six Common Market countries taken in February and March 1962:

"Would you say you are interested in political activity . . . ?"

From J. Meynaud and A. Lancelot, *La Participation des Français a la Politique* (Paris, 1965), pp. 9–10, 42–46, 47–51. Reprinted by permission of Presses Universitaires de France. Editor's translation.

	GERMANY *percent*	BELGIUM *percent*	FRANCE *percent*	ITALY *percent*	LUXEMBOURG *percent*	HOLLAND *percent*
Very much	16	7	10	7	9	11
Moderately	31	23	33	26	30	43
A little	32	31	28	23	32	30
Not at all	20	39	28	44	29	16
No reply	1	—	1	—	—	—

These general indications tally with findings in a number of community studies, notably the 1950 study of Auxerre by Charles Bettelheim and Suzanne Frère. Seventy-two percent of those questioned in the town stated that they had no interest in politics (61 percent of men and 80 percent of women).

* * *

Although citizens in general take little part in political life, this characteristic is not spread uniformly through the population. It divides along several lines of cleavage into groups whose interest in public affairs is variable . . . .

INDIVIDUAL FACTORS

This category includes the immutable characteristics which distinguish individuals — such as sex, age and race. . . . Let us first consider differences arising from sex. Men and women do not participate in politics with equal intensity. The replies to the question put by the Institut Français d'Opinion Publique, in 1953, "Are you interested in politics?" broke down as follows:

	MEN *percent*	WOMEN *percent*
Yes	36	13
A little	36	27
No	28	60
	100	100

This difference in attitude is reflected in electoral participation. Using data relating to some 130,000 voters in the 1951 elections, Mattei Dogan and J. Narbonne were able to discover with a fair degree of accuracy the comparative abstention rates of the two sexes. There were more women than men

on the electoral rolls, but since two-thirds of those abstaining were women, men in fact cast a majority of the votes.

A 1958 survey by Georges Dupeux agrees with these findings.

INDEX OF ELECTORAL PARTICIPATION

	MEN *percent*	WOMEN *percent*	ALL *percent*
High participation	28	10	18
Average participation	41	31	36
Low or no participation	31	59	46
	100	100	100

Other enquiries have revealed women to be less likely than men to join political parties . . .

Age also has a marked effect on participation, which is lowest among the oldest and youngest. The Auxerre enquiry revealed that the highest interest in politics lay in the 55–60 group for men and 45–50 for women. An enquiry among young people between 16 and 24 showed that among males at least interest increased with age. However, it remains below the levels of mature people, and it is not surprising to find 68 *percent* of the young people in this sample opposing the lowering of the voting age to 18 . . . Among older people political apathy is the rule, though some remain marked throughout their lives by the circumstances which awakened them politically (for example a great upheaval like the Dreyfus Affair). This historical factor explains the relatively low rate of abstention in certain age groups . . .

SOCIAL FACTORS

While the best known social factors are economic and occupational, the influence of cultural factors like educational level and

131

religion cannot be overlooked. It is sometimes said politics is a "rich man's luxury." Does observation confirm this assertion? . . . . In France it is difficult to discover this because researchers find it impossible to obtain information about incomes. In the survey carried out during the 1958 elections, there was an attempt to solve this problem by asking respondents if they felt they earned enough to meet their own needs and those of their families. The replies showed a positive correlation between the degree of economic satisfaction and electoral participation.

Participation	SATISFIED *percent*	FAIRLY SATISFIED *percent*	DIS- SATISFIED *percent*
Strong	27	17	16
Medium	32	42	35
Weak or Nil	41	41	49
	100	100	100

Though these indices are interesting they cannot be considered wholly conclusive. Furthermore, income is not an adequate indicator of social status. Occupation is also an important factor. Unfortunately the study of the influence of occupation is complicated by the lack of standard definitions relating to the various jobs, and the absence of any agreed hierarchy of social esteem. However, various enquiries make it possible to postulate that in France (as in comparable countries) those engaged in occupations which allow some form of independence or enjoy a degree of prestige are more likely to participate in politics. According to the Auxerre enquiry men in the "liberal professions," "technicians and supervisory grades," and "heads of businesses" were most likely to be interested in politics. "Craftsmen," "workers," and "laborers" were at the opposite end of the scale, with "small shopkeepers" and "white collar workers" in between. It should be noted that there is a particularly wide spread between "liberal professions"

at the peak (with 66 percent interested in politics) and the groups at the bottom of the scale ("workers" 27 percent and "laborers" 18 percent).

In a study of the 1951 elections M. Dogan and J. Narbonne came to rather different conclusions. Ranging male occupations by decreasing order of abstentions they find liberal professions, industrialists and supervisors at the top,[1] which tallies with the Auxerre enquiry. But workers take second place, preceeding in that order, white-collar workers, shopkeepers, craftsmen, public employees, farmers and agricultural workers.

There is not necessarily any contradiction between these two sets of data. As has already been emphasized, voting does not imply any sustained political interest or regular activity. Elections are held on a Sunday or a public holiday: accordingly the elector does not give up "useful" time to them. The motives which — superficially at least — explain manual workers' low interest in politics ("lack of time") are not as compelling when it comes to voting (which may in fact be encouraged by a feeling of solidarity with members of their group). Such an explanation is not unlikely but we have not sufficient data to reach any firm conclusions.

Social status cannot be considered purely in economic terms. Cultural features, particularly religion, are very important. The exhortations of the Church doubtless explain the high electoral participation in Eastern and Western France despite their scattered population. Abstentions among women would certainly be higher if it were not for the hold of Catholicism on the female electorate. Further, the Church is carrying out important work in civic education; directly or indirectly through the specialized movements and papers it runs or inspires, it struggles to bring a growing number of the faithful into political life.

[1] i.e. most likely to vote. [Editor's note.]

Emeric Deutsch, Denis Lindon and Pierre Weill

THE "POLITICAL FAMILIES" OF CONTEMPORARY FRANCE

One of the characteristic features of French politics has always been the rapidity with which political parties have come and gone, making a bewildering alphabet soup of initials to remember. Here Deutsch, Lindon, and Weill have attempted to go beyond the parties to the nature of the electorate which underlies the party structure. Having first shown how the voters' preferences divide along the familiar left/right scale, they take their analysis further by imposing on it the sort of data on political interest and participation which we have seen already in Meynaud and Lancelot. The result, they suggest, is to reveal the basic nature of the 'political families' in the French electorate—characterized by the great amorphous *Marais* (Swamp) in the middle, which is the electoral arbiter.

When one asks French voters to sum up their political views by indicating their position along an imaginary left-right spectrum, almost 90 percent are able to do so. The following question was put to a representative sample of over 10,000 voters: "People's political opinions are usually classified in relation to a scale like this:

EXTREME LEFT			RIGHT	EXTREME RIGHT

As you see, there are two main groups, the left and the right. People may look on themselves as being more or less right-wing or more or less left-wing. Where would you place yourself on such a scale?". . . In April 1966 the division of replies was:

TABLE I: THE DIVISION OF VOTERS ON THE LEFT-RIGHT AXIS

16%	19%	31%	17%	7%	10%
EXTREME LEFT	LEFT	CENTER	RIGHT	EXTREME RIGHT	DON'T KNOW

These findings give rise to three main comments. In the first place it seems most voters do find the notions of right and left meaningful. Only 10 percent say they cannot locate themselves along a left-right spectrum. In the second place, although few politicians readily admit to being on the right, many electors have no hesitation in doing so; 24 percent place themselves on the right against 35 percent on the left. Finally the central section of the spectrum seems to exercise a strong attraction for electors, since 31 percent put themselves there.

Can one deduce that between the two camps of right and left there lies a sizeable center which can be considered as forming a tendency in its own right? May this not rather be a purely psychological reaction resulting from some voters' inability to assign themselves to one of the two camps, or from a profound indifference to politics? In other words, does putting oneself in the center amount to a real choice which would justify acknowledging the existence of an autonomous political family in the center, or a covert refusal to choose, which would

From E. Deutsch, D. Lindon and P. Weill, *Les Familles Politiques en France* (Paris, 1966), pp. 13–19. Reprinted by permission of Editions de Minuit. Editor's translation.

lead one to classify these centrists with the 10 percent of voters who were unable to place themselves along the spectrum at all? To decide this we require a second criterion of assessment, taking into account interest in politics or the extent of political participation.

Interest in Politics

In order to measure the extent of a voter's interest in politics one can ask him several questions: "Do you ever talk about politics with members of your family, friends or colleagues?" "Do you read the political news in your newspaper?" "Do you follow radio or television news broadcasts?" One can also apply "information tests" which provide a measurement of respondents' political knowledge. Finally, one can put a wider and more subjective question: "Generally speaking, would you say that you are very interested, quite interested, slightly interested or not at all interested in politics?" Experience has shown that this last question very satisfactorily summed up a whole range of more precise and objective questions. Thus one can legitimately use it to classify voters in relation to their political interest.

Using the replies given, voters can be assigned to two large categories: the "participants"—those who say they are very or quite interested, and the "isolated"—those who say they have little or no interest . . . . The participants thus defined represented 37 percent of the voters in 1966, and the isolated 63 percent.

The participants are clearly distinguishable from the isolated so far as political information goes: thus 67 *per cent* of the

TABLE II: DIVISION OF VOTERS ACCORDING TO THEIR POLITICAL INTEREST, 1966

		EXTENT OF INTEREST
participants 37%	8%	very interested
	29%	quite interested
isolated 63%	29%	little interest
	34%	no interest

participants read "sometimes" or "frequently" the political news, while 73 percent of the isolated "rarely" or "never" read it. They are also differentiated by their overall attitude to "politics." Even when the "participant" does not take an active part in politics, he is interested in it, appreciates its importance and tries to fit together the information he receives and the problems he is aware of into a structured and coherent whole. The isolated voter on the other hand is ignorant of or even scornful of politics and politicians, and perceives political problems only when they directly affect him, without attempting to integrate them into a coherent picture even then. His attitude is expressed by declarations like these, noted during interviews:

—"Politics disgust me; they don't interest me at all. You earn money to pay taxes and your money's poured out on other countries . . . I don't get mixed up in politics, I'd rather stay honest."

—"The best politics is steak for dinner, and the bigger the better."

—"So far as I'm concerned, everything's fine; I'm not married and I'm looking for a suitable wife . . . I'm putting all my efforts into improving my position . . . As for the general state of France, I'm not really interested, I couldn't care less. Who cares about political debates? The housing situation's bad? Well, let them sort it out then, it's nothing to do with me"

—"I've no time to read the paper, just sport and the local news. And after all if you take different papers they don't tell you the same story. One says black and the others say white and which are you to believe? Radio and T. V. are just the same, trying to throw dust in our eyes."

These quotations give a good impression of the general attitude to politics of the 63 percent of "isolated" voters. But the percentage varies appreciably from one group of voters to another. The tendency to participation and isolation appear in the first place to be strongly linked to certain socioprofessional groups. The proportion of isolated voters is much higher among women than among men, among the old rather than the young, among those living in the country rather than citydwellers, and among white- and blue-collar workers, peasants and small shopkeepers than among supervisors, managers and the liberal professions. The degree of participation also increases with the educational level. Finally, it varies according to the declared political tendency:

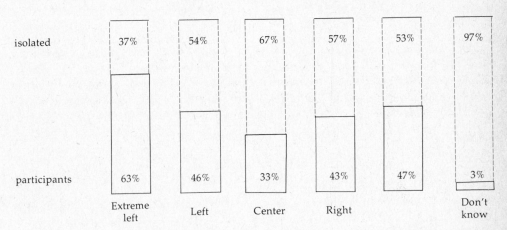

TABLE III: VARIATION IN THE EXTENT OF POLITICAL INTEREST ACCORDING TO POLITICAL SYMPATHIES.

	Extreme left	Left	Center	Right		Don't know
isolated	37%	54%	67%	57%	53%	97%
participants	63%	46%	33%	43%	47%	3%

This table shows firstly that almost all the voters who are unable to place themselves on a left-right axis are isolated. It shows next that the percentage of participants falls regularly from the extremes to the center. Finally it shows that the degree of participation is on average higher among voters who say they are on the left than among those who say they are on the right.

[The authors continue to analyze their material further, noting there is little difference between the attitudes and behavior of, for example, the participating and the isolated extreme left, and concluding that in fact there are effectively six political families in France today. Four of these follow fairly straightforwardly from the preceeding analysis: they distinguish between extreme-left, left, right, and extreme-right. But they argue that a distinction becomes necessary between the participating "centrists" — constituting one third of those who assigned themselves to the center — and the isolated centrists. They assign these "false centrists," that is, those who declared themselves to be in the center but are not interested in politics, to a sixth group in common with those who are unable to place themselves on the political spectrum at all. This group they term the Marais (Swamp). These, they insist, are not "floating voters" but voters who have no sure political interest or identification and who consist of a group which is fluid, unstable and inconsistent. Redrawing the table on the basis of this new classification, they argue that the true nature of the French electorate is as follows:

IV: THE SIX POLITICAL FAMILIES IN FRANCE IN 1966

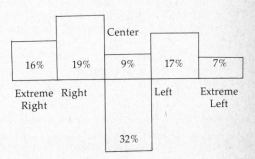

		Center		
16%	19%	9%	17%	7%
Extreme Right	Right		Left	Extreme Left
		32%		

Thus the Marais is the largest single political element, dominating the political scene, for even with the aid of the committed center neither the right nor the left can claim the majority of the electorate.

Nathan Leites

THE UNIMPORTANCE OF DOCTRINE

One familiar stereotype about French politics, which is as dear to Frenchmen as to foreigners, is that they are peculiarly intellectual and ideological in content. But to Nathan Leites the fact that party utterances so often abound in historical allusions and ideological phrases is not conclusive; politics is what the parties actually do rather than the language with which they clothe—or hide—their actions. To him, French politics is uncommonly elastic and pragmatic in character rather than narrowly rigid and ideological. As the next extract will show, not everyone finds his arguments conclusive.

In France, one often hears, politics is "intellectual," "theoretical," "abstract," "ideological," even "idealist." According to the most important contemporary commentator on parliamentary activities (Jacques Fauvet), "ideological quarrels" occupy "an eminent place" in politics. They invade everything: "We always start by conferring on our most trite discussions the dignity of philosophic disputations," for "the French people prefer pure ideas in all circumstances."[1]

In the preface to the book which contains these assertions—the only recent essay on French politics by an observer close to the political class—the author announces that he is "liberating himself for awhile from the constraints of day-to-day events," and proposes to regard the "landscape" which he is usually viewing at short range "from a greater distance."[2] In so doing he seems to have turned his eyes toward an imaginary world, where "sordid" facts have been replaced by "pure" ideas that may appear out-dated but do not lack dignity . . .

It is, in fact, not easy to find doctrines in French politics, though politicians frequently talk about them; less frequently, by the way, than they are often believed to do, and less emphatically than they used to do in the Third Republic.

Let us consider from this point of view the main groupings in French politics (always with the exception of the Communists and of the extreme Right.)

The initials usually employed to designate the Socialists, SFIO, stand for "French Section of the Workers International;" but one wonders how many among those specialised in politics are in any way aware of the antiquated ideological words behind the familiar abbreviation. Though the Socialists are particularly inclined to talk about their "doctrine," the commentator cited before, who stressed the role of "ideology" when he makes overall statements, admits that the Socialist Party "has no doctrine any longer."[3] Still, it is "one of the rare political organizations which still possess a certain modest number of eco-

[1] Jacques Fauvet, *La France déchirée* (Paris 1957), pp. 14, 38.
[2] Ibid. p. 8.

[3] Fauvet, *La France déchirée*, p. 128

Reprinted from *On the Game of Politics in France* by Nathan Leites, (1959), pp. 7–11, with the permission of the publishers, Stanford University Press. © 1959 by the RAND Corporation.

nomic and social conceptions of their own."[4] These "conceptions" include a favorable attitude toward the maintenance and extension of governmental activities in economic affairs, and an advocacy of what are regarded as the interests of lower-income groups, whether salaried or not. On the other hand, words such as "socialism," "nationalization," or any other terms referring with an air of specificity to a radical transformation of the present order are, on the scale of national politics, not too frequently employed by the Socialists. Demanding that all nuclear fuels be owned by Euratom, a Socialist speaker in the Assembly, a former Premier, added: "If we regard this measure as desirable, it is not, ladies and gentlemen, please believe me, because of any sectarian ideology hostile to private property."[5]

When a Socialist Premier wants to "fall leftward," he may suddenly come out with vague demands for workers' participation in the conduct of business, so that the Moderates may cry "Sovietization!" Nobody will have known that the Socialists were particularly intent on this reform, and few will wonder about the disappearance of the demand once it has served its function. Suppose that *Le Monde*, the newspaper most widely and thoroughly read by the political class in Paris, wanted to describe in detail the program of the Socialists: many of its readers, though specialized in politics, would feel that they were being led into rather unknown territory, though they would also be sure that there were no major surprises in store for them.

If teachers are part of the "intelligentsia," the Socialists represent that stratum to a higher degree than any other party; but among the intellectuals who are Socialist militants, functionaries, parliamentarians, exceedingly few are known on nonpolitical grounds or as contributors to "doctrine."

"The doctrinal effort which the appearance of the Communists ought to have imposed on the other parties, and particularly on the Socialists," observes Jacques Fauvet, "was not made until shortly before the war."[6] I should rather say that it was not made at all, as far as the Socialists are concerned, despite a few essays by Léon Blum and one book by Jules Moch. If that book, *Confrontations*, appeared to be followed by some difficulties for Moch in the party, this was not because of any excessive deviations from Marxism which it may have contained, but rather because the author envisaged raising the age of retirement—a suggestion unwelcome to public employees forming a decisive part of the Socialist clientèle. It would, indeed, be difficult to define the precise relationship between the alleged Socialist doctrine and Marxism, which Socialist leaders have not renounced but which they claim as their own quite rarely and only in very brief affirmations. The few persons who are held by party members to be "theoreticians" because they write in the party's monthly are quite unknown outside the limited circles of its readers, and so is the monthly itself.

When somebody talks about "the doctrine of the Radicals," others immediately think of the philosopher Alain. On the other hand, one often hears the following anecdote retold: having written a book called *Elements of a Radical Doctrine*, Alain had it placed before the seat of every Radical minister at the table of the Council of Ministers. One of the recipients, upon looking at the book, remarked: If a Radical doctrine really existed, would we not be the first to know it? "To my mind," declared an important Radical (Edgar Faure), "Radicalism is a method for solving problems rather than a set of solutions."[7] (He went on to suggest that the facts outside of parliament and the distribution of party strength within it imposed about the same "method" on every reasonable man.) "The Radicals conceive of themselves as Socialists," alleged Jacques Fauvet.[8] But if the full

[4] Fauvet in *Le Monde*, October 31-November 1, 1954.
[5] Félix Gouin, Assemblée Nationale (AN) July 5, 1956; Journal Officiel (JO), Débats parlementaires, Assemblée Nationale, p. 3257.
[6] *La France déchirée*, p. 44
[7] *Combat*, February 3, 1958.
[8] *La France déchirée*, p. 31.

name of the party is "Republican Radical and Radical Socialist Party," the words "Socialist" and "Socialism" are almost never applied by Radicals to themselves on the level of national politics; they almost never claim allegiance to any doctrine called "Socialist."

Lately an effort has been made, in the group around Pierre Mendès-France, to create a new Radical doctrine. But this is indicative of the breakup of the old Radical Party into various fragments rather than of its continued vigour. Among the eighteen members of the directing committee of the periodical which attempts this creation of a new doctrine (*Cahiers de la République*), there are at least two Socialists, two "Left Catholics," and one Left Gaullist.

The Christian Democrats, too, used to have a periodical supposedly oriented on doctrine (*Terre Humaine*), edited by a man viewed as the "theoretician" of the party (Etienne Borne); but it ceased publication for lack of readers. Jacques Fauvet admits that "the principle of unity" of this "movement" is "emotional rather than intellectual:" "being faithful to a tradition,"[9] that of the anticonservative trend in French Catholicism between the 1830s and the Second World War. "If one had to indicate the aims of the Christian Democrats ten years after the foundation of their party," another journalist remarks, "all one could do would be to name a few chapter headings of a program which was never developed."[10] It is known, for instance, that the Christian Democrats do not like "capitalism." But as to the vague formulae about the "new institutions" through which the "reign of money" is to be replaced by "a more humane order of things," only the authors of doctrinal reports prepared for national party congresses would be able to repeat their texts even approximately.

Even those who believe that "doctrine" plays a dominant role in French politics agree that there is little of it among the Moderates, where one is usually content with rejecting Socialist errors, without, however, seriously attacking the social-economic status quo on behalf of less government interference.

In his famous speech in Bayeux in 1946, de Gaulle furnished his followers the bases of a political doctrine by sketching a "presidential" constitution for France. In addition, there was the idea of an "association between capital and labor" as well as "federalist" words concerning the French Union. But during the years when Gaullist or ex-Gaullist movements were of importance in French politics (1947–1955), doctrine was shrinking rather than expanding. The major postulates of Gaullist ideology only rarely appeared in parliamentary speeches or in actual proposed legislation. It became unusual to hear a Gaullist leader say in the Assembly, "We continue to strive for a presidential regime."[11]

On the whole, Gaullist speakers came to limit themselves to the affirmation that existing institutions were in need of radical revision and that the salvation of France depended on the General's return to power. The only Gaullist periodical that had a somewhat doctrinal air ceased publication in 1953. At the same time the Gaullist criticism of the "regime" ceased to be peculiar to that group and became what was widely felt to be a set of commonly accepted and predictably inoperative truisms.

Though there is little "doctrine" in French politics, what does, of course, exist for each major political tendency, and what often gives the impression of "doctrine," is a set of somewhat special and more or less emotion-laden phrases. (These are at present more important on the local level and in elections than in parliamentary politics. The decline of party vocabularies in Paris may foreshadow a similar development in the provinces.) "Every major political tendency has its pantheon and its vocabulary."[12] This is true, as I said, though less so for the Moderates than for the other

---

[9]*Ibid.*, pp. 128–9.
[10]Raymond Barillon in *Le Monde,* January 9, 1954.

[11]Raymond Triboulet, *A.N.*, March 2, 1956; *J.O.*, p. 639.
[12]Fauvet, *La France déchirée*, p. 42.

parties: there seem to be no commonly accepted heroes of the Moderates after Henry IV. Often, by the way, the words to which adherents of a party are attached and which differentiate them best from partisans of other movements are not those by which the party would characterize itself; an instance would be the use of the adjectives "human" and "new" by the Christian Democrats. Also, the pantheons of the various tendencies are sometimes a bit strange. "Neither Montalembert . . . nor La Tour du Pin . . . deserves to figure in the genealogy of the Christian Democrats,"[13] remarked, correctly, Jacques Fauvet in speaking of two prominent French Catholics of the nineteenth century. If they are nevertheless claimed by the Christian Democrats, this is not by virtue of the efforts made by ingenious "theoreticians" who have interpreted them in the desired sense, but rather because one knows them little and cares less, and because their names appear mostly on ceremonial occasions, when words are not taken too literally.

François Goguel and Alfred Grosser

THE SIGNIFICANCE OF METAPHYSICAL DISAGREEMENTS

The fact that party leaders say one thing and act otherwise does not of course mean that ideology and doctrine are unimportant in a country's politics. Leites was concerned with the "parliamentary game." Goguel and Grosser, on the other hand, argue that one cannot understand the political history of France in the recent past without grasping the impact of metaphysical disagreements, and that even today, despite the "end of ideology" and the spread of secularization, the religious dividing line can by no means be discounted.

The second characteristic of the traditional French political behaviour is the major part played by disagreements of a metaphysical nature in drawing the lines between political parties. In more concrete terms, the fact that for a long time the problem of attitudes towards the Catholic Church was the most important and the most significant in political life. "No militant member of the Left," wrote André Siegfried in 1930, "has yet learned to believe that the Church can work sincerely for the Republic." At the time nothing was more true.

Why is it that religious questions were so long of prime importance in French political life? Should the chief responsibility for this be put at the door of the Catholics or their opponents? There is no simple answer. When the members of the National Assembly voted for the Constitution Civile du Clergé on 12 July 1790, their aim was simply to reorganize ecclesiastical administration while increasing, to the benefit of the State they were in the course of creating, the means of controlling the Church which up to then had belonged to His Most Blessed Majesty; or were they setting out, by subordinating the religious power to the civil power more closely, to prepare the future triumph of "light" over the "darkness" of Catholic dogma? In other words were they consciously and determinedly beginning the ideological conflict whose

From François Goguel and Alfred Grosser, *La Politique en France* (Paris, 1964), pp. 23–26. Reprinted by permission of Librairie Armand Colin. Editor's translation.

effects were to dominate French political life through one and a half centuries? At all events, the reaction that the Constitution Civile du Clergé stirred up among Catholics after it was condemned by the Holy See put the Church of France in the counter-revolutionary camp and, by the same token, the supporters of the principles of 1789 in the camp of the opponents of the Church — for almost one hundred and fifty years. As the historian of the Revolution Georges Lefebvre has written, "The schism gave an extraordinary impetus to counter-revolutionary agitation. Many people refused to risk their salvation by renouncing the "good priests"; so without having any thought of re-establishing the Ancien Régime they were nonetheless dragged into opposition . . . On their side the revolutionaries treated those who refused to submit as public enemies . . . The sickness was without a cure."

To show how and why the problems of the place of the Church in French society and the attitude of the State towards it for so long played an essential part in differentiating between French political parties one has to recapitulate the whole history of France in the nineteenth century and the first part of the twentieth, from the law on sacrilege to the Debré law of 1959 on State aid to religious education.

During the Third Republic the key fact, which may simply be recalled without exploring the reasons for it, was that the Church of France — hierarchy, clergy and a great number of its most zealous adherents — opted for the restoration of the monarchy after the war of 1870. This is why Gambetta issued his celebrated watchword to republicans in 1876, "clericalism — that is the enemy," and why several years later Jules Ferry and Paul Bert presented their new organization of compulsory public secular education as a means of freeing the minds of future citizens from Catholic influence. Inevitably this brought its reaction; the support given by the Church to Boulanger's attack on the Republic; the anti-Catholic legislation voted in 1901 and 1905

by the republicans who had emerged victorious from the Dreyfus affair; finally the participation by bishops and clergy in the attempt by Action Française to group the forces hostile to the Republic under the banner of all-out nationalism.

This succession of events explains why a cleavage between parties almost wholly determined by the attitude of the candidates on questions of religious policy appeared in electoral contests from the earliest elections in the Third Republic and subsequently consolidated itself in a highly durable manner. There is no doubt that the existence of single-member constituencies with two ballots contributed to this consolidation of a political frontier along a border relating to the religious question. The second ballot coalitions implied by such an electoral system can be arranged more readily against a common enemy than in favour of an agreed programme. The republican coalition of the early years of the Third Republic could only be formed on a basis of opposition to the monarchy and on the common determination of its members to guarantee the independence of civil society in relation to the church and reduce the influence of the priests over the minds of its citizens. Conversely the legitimists, orleanists, bonapartists and later the nationalists could only justify their agreement at elections by their favorable attitude to Catholicism. In this way habits were formed which quickly became almost second nature to the voters: the opposition between right and left tended to boil down to the opposition between supporters and opponents of the Catholic Church. . .

Up to 1914 the dividing line laid down in this way by religious problems between voters and candidates was scarcely altered when a majority had to be formed in Parliament to support the government. Whoever "made a deal" with the Church, that is, with "reaction," was automatically excluded from power. When circumstances forced a republican government which was under attack from its left to accept or even seek the support of Catholics . . . it did so with great reticence and pledged itself frequently to remain in power only as long as it kept the confidence of the majority of "republicans," that is, the supporters of the secular State. Catholics were cast into a sort of political ghetto, not very much different from the one which in more recent times has so frequently isolated communist members in Parliament.

It was the war of 1914–1918 which, thanks to the "Sacred Union," put an end to the ostracism which had struck at Catholics within the Republic. The new conditions of political life created by the conflict were subsequently to prevent that ostracism making a complete reappearance in parliament and in the government. But on the electoral level the traditional split was much more difficult to close. Thus, while the radicals had more than once between the two wars to agree to join with Catholics in forming governments, up to the last elections of the Third Republic almost everywhere they maintained their traditional attitude, founded on the union of the entire left, defined by a certain conception of the secular state, against all those who, whatever their political, international or social welfare programme might be, would not consider the "secular" laws of the 1880s on schools, of 1901 on religious communities, of 1905 on the separation of Church and State to be untouchable.

Again after the second world war, but this time most often on the initiative of the extreme left, the religious problem more than once threatened—sometimes successfully—the unity of parliamentary majorities which included socialists, radicals and the Christian Democrats of the Popular Republican Movement. But it has become increasingly clear that while the attitude of the parties to religious questions retained a considerable importance in determining electoral alliances in rural areas, things were quite different in cities and urban areas. All in all, one can say that while the absolute predominance of a criterion of a politico-religious character in fixing the demarcation line between parties is today in a large measure a thing of the past, this predominance lasted too long for it to have ceased completely to show itself in the reflexes of voters, members of parliament and party leaders. The invasion of political life by preoccupations of a different order, whose character is more immediate and concrete, has played a decisive role in the incursions that have taken place in traditional behavior.

But even today one cannot fully understand French political life unless one remembers the place that considerations of a religious nature took for so long in the party struggle, a place which is due both to history and to the French habit of translating political disagreements into doctrinal or ideological terms. For this is the quasi-philosophical level on which republicans long put themselves in order to refuse full equality to Catholics in a régime which they conceived as not merely a legal and social mechanism, but the affirmation of a certain conception of human nature, the world and history.

Emeric Deutsch, Denis Lindon and Pierre Weill

THE END OF IDEOLOGY?

Earlier sections have presented de Gaulle's sweeping dismissal of political parties as outdated relics representing nothing, and the parties' own presentations of what they stand for. Nathan Leites has argued that to practicing politicians at least doctrinal considerations have ceased to be significant; Goguel and Grosser have insisted that they cannot be dismissed out of hand. Finally Deutsch, Lindon and Weill look at the electors themselves. Here they comment on the decline of ideological factors and show the blurring of the old distinctions between left and right. Yet in the end differences of political temperament do remain between the various "political families," and some of their varying characteristics are documented here. Perhaps in these persistent differences we see one explanation of why the political parties which so many gaullists believed were doomed to be swept away have so tenaciously clung to life despite all the General's anathemas against them.

The word ideology is often used to designate a coherent and tightly structured conception of society, history or even the universe. That is not the way we use the word here. In asking whether the political families have an ideological content, we shall limit ourselves to trying to find out whether the voters constituting each family have certain political opinions and attitudes which distinguish them from those in other political families.

Accordingly, in the course of several enquiries, we asked voters their opinions on traditional problems, such as aid to church schools, nationalization, socialism, communism, the right to strike and the army, and on certain current problems like the Common Market, the nuclear strike force, aid to under-developed countries, the Atlantic Alliance and the political system . . . Five main findings emerged: in the first place the traditional indicators of the left and right—questions which used to provide a sure means of distinguishing between them—have almost all ceased to play this role; yet despite this absence of clear-cut differences on certain key problems, appreciable differences of political "temperament" still exist between the political families; the two right-wing families appear much closer to each other than the two left-wing families; the center is much closer to the right than to the left; finally the Marais[1], as one would expect, is notable for its lack of political opinions and temperament.

There is no doubt that at certain periods there have been certain "key" political problems in France which produced clear-cut distinctions between right and left. The problem of the Republic and the Monarchy in the nineteenth century, rela-

[1]The authors' expression for the section of the electorate which has no sure political interest and position. [Editor's note.]

From E. Deutsch, D. Lindon and P. Weill, *Les Familles Politiques en France* (Paris, 1966), pp. 26–32. Reprinted by permission of Editions de Minuit. Editor's translation.

tions between church and state and the Dreyfus case around 1900, nationalism at the beginning of the century, and nationalization at the Liberation, were to politics what litmus paper is to chemistry; they provided an almost infallible indication of whether a man was on the right or left . . .

This is true no longer. It seems there are no longer "key" political problems providing a sure distinction between left- and right-wing voters: we did not find one political theme on which three-quarters of the voters classing themselves on the left had one opinion, while three-quarters of those considering themselves on the right held a different opinion.

The only problems producing fairly clear-cut opposing majorities between right and left are governmental authority, the right to strike, the army and the nuclear strike force. But even where the opposition between the right and the left is the most marked – over the question of governmental authority – there is no unanimity, nor even a very great homogeneity of opinion in each of the families, particularly among the moderate right and left:

ATTITUDE TOWARDS GOVERNMENTAL AUTHORITY

	EXTREME LEFT percent	MODERATE LEFT percent	MODERATE RIGHT percent	EXTREME RIGHT percent
Governmental authority should be maintained	19	30	54	62
Government should be made less authoritarian	73	58	30	26
No opinion	8	12	16	12

Other problems show no clear-cut opposition between the right and the left, for a variety of reasons. In a number of cases it seems that the left has moved closer to the right, in the sense that a sizeable fraction of the left, and particularly the moderate left, holds views which were traditionally considered as belonging to the right: this is particularly the case with aid to the church schools and nationalization:

"AID TO CHURCH SCHOOLS SHOULD BE SUPPRESSED"

	EXTREME LEFT percent	MODERATE LEFT percent	MODERATE RIGHT percent	EXTREME RIGHT percent
Agree	63	31	8	12
Disagree	33	54	82	82
No opinion	4	15	10	6

"LARGE PRIVATELY OWNED COMPANIES SHOULD BE NATIONALIZED"

	EXTREME LEFT percent	MODERATE LEFT percent	MODERATE RIGHT percent	EXTREME RIGHT percent
Agree	58	34	25	29
Disagree	22	42	50	47
No opinion	20	24	25	24

On the other hand, there are other cases where the right has come closer to the left; for example right-wing voters are more likely to approve than disapprove of the opinion "Socialism must be built."

"AN EFFORT MUST BE MADE TO BUILD SOCIALISM"

	EXTREME LEFT percent	MODERATE LEFT percent	MODERATE RIGHT percent	EXTREME RIGHT percent
Agree	84	69	38	32
Disagree	6	11	21	31
No opinion	10	20	41	37

143

Other problems which are relatively recent, on which one might have expected temperament or tradition to produce opposition between left and right show more division within the political families than between them. This is the case with aid to under-developed countries which left-wing electors, despite their traditional "generosity" are no more ready to approve than those on the right:

ATTITUDE TOWARDS AID TO
UNDER-DEVELOPED COUNTRIES

	EXTREME LEFT *Percent*	MODERATE LEFT *Percent*	MODERATE RIGHT *Percent*	EXTREME RIGHT *Percent*
Expenditure on aid to under-developed countries should be reduced	**51**	**57**	50	53
Expenditure on aid to under-developed countries should be maintained	39	36	38	37
No opinion	10	7	12	10

It seems therefore that there are currently no problems which provide a means of discriminating readily between a left-wing elector and a right-wing one. The terms left' and 'right' no longer have a simple and precise content as once they had. Does that mean that they stand for nothing and that the political families we have defined are objectively meaningless? Not in the least, for while there is not a clear line of demarcation between the right and the left, there are nevertheless real and perceptible differences of "political temperament" between each of the six families.

This difference appears clearly if, instead of considering the opinions expressed by the voters of the different families on each individual problem, one examines the proportion of left-wing and right-wing opinions expressed over the whole range of political problems[2].

The results of this analysis are presented in the accompanying table which indicates how many voters in each political family hold a strong majority of left-wing opinions, a slight majority of left-wing opinions, about as many right and left opinions, and so on.

It will be seen that each political family has a different propensity to react to political problems. From the electors of the extreme left who almost all show a majority of left-wing opinions to those of the extreme right who in general have a clear majority of right-wing opinions, there is a regular evolution. Only the Marais puts itself outside this continuum—a high proportion of voters belonging to it express no opinion on most political problems. Thus, while one cannot say with certainty of a moderate-right-wing voter that he is opposed to nationalization or socialism, or of a center voter that he favours church schools or is opposed to strong government, on the other hand, for the voters of each family one can forecast the proportion of right-and left-wing replies they will make to a range of questions on political problems. These results show that the political families, defined on the basis of the political leanings declared by the voters themselves, do retain some meaning. They do not amount to well-defined ideologies or even to precise opinions on certain specific problems, but to a temperament or perhaps to an implicit scale of values, which are expressed by a tendency to react most often on the left or on the right when confronted by political problems. Defined in these terms, the differences between the left-wing and right-wing families as a whole are striking.

[2]For each problem studied an opinion may be considered as a left-wing opinion if it is expressed more and more frequently as one moves to the left on the left-right spectrum, and conversely for a right-wing opinion.

Proportions of left- and right-wing opinions
expressed by voters belonging to the various families

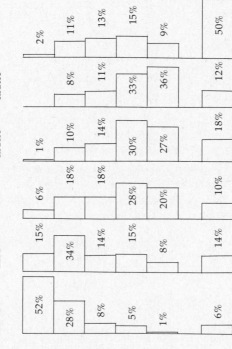

	Extreme Left	Moderate Left	Moderate Center	Moderate Right	Extreme Right	"Marais"
Big majority of left-wing opinions	52%	15%	6%	1%	2%	
Small majority of left-wing opinions	28%	34%	18%	10%	8%	11%
Almost equal number of left- and right-wing opinions	8%	14%	18%	14%	11%	13%
Small majority of right-wing opinions	5%	15%	28%	30%	33%	15%
Big majority of right-wing opinions	1%	8%	20%	27%	36%	9%
Big majority of "don't knows"	6%	14%	10%	18%	12%	50%

X.   Referenda and Elections

Henry W. Ehrmann

THE REFERENDUM IN THE FIFTH REPUBLIC

One of the most widely remarked features of the early years of gaullist rule was the General's predilection for direct resort to the people in national referenda—in 1958, 1961 and 1962. The referendum was portrayed as a regular feature of political life under the new regime. Yet since 1962 it has faded into the background. The explanation would seem to lie less in the absence of great issues worthy of being submitted to referendum than in de Gaulle's failure to separate his mortal enemies, the party leaders, from their followers. Even so the referenda have been major occasions in the Fifth Republic's political history. Henry Ehrmann here analyses de Gaulle's use of the referendum in those early years when it could still be used simultaneously to demonstrate triumphantly support for his policies and to put his foes in the parties to rout.

Incessant discussions of institutional changes marked most of the first years of the Fifth Republic. The debate in which critics of the regime as well as its spokesmen participated, pertained primarily to the presidency whose character and functions had been so totally transformed by political realities. The carefully spaced and frequently oracular statements of General de Gaulle were marked by an acknowledged pragmatism, obviously designed to keep all institutional arrangements flexible until they had been tested by experience. There was, however, little doubt that in de Gaulle's eyes those aspects of the constitutional experience had proven most viable which had long suited his own temper. Upon his return to liberated France he had

been careful, or so he said later, to "accept for my power no other investiture than that which the voice of the masses would give me directly." Since 1958, the presidential trips to the provinces have been turned into manifestations of undifferentiated popular acclaim for the leader who found in them psychological encouragement when the political climate in the capital had proven oppressive.

The unforeseen development of the referendum did much to give the regime its increasingly plebiscitarian texture. De Gaulle's memoirs had lauded the consultation of the electorate by referendum. To the contrary, in his early comments on the constitution, M. Debré's defense of the referendum had been half-hearted: he appar-

Summarized and adapted from "Direct Democracy in France," by Henry W. Ehrmann, *American Political Science Review*, LVII, 4 (December: 1963). Reprinted by permission of the American Political Science Association and of the author. Footnotes omitted.

ently realized that the new institution was structurally alien to the parliamentary system which he wished to erect. The language of Art. 11 dealing with the referendum seemed to assign to it a less than secondary place; most French and foreign commentators doubted that it would open opportunities for practices of direct democracy. Already, however, the constitutional referendum of 1958 had proved far more useful to the regime than the subsequent national and local elections which, by a varying degree, attested the resilience of traditional political structures.

The greater his impatience with the representative features of the new régime, the more General de Gaulle became convinced that his was indeed the role of the *"guide"* in the sense in which Rousseau had used the term. The *Contrat Social* had assigned to the leader the task of formulating correctly the few questions which were to be put before the people in such a way that the general will may "see things as they are [and] sometimes as they ought to appear to it." Accordingly, the two referendums held on January 8, 1961 and April 8, 1962, asked the sovereign to manifest the general will by approving de Gaulle's Algerian policies.

Both consultations bore the earmarks of plebiscites. Each time the voters were invited not to arbitrate between equally available solutions but to endorse an already established policy from which no return to the *status quo ante* was possible. An act of faith was demanded from the electorate in order to isolate the opposition and to discourage rebellion. At the same time, the providential leader declared that he could not continue in office without a massive vote of confidence, thus raising the spectre of unending war in Algeria and of political chaos at home. As in the case of other plebiscites, the bills that were submitted to the electorate wrapped several propositions into one. This not only maximized the chances for approval but tied the sanction of the past to an acceptance of the future, as when the referendum of April 1962 asked for a new grant of almost un-

limited presidential powers. In both campaigns de Gaulle stressed that he was appealing to each citizen as an individual, "above all intermediaries," that the referendum was a "personal affair" between himself and the nation. With such assertions as to the nature of what he called "the clearest, the frankest, and the most democratic of procedures," came the announcement that in the future direct appeals to the people would multiply and "mark profoundly the character and functioning of republican institutions."

Party and group leaders realized fully that the deliberate shift to a plebiscitarian form of government violated the rules of the game as they had understood them when they approved the constitution. Moreover, the referendum on the Evian accords also violated Art. 53 of the constitution, and it was widely known that the Council of State had reported adversely on the legality of the new presidential powers. Nonetheless, it was left to the discredited protagonists of *Algérie Française* and to some tortured expressions of individual doubt, to voice protests against the unconstitutionality of the referendum. Outright violations of the constitutional text had occurred before and had been challenged only weakly so long as the war lasted. The absence of an effective constitutional jurisdiction and the rapid transformation of power relations between governmental organs, gave to the President, as if by default, the position of guardian of the constitution. His discretionary interpretation of an often obscure text had met with little resistance in the past. When the Evian agreement promised the end of the seven years war, constitutional scruples carried little weight.

The large majorities of "yes" votes in the first three referendums of the Fifth Republic were not the only indication that the electorate looked favorably on the referendum as an institution. In opinion polls held in 1961 and 1962, 57 percent and 65 percent, respectively, of the voters approved of being consulted directly on the Algerian policy. If in October 1962 the popularity of the "repeated use" of the referendum had decreased, more voters endorsed the idea of a direct consultation than there were to be "yes" votes (51 percent as against 46 percent of votes cast).

A historical situation in which representative institutions were discredited and in which there seemed to be available no reasonable alternative, was undoubtedly the principal reason for the popular acceptance of a fairly novel and hitherto widely distrusted device. Normally the regime held public opinion at arm's length and provided a "counter-pedagogy" rather than the political education for which Debré had called before 1958. But the referendum, not unlike the provincial visitations of the President, provided a temporary mobilization of the citizenry. If the direct appeal is flattering, the commitment exacted is fleeting and maintains the distance between the leader and his followers which appears particularly desirable in a society characterized by a dislike of face-to-face relationships.

In the 1961 referendum, only 18 percent of the registered voters had cast a "no" vote, although the parties and deputies that urged a negative vote had mustered a combined strength of almost 40 percent on the first ballot of the preceding elections. This goes far to explain why after Evian none of the traditional political formations recommended the outright rejection of the referendum. The acceptance of the peace settlement in 1962 by 90 percent of the votes cast was easily interpreted by the government as a popular verdict rejecting "legalistic" wrangles. It was, nevertheless, short of satisfactory to de Gaulle. This time, the approval of peace in Algeria had submerged the vote of personal confidence for which the President had called once more. The deliberately authoritarian style of his addresses had failed to drive even the communists off the bandwagon.

If elections were held before the régime was able to differentiate itself in some dramatic fashion from the traditional parties, there was danger that the parties might reestablish their identity and their habitual clientele. Therefore, de Gaulle refused to dissolve parliament and to call for the new elections which had been generally expected to mark the start of a new phase for a parliamentary regime at peace.

The nearly successful attempt on the President's life, in August 1962, precipitated his decision to seek the long debated and often postponed constitutional revision by the short-cut of an unconstitutional referendum. Art. 89 of the constitution had regulated the amending procedure by combining features of the two preceding republics. One of two alternative ways of revision provided for a referendum on an amendment which had been adopted in identical form by both houses of parliament. Hence the electorate had at best a veto, not the initiative in matters of constitutional revision. Since Art. 89 gave Senate and National Assembly an equal voice, the Upper House had more weight in the amending process than in ordinary legislation. In line with the general outlook of a "senatorial" constitution, the chamber of notables was to afford protection against an Assembly which might try to upset the reforms of 1958.

When four years later not parliament but the executive felt the need for constitutional revision, its project, which proposed presidential elections by popular suffrage, was certain to meet parliamentary opposition. At least the upper house would not readily endorse the liquidation of an electoral college which, in composition and character, was very similar to its own. Nonetheless, it would not have been impossible to obtain from parliament the desired constitutional reform which was known to be popular. The government could have made fullest use of the means at its disposal to discipline parliament, including dissolution and the threat of altering election procedures for the Senate by ordinary legislation. However, to seek the reform in the constitutionally prescribed manner would have required considerable time and seemed therefore unsuitable at a moment when the President had to reckon with the imminent possibility of violent death. Since after his demise a return to the traditional forms of republican government appeared likely, General de Gaulle might well have feared that his inability to leave a lasting imprint on the country's political institutions would mar his historical image.

Nearly all experts on public law agreed that the government was violating the constitution when instead of observing the amendment procedures it decided to submit a change in the method of presidential election (Arts. 6, 7) to a popular referendum, provided for in Art. 11. The spokesmen for the government retorted with a variety of arguments which, for all their nuances and internal contradictions, asserted that the *vox populi* was capable of vindicating any innovation. The popular verdict would have to resolve an alleged contradiction between Art. 11 and Art. 89. A constitution which had reasserted (in its Art. 3) the historical claim that "national sovereignty belongs to the people" could be changed by the people at any time.

The referendum debate thus echoed memories of 1789, when a *pouvoir constituant originaire* (constituent power) had been recognized as overriding whatever formalities might have been prescribed for the exercise of the *pouvoir constituant institué* (amending power). When Sieyès had declared that the constituent power knew no constraints, he seemed for a moment to revert to the principles of the *Contrat Social.* However, the constitution of 1791 stipulated that it was "in accordance with national interest" to exercise the "imprescriptible" right of constitutional revision only in ways prescribed by the constitution itself. Afterward, Napoleon was the first among many to manipulate with great ease the *pouvoir constituant originaire* incarnating the national will. But modern French constitutional theory has always denounced the argument that the sovereign people possessed an unalterable constituent power as "sophistry" and as an attempt to "legitimize almost permanent revolutionary action."

In 1962, the government's appeal was anything but a call for revolutionary action. Instead, the voters were admonished to insure the continuation of political stability and economic well-being by preventing the departure of de Gaulle, which would be inevitable if the referendum were to fail. In many ways, October 1962 reenacted the situation which had arisen when the enabling act of June 3, 1958 ignored the amending procedures of the preceding constitution. Then as now, de Gaulle symbolized a merging of constituent and constituted power. The majority of voters who each time sanctioned the constitutional text proposed to them, did so not because of the inherent value of its provisions but because they wished to see de Gaulle in power. Hence they were prepared to grant him the instrumentalities of power for which he asked.

Both the circumstances under which the first President of the Fifth Republic had been elected and the transformation of the Presidency which had taken place since then, reinforced the official argument that the electorate was asked merely to sanction a *de facto* development. In 1958, de Gaulle undoubtedly had been "the people's choice." To ensure governmental stability his successor would need the vastly broadened power which he would inherit. But then he too should be elected by the nation, not merely by 80,000 notables who might have a penchant to choose a man of minor stature. For such reasons, the question of the constitutionality of the plebiscite was still not a decisive factor for a majority of voters, even though at this time it had considerably more weight than during the preceding referendum. In an opinion poll taken in December 1962, 76 per cent declared that it would be "grave" if a government did not respect the constitution "integrally." Did the voters wish to ignore the fact that many of them had just endorsed the latest of many instances in which a French constitution had become the victim of French politics?

On the other hand, the fact that in the latest referendum only 46 percent of the registered voters cast an affirmative vote lent little credibility to the claim that the plebiscite had been a manifestation of the sovereign's constituent powers.

David B. Goldey

PRELUDE TO A PRESIDENTIAL ELECTION

The December 1965 presidential election was the first to be fought under the new system of electing the president by universal suffrage which was adopted in 1962 — a system intended both to confirm the strengthening of the presidency and bring about a simplification in the fragmented array of political forces which has plagued France. In the first of three items on the election David Goldey describes the manoeuverings and calculations which preceeded the opening of the actual campaign.

Partisans of direct presidential elections had argued that it was the only way to prevent a return to a Fourth Republic *"revue et non corrigée."* Competition for the presidency imposed a two-party system in the United States that was less clear and rigid than the English model, but serviceable nonetheless; the same device might help produce the same result in France. Enthusiasts who thought they had found a quick way of reforming the French parties were almost bound to be disappointed, however. The American institution was set in a very different political society. French parties, especially on the right, were small and weak; their unstable, shifting coalitions were incomprehensible to and unpopular with the mass electorate. Perhaps half the voters felt little attachment to any particular group; perhaps as many as a third were unable to situate themselves at all either in terms of tendencies or policies. The instability of this electorate, particularly on the right, provided the dissatisfied, transient voters who surged from one party to another in every postwar election.

General de Gaulle has always had a special attraction for these floating voters, and the party which depended upon and supported him, the UNR-UDT, benefited from their suffrages at the expense of all the parties of the right and centre — and even of the Socialists and Communists. But de Gaulle always claimed to be above party and refused to be committed to the UNR; by amplifying oscillations of opinion, de Gaulle's appeal complicates electoral strategy and makes party realignment both more difficult and more desirable. So long as the General looked invincible — but not immortal — it was only necessary to survive him; the painful task of adapting party structures hardly seemed worthwhile. Party bureaucracies, fearing structural unemployment, exploited old (if eroded) loyalties; most parliamentary leaders thought in terms of the general election of 1967. One of them, Gaston Defferre, tried to federate the left and centre parties, Socialists (SFIO), Radicals, and Christian Democrats (MRP), as the only credible way to challenge de Gaulle — and win votes from the Commu-

From David B. Goldey, "The French Presidential Election of 5 and 19 December 1966. Prelude to the Campaign," *Political Studies* (June, 1966), pp. 208–209. Reprinted by permission of The Clarendon Press and of the author.

nist Party. But since no one thought Defferre could win the presidential election, he could not easily use the occasion to force the party leaders to make sacrifices; rather, he offered them the uncertain compensation of a majority in the far future for the certainty of present difficulties. In June 1965, MRP and SFIO bosses combined to defeat the nascent Federation, and Defferre withdrew his candidacy.

While traditional spokesmen lamented the depoliticization of the country, reformers complained that voters were being offered the very alternative they had decisively rejected in 1962: a return to the parliamentary *moeurs* of the Fourth Republic. The parties seemed headed for an even worse fiasco than in that year; since 1963 de Gaulle had never fallen below 50 percent in the opinion polls, with a further quarter undecided. Under these circumstances Defferre had not seemed indispensable. But having torpedoed him, party chiefs suddenly noticed that they too were without lifeboats; in September 1965 there began an undignified scramble for candidates.

Guy Mollet (to protect his left) promoted the candidacy of the bourgeois politician most acceptable to the Communists, François Mitterrand — while smiling on the attempts of Radicals, MRP and Conservatives (CNI) to draft the hero of the older business conservatives, Antoine Pinay. When the "candidate of experience" finally declined, the 45-year-old senator Jean Lacanuet resigned as president of MRP to become the "candidate of youth" — or, claimed the gaullists, his party's sacrificial goat. So, from a month of tawdry intrigue there emerged two personable, intelligent nominees, both in their forties and both committed to reforming the parties à la Defferre — but with a difference. And behind the two candidates, who both ran as independents, there formed coalitions of parties and party leaders.

The volatility of important sections of French opinion was nowhere better demonstrated than during the campaign. In a September survey over 60 percent of the sample favoured de Gaulle, in December only 44 percent. At the end of October one of the two major polls registered the first signs of this shift: a marked rise among the "undecideds" and an equivalent fall in de Gaulle's total. Both polls recorded the gathering force of the movement after the General announced his candidacy on 4 November in a television speech in which he demanded another seven-year blank cheque from the electors, if they wished France to survive. It was a peculiar commentary on the much-vaunted institutional stability of the Fifth Republic; the President, in effect, dared Frenchmen to try and get along without him.

Of the five other candidates, disdainfully lumped together as the opposition by de Gaulle, four tried to convince the voters that they were suitable successors. Mitterrand was the "sole candidate of the whole left," including the Communist party, welcomed back from its exile "in the east" by Guy Mollet. Lecanuet, a man of the centre, drew more right-wing support than his two rivals — a decent conservative senator, Pierre Marchihacy, taller than the General but otherwise unexceptional; and J-L. Tixier-Vignancour, a clever, controversial political lawyer, running as the candidate of the extreme-right and especially of the million European Algerians now installed in France, the *rapatriés*. Finally, there was a dissident Fourierist, Marcel Barbu, who entered the campaign in order to get an interview with the incumbent President, but finished it by demanding free access to the television. Above all mere candidates, factions, and even Frenchmen, hovered the outgoing President, General de Gaulle, determined to remain the incarnation of national unity and the personification of the French state.

Philip M. Williams

THE PRESIDENTIAL ELECTION CAMPAIGN, 1965

For six months the parties, on Left and Right alike, had been busy with manoeuvres conducted in slow motion within a close circle of politicians, and reminding the bored or disgusted man in the street of the hated ministerial crises of the past. When Defferre had sparked some public interest, the machines had destroyed him. So with better-known figures keeping well away from the field, the opposition was represented by a left-wing opportunist who inspired confidence in no one; the unknown young leader of a party which had spent the year facing Left and Right in turn; a political adventurer with a fascist record; an obscure senator and a bizarre crank, both without serious backing. The parties had learned nothing and forgotten nothing; no wonder the result seemed a foregone conclusion.

Yet the General was wrong to believe his opponents would again do his work for him. In 1962 the Algerian War had only just ended. But in 1965 France had been at peace for three years, and Frenchmen were preoccupied with the domestic problems which had never seemed to command the great man's attention. After seven years, and at 75, their benevolent monarch was seeking reelection for seven years more. But he could not last for ever, and increasingly they were worried about "afterwards"; *l'après-gaullisme.*

If the parties had done nothing right before the campaign opened, the President did nothing right once it had begun. Confirming the contemptuous impression given by his long delay, his brief announcement of his candidature showed all the old hallmarks: before de Gaulle—nothing; under de Gaulle—perfection; if not de Gaulle—catastrophe. Indeed he acted as if he believed the critics who had charged him with reducing the French people to a state of civil slumber broken only by automatic reaffirmations of confidence in his leadership. Yet where was "depoliticisation" when local elections in March brought out masses of voters, Defferre's federation aroused great interest, and Tixier drew huge crowds to his meetings at the resorts? When the campaign opened in earnest even normally non-political citizens followed it with intense attention.

The usual methods of French electioneering were all brought into use: posters official and illegal, small local meetings (mostly for Mitterrand or Tixier), big rallies in the main towns at which—as in Britain in 1959—television unexpectedly stimulated interest and large and eager crowds attended. While Mitterrand's campaign was wholly traditional, except for the helicopter in which he flew about, his rivals employed some techniques less familiar in France. Tixier's summer "circus" and his propaganda film "Sept ans de malheur" were successful publicity stunts. Lecanuet also showed a film at some meetings, and at his final Paris rally a huge audience saw de Gaulle's television address and then heard the candidate reply to it. Lecanuet buttons, scarves and handkerchiefs were an innovation, and his campaign, financed by a few large companies, organised by a public relations firm—the same that man-

From Philip M. Williams, "The French Presidential Election," *Parliamentary Affairs* (Vol. XIX, no. 1, Winter 1965–1966), pp. 16–24. Reprinted by permission of The Hansard Society for Parliamentary Government and of the author.

aged James Bond—and advised by a market research organisation, provoked opponents to complain that he was being sold like a toothpaste.

Far more important were radio and television. The State radio gave the candidates two hours each, and on the private stations (which have a bigger audience) there were several debates between their leading supporters: the UNR and Socialist general secretaries; Tixier's campaign manager Le Pen and a Gaullist deputy, who almost came to blows; Pierre Mendès-France and Michel Debré, whose two two-hour debates aroused so much interest that a third was arranged on the spot. During the final fortnight each candidate had two hours on television, and it was the medium in which de Gaulle had so long been the unchallenged champion that did most to provoke—or at least crystallise—the opposition to him.

For years the government had systematically exploited ORTF (state radio and television). Clearly, it did not think two weeks of equal time for opposing candidates was a dangerous concession; its main concern was to give no handle to opposition criticism. The administrative arrangements were made not by the Constitutional Council (which should supervise election campaigns, but had been criticised as a Gaullist tool) but by an *ad hoc* Control Commission of senior civil servants; and for the two weeks' campaign ministers were formally instructed by the premier not to make public appearances except in case of "necessity." The Gaullists' confident expectations broke down by the second week, when "necessity" obliged the ministers to appear with unheard-of frequency; and when the controllers of features and news bulletins blandly ignored the Control Commission, which was punctiliously regulating the candidates' broadcasts. These infringements of impartiality (which were corrected for the second round) did not offset the impact of five speakers who came on television to say what they thought even if it was not what the authorities wanted.

Few if any Frenchmen were unaware how the medium had been manipulated; and every opposition candidate reminded them, promising that if he were elected he would naturally allow his opponents access to this public service. Yet the critics made all the greater impact (as a few intelligent Gaullists had foreseen) because opinion had not been "vaccinated" in advance against argument on the screen. But they were also far more skilful than the older politicians, who in previous referendum and election campaigns had regularly read in monotonous tones their dreary and platitudinous election addresses. Now for the first time two youngish and personable political leaders, who seemed quite capable of managing national affairs responsibly, were using the medium properly.

De Gaulle did not adjust at once his style or strategy to face this competition. Not being a candidate like the others he would neither campaign himself nor encourage his followers to do so. If ministers were told to observe discretion while the battle was on, the UNR was to be neither seen nor heard. Such activity as was permitted was directed by a "non-partisan" Civic Action Committee managed by one of his former secretaries. The President renounced his two hours of television time, except for a brief final broadcast; the one he made on November 30th was a belated admission of the opposition's success.

In announcing his decision on November 4th he sounded no new note, but repeated the old appeal against "the State abandoned to the parties and sinking into chaos . . . but this time without hope of redress." Every Gaullist spokesman took up the theme, which critics summarised in a phrase he never used, as *"Moi ou le chaos."* It was a poor advertisement for Gaullist stability, but the General thought "the five oppositions, five candidates—who agree only in wanting me to go" would reinforce it by exposing "their mutual contradictions, their irreconcilable clienteles, their divergent combinations." Instead they left their lesser rivals severely alone, concentrated their fire on the President and, to an astonishing extent, all exploited similar lines of attack.

They devoted much of their time to contesting the vaunted stability which had served the Gaullists so well. Mitterrand and especially Lecanuet stressed their youth, and referred discreetly to de Gaulle's age and "the moment of decision which must come eventually." There were warnings that the General might not serve out his term, but might try to choose a successor unknown to the voters. His decision to stand again, and his reasons, were called an open vote of no confidence in the UNR. All his opponents accused him of flouting his own constitution and promised to work it correctly, accepting — despite their initial hostility — that the President must be a national leader with a policy, and not a mere figurehead. All dissociated themselves from existing party organisations and discipline and stressed their personal independence, but none repudiated parties as such. Marcilhacy claimed (correctly) to be the only candidate not selected by himself. Tixier-Vignancour, Mitterrand and Lecanuet each said his personal campaign was only a beginning from which a new party should arise — on the Right, Left Center or Center — better adapted to the new world than the old decaying machines. Indeed the last two linked their own political futures to the success of party realignment, and Lecanuet made it the central note of his final television broadcast.

Even on policy issues there was agreement on the criticisms and sometimes on the alternatives proposed. All the oppositions called for an expanding instead of a stagnant economy and complained that France was lagging behind the rest of the Six. They all denounced the lamentable shortage of schools and cheap housing (the Gaullists had done much to meet the former, nothing for the latter). They all discovered (as the Gaullists had always known) that women had votes, and delivered appeals specifically addressed to them. The convergence even extended to foreign pol-

icy. Tixier's Atlantic loyalty was uncompromising, and his zeal for the United States startled those who recalled his previous vitriolic anti-Americanism. Mitterrand and Lecanuet both declared their support of NATO, but Lecanuet promised he would not be subservient to the U.S., and Mitterrand agreed with de Gaulle in favouring modifications of the alliance terms though not with the President's method of seeking these. All the critics attacked the President for changing foreign policies (Mitterrand claimed there had been fourteen), accused him of sabotaging European union, and condemned France's nuclear deterrent. Tixier, the old ultra-nationalist, even used one television appearance for a brief lesson in strategy illustrated by a carefully chosen map of the world reducing France to the smallest possible space.

This similarity of approach enabled the oppositions to capture one of the most telling Gaullist themes. The unity of the nation above the petty divisions of region or class or political faction had been a note which the General struck successfully in every appeal he made. But now his opponents, too, professed non-partisanship. Strident anticommunism seemed at last to have disappeared from the French political vocabulary; even Tixier hardly denounced the red peril and positively appealed for Socialist and Radical votes. Mitterrand hoped to conciliate Catholics by never referring to his orthodox left-wing position over the Church schools. Lecanuet made the abolition of "internal frontiers" (between Catholics and anticlericals) as well as external ones (among the Six) the main grounds of his call for a new party. Every candidate endorsed the demand for an amnesty for those in prison for Algerian war offences, and Tixier, calling for the release of generals who had plotted against de Gaulle or of students who left bombs outside left-wingers' homes, was unexpectedly echoed by pleas for national reconciliation from the Centre and Left.

The most conspicuous feature of the whole campaign was this interchangeability of topics by which everyone, seeking to win away their rivals' supporters, was drawn towards the centre. Subjects and attitudes peculiar to one candidate were remarkably few. Lecanuet appealed primarily to former Gaullist voters and claimed to be the heir of Defferre (whose federation he had helped to scuttle). Mitterrand made the most of the unwonted left-wing solidarity behind his candidature and stressed—notably in his final broadcast—the historical fears and glories of the French Left in the rhetorical tradition of 60 years before. Neither was above an occasional word calculated to please the critics of foreign aid or the supporters of *Algérie française*. But only Tixier thoroughly exploited the Algerian amnesty and the strong aversion to foreign aid, calling for the money to be spent at home and not on "nigger kings." He committed himself to the farmers' cherished demand for price parity, and to cutting taxation by 11 percent (10 percent would not have sounded sufficiently serious), cheered South Vietnam, and championed free enterprise. Lecanuet also attacked "collectivism and Marxism" and praised individual initiative—while the candidate of the Left said that some denationalisation was perhaps desirable. Lecanuet tried to tempt UNR politicians, many of them worried about "afterwards," by promising to work if possible with the existing parliamentary majority, but concentrated mainly on the need for a new "democratic, social, European" party of the Centre.

The old parties, after their feverish activity in choosing and endorsing candidates, took back seats for the campaign itself. None was asked to speak officially for a candidate on the radio or television, as the law allowed. Each candidate had an *ad hoc* committee of supporters running his campaign, and on these there was not much love lost between members of different political loyalties. The parties played little part at public meetings, though at Lecanuet's a Conservative and a Radical leader, Bertrand Motte and Maurice Faure, were prominent speakers. Mitterrand, in contrast, was somewhat embarrassed by Communist support, and appeared entirely alone, except in towns where the Socialist or Radical mayor introduced him (if the mayor was a Communist, he stayed well away).

Among other organisations, the Algerian refugee societies were the backbone of Tixier's campaign and the leading advocates of united Europe virtually formed Lecanuet's general staff. Trade union and professional organisations preferred not to endorse any candidate, so that only the Communist-dominated CGT and the anticlerical teachers came out for Mitterrand; but the influential Peasants' League (FNSEA) urged its members to vote against de Gaulle and so in effect did the CFDT, no longer officially a Catholic trade union.

The press gave good coverage to the campaign, including the television broadcasts. Editorially the principal provincial dailies were divided fairly evenly between de Gaulle, Mitterrand, Lecanuet and complete neutrality; but few were heavily committed like the *Dépêche* at Toulouse, and most avoided offence to their broad local clientele by not blantantly taking sides. Most Paris papers leaned to the opposition, but *France-Soir* was actively Gaullist and so in the end was *Le Figaro*. As the Communists were now subordinating foreign to domestic policy, *L'Humanité* did not publish a Tass communiqué which sounded too friendly to de Gaulle, and corrected "tendentious interpretations" of the party line in the "French and foreign" press—i.e. *Pravda. Le Monde*, while as usual giving space to everyone, at last ended years of editorial balancing by coming out (cryptically) for the opposition. The intellectuals' vote was treated as important news even by *Paris-Match*. Their extreme-Right minority divided between Tixier and Lecanuet, and the Left majority was thoroughly unhappy with Mitterrand and the party bosses behind him. A good many came out for de Gaulle, while *L'Express* gave half its endorsement to Lecanuet, arguing that if he came close behind Mitterrand the Socialist

Party would swing back to Defferre. On the same grounds J.-P. Sartre switched his advice at the last minute from abstention to voting for Mitterrand.

Such tactical assessments of the campaign's progress played a part in more influential quarters also, and were helped for the first time in France by regular opinion polls. These showed, as politicians sensed, that the battle was going badly for the General and well for Lecanuet (everybody underestimated Mitterrand). Soon the prospect of a second ballot appalled the Gaullists. Early in the last week meetings were multiplied, ministers and deputies mobilised, and a new and bitter note struck. Along with the familiar claims of constructive reform at home and assertive independence abroad, and warnings against the Fourth Republic's past impotence and the opposition's present divisions, there were now personal and violent attacks on the rival candidates—most vitriolically against Mitterrand but most intensively against Lecanuet. Radio and television (apart from the candidates' broadcasts) also reverted to their normal partisanship.

De Gaulle himself, though naturally never stooping to the excesses of his supporters, at last adopted a new tone. In his unexpectedly defensive "extra" broadcast of November 30th, his reminders of social reforms and nationalisations by his Liberation government seemed aimed at the Communist voter. His final appeal, instead of threatening "chaos," spoke warmly of his ministers as "a team of action and success." Lecanuet did not modify his tactics to meet the Gaullist attack; he had throughout stood more in the center in his broadcasts than in his addresses to right-wing audiences in the provinces. But Mitterrand did change, suddenly announcing himself a few days before the poll no longer as "the one and only candidate of the Left," but as "the candidate of the Left and Left Center."

The results of the first ballot on December 5th exceeded the worst Gaullist fears: the President had fewer than 44 percent of the votes cast. A second ballot was needed at which the law allowed only the top two candidates to stand (unless one chose to withdraw). So Mitterrand was now the sole opponent, and Gaullist spokesmen at once denounced him as the prisoner of the Communists—and Lecanuet as the man who had split the "national" vote (the Minister of the Interior even implying that he had been unpatriotic to stand at all). But this bitter outburst was quickly stopped. The Gaullists were firmly instructed that there was to be no demagogic anti-Communist campaign, that the second ballot was not to be fought as a contest between Left and Right, and that Lecanuet and his supporters were to be ignored, not denounced. For the General would not give up his claim to stand above factions and represent the whole nation, while the shrewder Gaullists feared to alienate potential votes—and the Control Commission now kept an eye on the news bulletins. The last two weeks of the campaign thus regained the seriousness and dignity from which it had momentarily departed.

Now the Gaullists mobilised for a serious contest. The most sensational change was in the General himself, who revolutionised both his approach and his style. Interviewed by an ORTF journalist, he answered questions not only on foreign policy but on the mundane problems of motorways and telephones with easy command of the subject and jovial familiarity. The historic de Gaulle having failed to win his customary electoral triumph, for the first time in his life and to the delight of most of his countrymen *le Grand Charles* became a candidate—and an appealing one.

His supporters followed their instructions, sometimes with bizarre results. Left-wing Gaullists were encouraged to claim that the General represented France's finest progressive traditions, and Malraux asked where Mitterrand had been when Republican Spain was fighting for its life—to loud applause from his elderly, bourgeois, Catholic Parisian audience. A

Gaullist weekly of limited circulation printed eight million copies of a "supplement," *France Avenir* (successor to the old *France Référendum*)—but at least one provincial UNR deputy did not send it out, since its references to Mitterrand as a young Catholic would have done him good, not harm. In a Paris suburb voters found in one envelope three leaflets attacking him as an enemy of the Church, a threat to the bourgeoisie—and a bogus progressive who never supported real left-wing causes.

The opposition was no less eager to steal the enemy's clothes. Mitterrand now called himself "the candidate of all democrats" (*républicains*) and, without changing his policies, specifically "welcomed" all votes coming over from his eliminated competitors. Most of them gave him cautious support. Barbu did so "without enthusiasm" and Marcilhacy only by implication: he agreed to Mitterrand's request to watch for electoral fraud in the overseas territories, where the General had won some majorities of Eastern European dimensions. Many of Lecanuet's voters would not support a man of the Left; knowing this, their leader advised them either to spoil their ballots or cast them for Mitterrand—but not for the General. Wholehearted endorsement of the candidate of the Left came only from the Champions of the Extreme Right: Tixier and his whole campaign committee, the Algerian refugee organisations, the exiled Soustelle and Bidault, and every former advocate of all-out war in Algeria or fascism in France.

Hatred of De Gaulle in these quarters had been plain for years. But it also affected responsible and moderate Conservatives —especially their most politically conscious and active representatives, among whom the Gaullist contempt for "intermediaries" was taking its toll. Jean Monnet and the European lobby led the way to the left-wing camp, followed by many bankers, generals and clerics astonished by the company they were keeping and the discovery that so many of their friends were doing the same. Thus while a good many left-wing spokesmen and some voters still preferred de Gaulle, a large fraction of the Right saw in him an enemy far more dangerous than Mitterrand.

THE 1965 PRESIDENTIAL ELECTION: THE CANDIDATES MAKE THEIR CASE

On the eve of the first ballot in the 1965 election, all the candidates appeared in turn, alone, on radio and television to make their closing appeals to the electorate. Each in his personal political style tried to sum up the substance of the case he was trying to put before the country and mark out the differences which separated him from his opponents. Below are the addresses of the three leading contenders, in the order in which they spoke, though—owing to pre-recording— the later candidates had not in fact heard the earlier ones before taking the air. This, then, in the candidates' own words, was what they argued was at stake.

GENERAL DE GAULLE

Men and women of France,
The decision you are going to take by your vote the day after tomorrow will doubtless commit the fate of our country far into the future. Therefore this is an overall decision which implies an overall judgment on the new Republic and on the Frenchman who has the honour to preside over it.

Where were we seven years ago? The

Editor's translation.

situation then could be summed up in these terms: the regime of the parties, horrified at its own failure, abdicated its responsibilities yet again and gave way to our Republic. I say this, as you know, from a full knowledge of the situation. That is why it seems particularly presumptuous of candidates who, whatever they may say, are inspired only by the bygone regime, who inherit the same divisions, who emanate from the same combinations, who misuse the same illusions, and who want nothing more than to begin again, to claim to teach lessons.

Where are we going now? Five basic problems, formerly hidden by pretences and ambiguities, since nobody was able to resolve them, are effectively settled. The country's institutions were formerly made for impotence, while today there is a Chief of State, a government which lasts and governs and a Parliament which exercises its legislative power effectively and worthily. Decolonization, which divided the French, turned the whole world against us and disturbed the army, is completed. Peace, which we had never known for at least half a century, is now restored. Inflation, which corroded the economy, public finances and the currency, and maintained a constant state of social insecurity and of perpetual injustices, is now choked off. Finally, independence which was formerly stifling beneath a pile of lying myths, has been regained.

This is the essential base from which we are advancing in many other important fields: adaptation and expansion of industry, agriculture, foreign trade, standard of living, investment, scientific research, education, housing, pensions, hospitals, sports, etc. As for tomorrow's stage; it is already traced out in the law of the Fifth Plan, the law of social progress decided by our Republic and which lays down for five years the aim, the path and the resources for the march of our whole country and each of its children towards prosperity. This charter for our progress must be carried through with the ardor of a people who are on the upward path while preparing what will come after, which must be better and more fraternal.

Abroad, it is our intention that the economic union of western Europe which is partially functioning, shall be completed between the Six on the basis of common sense and friendship and then, no doubt, one day it will be opened to neighboring countries. At the same time we want to carry through the vast enterprise of *rapprochement* with the East, which has begun so happily, to the point where fuller understanding and practical consideration are possible. Finally, what a task is and will be ours in developing the new or renewed links we are weaving with Asia, Africa, Latin America and the East! This is how France, who has become France again, with her humane ambition and her eternal genius, must aid the world to find its equilibrium, which is the only way to peace.

Men and women of France, in asking each and every one of you for the demonstration of your confidence, I offer you the decisive way of confirming the new Republic. If you do this, I am sure that the active and successful team that it has given birth to, to match our needs, and the profound mass of our people, who founded it on my appeal, will pursue under its auspices the magnificent effort we have begun. I am certain that the Republic will survive after me, lively and fertile, because the sovereign people will have made clear it is their Republic and that throughout the future they will choose men who are worthy of it to answer for its destiny.

Men and women of France! Once more I have shouldered my responsibility before each and every one of you. On Sunday, you will take yours.

Vive la République!
Vive la France!

JEAN LECANUET

None of us can be unaffected by the great voice we have just heard.

There is not a man or woman among us, whatever disillusions there may since have been, who can forget the appeal of 18 June;[1] the glory of great memories cannot be eradicated, but a presidential election cannot be a mere anniversary celebration. It is a decision—your decision, for the next seven years and beyond.

So there is no need for us either to deny history or to wrap ourselves up in the past with this history, we must rather lean on this to measure French greatness and show the French people their new way forward to the future.

This future is now assured, the new generation is ready to take over. This, I believe, is the great revelation of the electoral campaign which is now ending. You no longer fear "after-gaullism," you no longer fear a vacuum or an overflow, and you know the great aims which will be ours: to build Europe, to march resolutely forward defending French interests every inch of the way, towards the United States of Europe; to create prosperity, to see it shared by every Frenchman and particularly the most lowly; to revitalize our regions; to build a France which is generous and responsive to social needs: these objectives are so basic, so clearly necessary that I am convinced that if you elect me to the Presidency of the Republic, they will find agreement in the French Parliament, or if not a new majority would carry them through in stability.

Consequently, an orderly, calm succession is now possible, without any transition, upheavals or stoppages; let us seize this opportunity which cannot occur again, which is our common chance of constructing our future.

Some people say: "Later, a little longer." But why? The reason General de Gaulle decided to stand after a long hesitation was probably that he was convinced that no public figure, not even among the men closest to him, could get the French people to accept a policy which is no longer in keeping with their aspirations, because it

bars the road to Europe, because it compromises our alliances, because it fails to achieve rapid enough social and economic progress. The fact that General de Gaulle appeals to his legend to try and continue to maintain and impose this policy is one more reason for us to fight it, and this is the reason for my candidacy.

Why put off the inevitable reckoning and grant a reprieve? To add to the delays we have already noted and from which all of us suffer in relation to other Common Market countries? To jeopardize our last chances of saving a united Europe? Do you believe that from an internal point of view the succession will be any easier in a few months or years? Personally, I believe the contrary.

Difficulties and rivalries can only develop and aggravate the situation. Next Sunday, on the contrary, we have the opportunity of making our decision with a calm horizon untroubled by the threat of any political storm. We can therefore think of our future and build it. What is happening, what you yourselves can feel, is that the page of history is turning. The period of tragedy, war and the aftermath of war is behind us. A new period with new horizons is now opening before us, for a new generation which must prepare to take over the succession in order, calm and dignity. But, need I say, we will have to make great efforts—for peace is also an effort. But to construct, to build the happiness of men, we must have the courage to rally together, to break down the old divisions of the past, to overcome outdated quarrels and to forge together the great democratic, socially progressive, European force on which the majority and political stability of tomorrow will rest. These are the possibilities which lie open to us.

Ah! We must eradicate all the frontiers, not only those which separate the nations, but the internal frontiers within our minds. Those who are Christians and those who are not, Frenchmen and women of all religions, of all philosophies, must draw together, converge towards a social human-

[1] i.e. De Gaulle's appeal to continued resistance in 1940. [Editor's note.]

159

ism—not that they should abandon their convictions; on the contrary they should enrich one another with their faith and their view of the truth.

They must join together in the plan of action to give France of modern times a new vital impulse—of France which is fraternal, pacific and generous. That is where true greatness lies, in the well-being of men and the blossoming of freedom.

Vive la France et vive la République.

FRANÇOIS MITTERRAND

Men and women of France,

In putting myself forward for your votes I wish to attain two objectives: the first is to restore, to restore to you, your function as responsible citizens, sole masters of the future of our country. The second is to put to you a new policy which will define that future.

This is not, it seems, the opinion of General de Gaulle who, I regret to say, lingers in the quarrels of the past. Nor, it seems, is it the opinion of the Prime Minister who was still saying to the press yesterday evening, "For the great majority of people the problem on 19 December is not to choose a future but to choose the man who will be in charge of that future for a certain period."

Of course the choice of the person who will lead France is not a matter of indifference. But I would like to link two ideas immediately: can you choose a man without knowing his policy? And if you do not know his policy, for what reason do you choose a man?

Since the beginning of the presidential campaign, wherever I have gone I have made a point of saying and saying again for the benefit of all of you who are listening to me: the fundamental choice on 19 December is between personal power and the Republic and its citizens.

I have put questions to General de Gaulle, but I have heard no replies. Philippics against the parties and the condemnation of political organizations are not suf-

ficient to enlighten us. Of course the political parties made errors and mistakes, and they admit this. But can one really sum up the whole history of the Republic by assigning all the defeats, failures or catastrophes to one side and all our victories, successes and hopes for the future to the personal power of a few men?

Gambetta stood for a great moment in our history, as did Clemenceau, while, as nobody can forget, General de Gaulle was the embodiment of our country's resistance 25 years ago.

But neither Gambetta nor Clemenceau dreamed of cashing in on their battles for the survival of France to carry through a policy of their own.

To condemn the parties means going against the 1958 Constitution—introduced by the will of General de Gaulle—which provides for discussion between responsible organizations and the ability of the citizens to choose the one they prefer among these.

As for me, I am not the man of any party or any coalition of parties. I am the man of a struggle. This struggle was the struggle of the left, the generous left, the fraternal left, until the moment on 5 December when universal suffrage selected me to lead the fight of all republicans against personal power.

How should a President of the Republic be chosen? If I understand General de Gaulle correctly, he must not be chosen from either the left, the right or the center. The President of the Republic should not issue from any particular section of the population. Then I seek in vain. Should he be recruited from a royal house, or from the House of Rothschild[2], or from the Jockey Club? Must it be denied that families of thought have always existed in our Republic? Must the existence of groups, needs, interests, doctrine in society be denied?

All one should ask of a President of the Republic, once he has become the Presi-

[2]M. Pompidou was employed by the bank controlled by the Rothschild family at the time he became prime minister. [Editor's note.]

dent of all the people of France, is that he should respect the fundamental rules which make a democracy a democracy.

Now what has General de Gaulle been doing for the last seven years? He acts like a citizen above the laws, above even the supreme law called the Constitution.

The role of the Chief of State: this is what it is right for us to decide among ourselves while there is still time. What then is the role of the Chief of State as General de Gaulle understands it?

He and he alone is the master of our external policy, and he chooses our alliances; he and he alone is the master of our military policy and chooses our weapons. He and he alone is the master of the judicial system, and appoints judges, concerns himself with promotions, and punishes those who challenge his actions in the press, and chooses those prisoners who must remain in prison and those who shall be released.

He is the master of economic and social decisions and budgetary allocations, since he gives the atomic bomb priority over education.

The role of the Chief of State as conceived by General de Gaulle does not correspond to any republican tradition; and to say this is not to say the factions are right, or to show a preference for the past, or to say the Fourth Republic was right and the Fifth is wrong—all that is a form of argument which should be dismissed from the debates of responsible citizens.

What counts is to know what we will do tomorrow. In the name of all who have supported me and fought with me, in the name of the millions upon millions of men and women who have supported my struggle, I have made my commitments, I have said what I will do. I have asked you to bear with me the responsibility for our personal freedoms which are subtly threatened, and for our collective freedoms which have been won over the centuries and need safeguarding. I have asked you to help me in drawing up a foreign policy which is in the service of peace and which serves the entry of France, with all her

unique qualities, her strengthened prospects for the future, into the new communities.

I have asked you to break with decisions of a military nature which commit France to an infernal race in which the world will perish. I have asked you for an outline of an economic policy based on expansion, an acceptance of progress, confidence in the capacity for work, the will for full employment, the creation of new riches, the ability to compete with other nations in foreign markets. And I have told you that this economic policy would be meaningless unless its end was human welfare, that is the determination to improve the lot of men and women who work, suffer and hope.

I have asked you to give topmost priority to education by giving our children, to every boy and every girl equal chances in life.

I have set out for you a complete policy which must be accepted as it is, or else it is meaningless. I asked you to choose on the basis of the arguments I have suggested to you and those I would have liked General de Gaulle to have put forward.

But instead there are only threats and warnings of catastrophe, as if catastrophe was tied to the fate of one man rather than the will of an entire people which is capable, if it so wishes, of overcoming perils and passing through the centuries.

Can anyone really claim, then, that without him France would be nothing? No. General de Gaulle is wrong. France does not belong to him. France is identified with nobody except her people.

Looking back over the centuries which have served to mould her, to keep her, to let her survive and grow, it is clear—and I believe this with all my heart—that France has not grown old. Where does the youth of France lie? In the centuries that lie before her and the tasks which await her.

At the moment of leaving you, abandoning pointless comparison, outmoded struggles, and proclaiming the act of faith of a responsible man, calling on all republicans to serve and love the French Republic, let us look ahead then, let us believe in our-selves, believe in the people, believe in the future of our country, believe in the policy we have laid down. And we shall feel this evening, at the end of so much toil, and with so great a task ahead, that while the road ahead is still a long one, how fine it is to set out along it in step together.

Let us think, men and women of France, that from now on it is possible, if we be-lieve in it, to cry *"Vive la République et vive la France."*

Christian Pineau

WHAT THE VOTERS WANT

This somewhat cynical electoral vignette is, like the previous extract by Chris-tian Pineau, taken from his political novel, which draws on his own experience as a political candidate.

At the *A la Civette café* the two friends carefully examined the letters which vari-ous organizations in the department had addressed to the candidates. Generally these contained more or less detailed questionnaires. Each demand required a "Yes" or a "No."

"What am I supposed to do with all this?" wailed Victor. "Heaven knows how many billions it would take to pay for all this lot. Since I have to insist in my meet-ings that taxes are too heavy, I'm cor-nered."

Jules Bardet has a more realistic view of the question. "You're quite wrong," he said, "if you think that the voters see the slightest connection between income and expenditure. The Budget is nothing but a hole into which you throw *sous*, and from which you fish them out. Everyone be-lieves there is always a big heap left at the bottom, and that anyone who is smart enough can always get some."

"But I can't say 'yes' to everyone."

"Yet that's the simplest thing to do. When you're elected, you'll do what you can, and they'll give you credit for trying."

"It's dishonest."

"The dishonest part is the question-naires. Most of the people who draw them up are thinking about their members and not about the candidates at all. An election is a fine excuse for these people who run these organizations to demonstrate their energy and competence. But you do some-times get a serious questionnaire."

"Look at this one." Victor waved a paper covered with little boxes in which replies were to be indicated. "'Do you support a general increase in wages? 10 percent, 20 percent, 30 percent, 40 percent. Strike out the answers not favored.' In your opinion which one should I strike out?"

"You can't win with that one. The com-munist candidate will choose the highest figure. If he's crafty he might even strike out all four and write in '50 percent.' You can't beat him there. So, if I were you, I'd declare myself in favour of raising wages, and I would write in the first box 'in keep-ing with the situation.' They won't be able to complain at that."

"Jules," the candidate groaned, "this is a dirty game you're getting me into."

From Christian Pineau, *Mon Cher Député* (Paris, 1959), pp. 26–27. Reprinted by permission of Réné Julliard. Editor's translation.

A TRADITIONAL VILLAGE MEETING

In form and atmosphere the traditional rural election meeting still remains much as it has been for generations. The candidate in the account that follows is François Mitterrand, already a prominent political figure, campaigning in his home constituency in Nièvre in 1958. But though the circumstantial details tie the event down in time and place, this could be an account of a meeting almost anywhere in rural France at almost any election this century.

The mist has fallen, with the night, on the woods of Morvan. The municipal council's tiny meeting room is well warmed. In the corner a barrack-stove is roaring away. On the walls a coloured print of Sadi Carnot (President of the Republic, 1887–1894), and a chilly marble bust of Marianne, inscribed "Liberty, Equality, Fraternity," and draped in a tricolour.

The room fills quickly. There are only men. Real peasant types, short, thick-set and swarthy. All generations are represented. The young men in muddy gumboots and leather jackets, the not-so-young in wooden sabots and old-fashioned hunting coats, with ornamental buttons. Twenty-five persons in all.

The mayor, fresh from the fields in his working clothes, explains:

"*He* always gets a big audience. *He*'s always late, but they all know that. He likes a man-to-man chat."

"You're one of his supporters?"

"Oh no, I'm Communist. But he certainly knows how to put things across."

Here is M. Mitterrand at least, sober and elegant, as at the National Assembly. He shakes hands with all those present, takes his place behind the simple table.

The mayor presents him; he begins his speech. First, local matters. He has long been deputy for this region. How much he cares for it! Formerly he loved the whole department. Now he loves above all his constituency, from Château-Chinon to Clamecy. So much so that those friends he still keeps in Nevers and Cosne reproach him. So much the worse for them. Mind you, he thinks highly of Cosne and Nevers, but not as much as this land round Clamecy. He *adores* Pousseaux, Grenois, Trucy, Villiers, Oisy, and Dornecy. He wants every village in the Morvan to live better, to have water, electricity. He will see to it . . . This is a family chat, a word whispered in your ear by the fireside . . . He recalls the hardships of these neglected Morvan-ites, the meetings he had held in the glow of an acetylene lamp, when he could scarcely see his questioners' faces . . . And so to national questions. To the rise of Black Africa, to the crisis of May, and finally to his NON, and the new constitution.

And then the questions. A stocky farmer rises to air his bitter complaint. In the past month the price of meat has dropped 100 francs a kilo. "Think of it, Monsieur le Ministre, we lose 30,000 francs a carcass. This constitution's all very well—but we've got veal to sell." He sympathises. It is the government's fault, of course. Another questioner insists—for no apparent reason—that General Leclerc died in Paris. "No, no," says Mitterand, "in an aeroplane accident at Colomb-Béchar." Unconvinced, his questioner grumbles quietly in the cor-

Le Figaro, 15–16 November, 1958, by permission. Editor's translation.

ner, while the final point is raised. "How many votes did Pflimlin get in the National Assembly?" "Four hundred and four," Mitterrand replies, but adding courteously, "though I could be wrong."

The meeting is over. M. Mitterrand shakes hands yet again, and climbs wearily into his car. Clamecy is eight kilometres away, and his tenth meeting of the day is waiting. He is already late.

Pierre Viansson-Ponté

NEW TRENDS IN ELECTIONEERING

The "traditional" election campaign has shown rather greater resilience in France than in many other countries, a result perhaps not simply of custom and political temperament, but also of the absence until recently of well-financed centrally organized parties and the high proportion of rural voters, combined with the slowness with which television has spread—paid political advertising on T.V. being banned. Yet gradually patterns are changing, though for all but a handful of candidates the 1967 campaign was still predominantly traditional in the constituencies. What Pierre Viansson-Ponté describes here, therefore, is the form of campaign which exists already in small sectors, and which some politicians are seeking to generalize; French elections of the future may look rather more like this, and less like the traditional gathering described in the previous extract.

The old-style meeting in a schoolroom or the *salle de marriages* in the town hall has long ceased to attract more than a handful of the curious or a few active members "doing their duty." The official poster panels pass almost unread and often remaining virgin of all proclamation, particularly in the towns. While the traditional "statement of beliefs" is still sent out to registered electors along with their ballot slips,[1] this is chiefly because candidates winning five per cent of the vote are reimbursed for the cost of this expensive operation—and of poster-sticking. But the carelessness with which these "official" leaflets are drafted and laid out shows that this is merely an outmoded ritual.

What counts nowadays lies elsewhere and takes different forms. Today the candidate will give first priority to laying siege to regional television or state or commercial radio stations, the local daily and the Paris papers, so that however slim the pretext his face or voice will be widely broadcast, his name spoken or printed frequently. If he can afford it he will try to rent poster sites before the official opening of the campaign to impress his face and name on every passer-by. If he issues leaflets they will be short, striking and direct, and will be distributed outside factory gates, office blocks, sports stadiums, movie houses—even churches. He will employ professional publicity advisers and recruit men paid by the day to put up his posters and distribute leaflets. Except in extremist organizations volunteer party workers are increasingly rare.

Experts will produce precise analysis of

[1] Before polling day every elector receives an envelope containing a "statement of beliefs"—i.e. a dreadfully printed election address —and a ballot slip for each candidate. [Editor's note.]

Le Monde, 6 July 1966, by permission. Editor's translation.

the electorate, providing exact details of its composition by age, sex, occupation, education and income. It will be more useful to know how many children there are in each home, the number of inhabitants per car, and the number of people waiting for the telephone[2] than to know voters' views on NATO or the organization of the French Radio and Television Office. This will make it possible to decide the psychological approach — spectacular moves or persistent solicitations — appropriate to each group. In the towns telephonists with persuasive voices will call women voters during the day and men in the evening at the rate of thirty calls an hour to extol the candidate's merits. Richer candidates will go in for such gimmicks as phosphorescent posters and distributing ornamental key rings.

While the candidates are making their first timid acquaintance with modern propaganda techniques, the big parties have no hesitation. Unexpected partners have joined the political game. A publicity firm specializing in marketing, Services et Méthodes, who had a few months earlier launched James Bond 007 products in France, was commissioned by M. Lecanuet to "sell" his candidature in the 1965 presidential election. This company suggested that on a given day he should put fluorescent dye in the water of the rivers and fountains of the big cities, that he should use aircraft to scatter clouds of green confetti bearing his picture over the same cities, that he should fly an immense green pennant from the Eiffel tower; that he should parade down the Champs-Elysées dressed in green in a green car with an escort of green outriders. When the whole of France was thoroughly curious and baffled the candidate would have appeared — the candidate of Europe whose flag, symbol and colour is green — the focus of attention. Deciding that barn-storming in the American style has not yet become a part of our political habits, and finding the whole operation far too expensive, M. Lecanuet

turned down the plans. After this brilliant suggestion and others no less spectacular, the James Bonds of political propaganda, whose contract ended on election day, signed another large and more promising one — with the UNR. This time the problem was not to "publicize" one candidate but 470, since Services et Méthodes' job is simply to suggest ideas and events for the majority's campaign throughout metropolitan France.

At all events, a candidate for one of the big parties will receive assistance in cash and materials to supplement any money he may be able to spend personally or collect himself for his campaign. The operation will be costly . . . .

The best informed experts estimate that a respectable parliamentary election campaign costs at least $50,000 in a Paris constituency and at least double that in suburban Paris or the provinces. The difference is due to the rural and suburban electorate being scattered, which makes it necessary to cover places which may be widely separated, involving more party accommodation and receptions, and heavier travelling costs, and it is often necessary to follow custom by presenting influential electors with small gifts, ranging from a cigarette holder stamped "National Assembly" to a key-ring or ash tray, and this is not done in the capital.

A quick calculation shows that a party which wishes to have candidates throughout the country will therefore spend, without counting the cost of its publications at national level but including sums raised or paid by the candidates personally, at least $4,500,000 to $5,000,000. This is a minimum, because it will pay for a few receptions, a few posters, expenditure on party rooms, secretarial help and postage, the dispatch to electors of propaganda and at best the issuing of a small local electoral newspaper. But it will not run to taking an opinion poll in the constituency or to posters outside the official panels two or three weeks before the official campaign — which can easily cost a further

$100,000 to $120,000. The example is quoted of an unsuccessful candidate in Paris who spent over $300,000 in 1962 simply to impress voters with his face.[1]

That a proposal such as the one presented by Services et Methodes to M. Lecanuet should even be put forward . . . measures the ground that has been covered. Indeed the UNR has been in the vanguard; it was certainly not interested in the internal politics of the United States, Britain or West Germany that led it to send observers to watch the 1964 Johnson campaign, those of the German parties in 1965 or the British in 1966. Again it is the UNR which for the first time has commissioned local polls to discover as far as possible the views of the electorate about its retiring deputies. Almost fifty constituencies were surveyed in this way before the 1966 meeting of the National Council. None of the deputies whose fame, popularity and electoral chances were measured had been warned, which inevitably provoked protests, some of them heated.

Moreover, the majority can use the machinery of the State as it pleases and makes no secret of this, since the Minister of In-

formation—echoing the chief of state—has even been heard to declare urbanely that the partiality of the "official" radio and television were only a modern counterbalance to the hostility of the written press to the régime. In the field of broadcasting the experts' advice has been listened to. Many candidates or political organizers consider the public does not always grasp something which is understated, and that one has to be "larger than life" to come across. In other words, they imagine that unless one says baldly "Vote for X" the effect will be nil. Yet the image's power of suggestion is quite sufficient, while too heavy an emphasis might well prove inappropriate. Better to organize a serious debate with a candidate—even if it is over the viewers' heads—or give him an opportunity for a discreet display of his achievements, his ability and his good appearance, than openly to offer him an electoral platform. The program will not make a direct approach to uncommitted voters, simply leaving them with the feeling of having been in direct touch with one of the candidates, who has proven to be a strong and sympathetic character. Thus the entry into action of the propaganda bulldozers is accompanied by resort to more subtle and scientifically calculated procedures.

---

[1]As the article implies all of these sums are extremely high by the traditional standards of French politics [Editor's note.]

ORGANIZING AN ELECTION CAMPAIGN

Although national campaigning is developing slowly, the strictly limited role assigned to television during French parliamentary elections helps preserve the importance of the ordinary candidate's campaign in his constituency. These extracts from the Popular Republican Movement's instructions to candidates in the 1962 parliamentary elections give a good impression of how things are often run.

VISITS AND CONTACTS

As soon as he is nominated the candidate should contact the leading figures in his constituency. This is particularly true of a

candidate standing for the first time.

In the early days of the campaign he should visit mayors, assistant mayors, other local leaders, possibly the priests in the various cantons. It is preferable for him to be accompanied by a senator if one is available.

Committees of support can be set up. People who cannot help by putting up posters or distributing leaflets can at least give moral support. In the last week of the campaign they will issue a communique declaring their support for our candidate. This communique can be printed on a poster and put up on electoral panels.[1] It can also be published in the local papers if they will accept it. The importance of person to person propaganda should not be underestimated. This quiet propaganda can be extremely effective if the candidate has a network of friends who make an effort to recommend him to their acquaintances.

One innovation in this field which is worth mentioning, since it can have a considerable impact, in the towns at least, is a telephone campaign. This requires considerable organization. Voters should be classed in categories, then the town should be divided into sectors which are allocated to teams of five or six people who will undertake to telephone people selected previously from the directory. Be very careful not to telephone the same person twice . . . .

Once the date of the election is known and before the opening of the campaign it is very important for the candidate and his friends to take a rapid opinion poll to discover which questions electors consider the most important . . . . According to the information obtained the candidate will draft his outline of policy and dwell on the most important points for the constituency.

MEETINGS

Three kinds of meetings are possible.

Public Meetings

These are addressed to the largest audience. They are advertised by means of posters, and often time is allowed for opponents who may wish to come and join debate.

Looking for a chairman, the candidate should ask either the mayor of the locality if he is a sympathiser or if he will accept anyway, or a friend, preferably one who holds some municipal or cantonal office.

The candidate should speak for less than three-quarters of an hour, and do his best to see that people who come to argue or who want to put questions do so after he has spoken.

During the electoral period he has a right to hold the meeting at the *Mairie* (town hall) or the Salle des Fêtes. However, before the campaign has officially opened the mayor may refuse to allow use of his *mairie*. The best thing is to draw up a very detailed plan of meetings in each locality during the week before the opening of the campaign and book the available halls as soon as possible.

Information Meetings

Experience shows that public meetings of the sort described above are not as popular with the public as they once were. There is another more effective formula. In important towns, or cantons which have a very large number of small communes, the candidate may not be able to make a personal visit to every influential figure. In this case he can hold an information meeting for certain specialized groups: farmers, those engaged in industry, women, etc.

Invitations are sent to a number of people who are considered to have the greatest influence on public opinion. The list is drawn up by the [party's departmental] federation. Invitations should arrive at least five days before the day of the meeting.

In the letter of invitation the candidate excuses himself for not being able to visit every district in the city, or every commune, and states his intention of holding a series of information meetings on a series of problems which particularly concern the social or occupational group he wants to

[1]In France a number of special electoral poster panels are made available free to all candidates. [Editor's note.]

reach. An announcement of the meeting is inserted in the press the day before the meeting. Everyone will read it, and anyone who is interested will come. The advantage of this formula is that the orator speaks to a selected and almost always sympathetic group within a larger audience of people who are not known to him.

Invitation-only Meetings

This is the same as the previous formula but more restricted. This involves an outline of general policy rather than a lecture on a specialized subject, and is addressed to people who hold responsible positions in business, the unions, the municipality, etc.

Even if this meeting attracts only a third or a quarter of the people invited, these will talk to other people and can contribute to very effective word of mouth propaganda.

However, one danger must be avoided: of overlooking important people when sending out the invitations. The list must be established carefully at the very beginning of the campaign with the help of friends in the canton or town. Further, the person invited should be asked to bring his friends.

Regional Meetings

A regional meeting is held in the regional capital during one of the three weeks of the official campaign, with a member of the movement who has a national reputation.

This leading figure will be surrounded on the platform by retiring deputies or candidates in the department who will each say a few words. The meeting may be preceded by a discreet press conference which will allow journalists to cover it more fully and prepare their reports.

The exact date of these regional meetings must be settled very early so that the Movement's speakers will be free. Contact the general-secretary's office about this.

During the election campaign it is desirable that influential circles and professions be informed of the activity of the MRP on their behalf. To do this a series of letters will be sent to you in the days preceding the election campaign.

You should see that the list of people to whom they will be addressed is drawn up as soon as possible. You will be able to refer to lists held by various industrial and occupational groups if we have sympathisers there: the local farmers' union, the Chamber of Trade, family associations, commercial travellers' organizations. You can also find lists of the liberal professions: doctors, lawyers, druggists, etc. in the prefectures.

To give a rough indication, in a constituency containing 100,000 inhabitants, 110 communes, 9 cantons, here is the list and the number of letters sent out:

letters to travellers and sales representatives	150
'' '' hairdressers	200
'' '' leaders of family associations	100
letters to rural leaders	100
'' '' workers	500
'' '' farmers	1,500
'' '' young people	1,000

This list could be extended. It could be increased as appropriate to include administrators of public authority housing, war widows, tenants, administrators of Social Security funds, leaders of youth movements, Catholic women, committees formed to fight alcoholism, veterans and war victims, associations of parents of pupils in free schools, finally shopkeepers.

To this may be added:

— an appeal for a campaign contribution from an electoral committee favouring the candidature of our friend. Do not forget to mention the Postal Check Account which will receive the funds.

— a letter from the president of a national

confederation such as the self-employed craftsmen, or the organization of small businessmen, to one of our members of parliament expressing his appreciation of the MRP's activity.

—a letter from an MRP leader expressing

support for our candidate. Finally at the end of the campaign a letter may be sent:
—thanking the candidate's friends in the constituency
—thanking friends in other constituencies.

Services et Méthodes

THE CANDIDATE'S VADE MECUM, 1967

Much was heard in the 1967 elections about the advent of new-style campaigning inspired by *Services et Méthodes*, the Gaullists' P.R. consultants—who were hailed by believers in "modern, efficient" electioneering and denounced by traditionalists. Some idea of this "new-look" advice can be gleaned from this extract from their circular to candidates six months before polling, describing the first preparations for the campaign. While unfortunately space prevents inclusion of the specifically organizational side, with its multiple injunctions such as "don't forget lunch," in this advice on campaign themes the careful reader might feel that behind the neologisms much of the new-style advice looks remarkably like unreconstructed old-time politicking.

A campaign is, of course, built on men and resources. But first it requires arguments which will attract and convince the readers. For this attraction to take place, and this conviction to be carried, time is an absolute essential:

"TIME DOES NOT FORGIVE WHAT IS DONE WITHOUT IT"

This is why we think that your activities should develop on four levels:
1. Prepare your stock of arguments
2. Form your team
3. Muster your answers
4. Launch or develop your campaign

PREPARE YOUR STOCK OF ARGUMENTS

What does this mean? It means, defining:
a. What will be the main AXIS of your campaign (concentrating opinion)
b. Around which the various THEMES

will be articulated (attracting opinion)
c. Themes developing through ARGUMENTS (convincing opinion)
d. And resting on striking SLOGANS (making a mark on opinion).

a. The Axis

In principle this is the axis of the national campaign, common to all candidates supporting the government.

b. Themes

Choice of these will in part depend on your analysis of the local situation and, among others, of the quality of the opposition. Depending on the circumstances you will pay greater or lesser attention to:

a plea for the Fifth Republic, the value of its achievements, the competence of its leaders, in short, the effectiveness made

---

Editor's translation.

169

possible by a faithful parliamentary majority on the national, international and regional levels. These themes should further be presented on two levels: THE RECORD, THE PROGRAM.

or, conversely:

the attack on the remnants of the past, everything about which shows that they have understood nothing and they are simply a bundle of contradictions. In this field too, the record should be mentioned (that past we never wish to see again) and also the program (in the inconceivable event of the opposition actually winning). It is quite clear, for example, that if your opponent is a sitting member known mainly for his political work on a national level, and who has not done all he could on a constituency level, that you will focus your entire campaign on local matters and keep partisan politics to a minimum. But if, on the other hand, your opponent is mayor of the largest commune and is clearly effective in the job, you will focus your campaign on the major national themes; thus according to circumstances you will move from a campaign based on constituency matters to one centered on the major national themes.

Let us mention one further criterion which may guide your choice. Depending on whether the constituency sided with the majority or the minority in the presidential elections, it will be in your interest in the first case to politize the campaign (confirm your vote) and in the second hypothesis to base it on local matters.

c. The Arguments

Here you must seek out and arrange permanently and systematically the argument which will allow you to convince the electors of the rightness of your chief themes. So far as national and international matters go, you will receive a candidate's file and dictionary of quotations at the beginning of October which will provide the arguments you need.

But on the other hand, at the national and regional level, this depends chiefly on yourself.

We cannot advise you too strongly to begin this inventory now, on two levels:

(1.) your constituency and the Fifth Republic

Record: make a list of everything that has been done at every level: social, economic, industrial, agricultural, investment, leisure, sports, education, hospitals, tourism etc., for all sections of the population, young people, elderly people, women, supervisors, white collar workers, blue collar workers, farmers, shopkeepers etc.

Program: analyse the Fifth Plan and look at everything involving your region. Enquire among the voters to discover their concerns or needs, see that your program can be based on these needs and concerns as well as on the Plan.

(a.) *your constituency and the opposition*

Record and program again: to do this begin to build up a collection of your opponent's gaffes, be ready to recall everything that went wrong in the past; dig out all the figures relating to the situation in 1958, mistakes that were made etc., scrutinise all their speeches and votes, (whether they were greatly or little involved in parliamentary activities, in either event you have an argument. If he attended parliament assiduously show that he has not looked after his constituency; if one the contrary he has paid a lot of attention to his constituency, show that he has not done his parliamentary duty) — to show their incompetence and incapacity which are only an indication of what France and their constituency would be in for if they were elected.
SLOGANS

You know that a striking phrase is often worth a thousand arguments. But one must take the time and trouble to perfect it and check its effectiveness.

To do this, invite your friends and helpers

to join in the effort and to try out the slogans on one another.

Here again we cannot say too forcefully:

START NOW. MEET. FIND THEMES. TELL US ABOUT THEM. THANKS.

Pierre Viansson-Ponté

THE GAULLISTS OPEN THEIR CAMPAIGN

Little by little political campaigning is changing, to become more spectacular and national in character; this mildly ironical account of the gaullists' opening salvo in the 1967 campaign gives the appropriate impression of mildly disordered change.

In the middle of the front rank, his arms folded, a satisfied expression on his face, Professor Pompidou seemed to be posing for the traditional end-of-year photograph. One could just see the yellowing print in the family album, with its finely printed caption "Class Five 1967." A fine class with no fewer than four hundred and sixty pupils even though twenty or so were absent. They had docilely taken their places in the fifteen rows of seats and waited patiently on the huge stage for the curtain to rise and reveal them to the gaze of some eight thousand spectators, most of them members of the various branches of the [Gaullist] family. Such was the curious ceremony of presenting the candidates, unknown in national political life before the present campaign, which took place at the Palais des Sports on Tuesday evening. After those of the Federation of the Left, and of the Democratic Center on Sunday, the Fifth Republic's standard bearers for each of the constituencies in metropolitan France and the overseas territories were thus exposed to the admiration of the populace.

On the prime minister's left were ranged, in order, MM. Chaban-Delmas, Joxe, Billotte, Frey; on his right MM. Malraux, Debré, Faure. Together with them the members of the Action Committee for the Fifth Republic took up the entire front row. In the second, ministers and dignitaries mingled with the rank and file. As always happens one or two preoccupied or undisciplined people did not take the place of honour to which they were due; thus M. Giscard d'Estaing, though a member of the Committee, hid himself in the tenth row.

Before the astonishing raising of the curtain, people had spent long periods marking time in the area round the Palais des Sports which was in a state of siege; then they were carried by the maelstrom to the heart of the immense building; and had to use their elbows determinedly to find even the smallest seat. Three dozen young and charming hostesses, for the most part daughters or nieces of ministers or members of parliament, distributed brochures, discs, novelties and smiles. Their turquoise blue dresses were neither "mini" nor "maxi". The service was pleasant even if method was rather lacking in the organization arranged by the specialists of "Services and Methods,"[1]

Even then still more patience was needed. But 45 minutes after the hour printed on the invitations this patience was amply rewarded. The projector, the heavy

---

[1]Public relations consultants

Le Monde, 2 Feb. 1967, by permission. Editor's translation.

artillery of propaganda, had suddenly begun to thunder in front of a giant screen which slowly arose, while 18 loudspeakers hammered out the opening bars of the Rite of Spring and spotlights, skimming and plunging, swept over the crowd, revealing it to itself.

Amid the clashing of cymbals, dazzled, jostled, blinded, one had to strain one's ears to hear the explanations, bawled in a staccato monotone, which accompanied every 60 square yard transparency. "The Successes of France" — which was the title of this spectacle — dragged in, higgledy-piggledy, Jean-Claude Killy[2], Pierrelatte[3], the Oléron bridge and Christine Caron[4], the submarine Gymnote and Jazy[5], ending in gaullist acclamation of the picture of Professor Monod — who had been applauded in flesh and blood only two days earlier at the side of M. Mendès-France. The three other Nobel prize winners, MM. Kastler, Lwoff and Jacob, had also been mobilized, willy-nilly, in service of a cause which, it seems, is not theirs.

Then came the hour for speeches. The "star" of the evening, Professor Mathé, performs the astonishing feat — for a specialist in leukemia — of raising applause for the atomic bomb. M. André Malraux was as

[2]Champion skier
[3]French atomic separation plant
[4]Champion skier
[5]Champion runner

lyrical, direct and incisive as the crowd had hoped, mingling poetic imagery and anathema with that moving yet syncopated rhythm which makes his very individual sort of eloquence a sort of glittering breathlessness. On this evening his task was to give a good conscience, and he carried it out to perfection, explaining everything away: when he left the rostrum no gaullist could still believe himself on the right, on the left or even in the centre "which is not in fact the middle;" the concept of the nation had suddenly nothing to do with nationalism; the idea of personal power lay in ruins; and "unconditionality," subtly ridiculed, was left a mere outdated myth.

M. Pompidou has made enormous progress as a speaker at meetings. His task was not difficult since he only had to pause for breath to be applauded; but one felt him capable of handling any situation. Methodically he painted the background, trampled every adversary under foot, crushed yet again the late Fourth Republic, several of whose achievements had just been applauded, and several of whose chiefs were sitting close at hand in the first row of candidates; then he raised the tone to give a glimpse of the future, that future which one of the slogans projected on the screen a few moments earlier had summarised in these terms for the benefit of those present: "The majority is — you."

XI. *Grass Roots Politics*

More often than not local politics in France is, almost literally, politics at the grass roots. For despite the steady spread of industrialization, the ever-extending sprawl of the conurbations and the spread of the media of popular culture to every corner of the country, even now almost one Frenchman in five is employed in agriculture, a third of the population live in communes with under 1500 inhabitants and a half in communes with under 10,000 people. No matter how small its population every one of almost 38,000 odd communes (for a population of just over 50,000,000) has its mayor, its municipal council and its *mairie*. The *mairie* is the place where one's birth is registered and one's death, where every man signs on for his military service, where everyone is married — since a civil ceremony is obligatory in France — where the endless identifications and certifications so beloved of French administrators must be obtained and countless other administrative formalities carried out in the course of a lifetime. Thus, both emotionally and administratively the *mairie* tends to mean more to the ordinary Frenchman than the town hall does to his British or American counterpart. He is in fact rather more likely to serve as a local councillor during his lifetime and, not surprisingly, he is considerably more likely to turn out to vote in local elections. Though France today is largely an urban and industrial country, the items which follow deal largely with the smaller towns and villages, reflecting the nature of published studies. Nevertheless they not only communicate the atmosphere of what has been, and still is for many Frenchmen, the norm in local government, but collectively they illuminate many of the problems created by the existence of this venerable system of local institutions in a period of rapid economic, social and demographic change — problems which in rather different forms are only too familiar in most other western democracies.

Gordon Wright

POLITICS IN ST. PIERRE-TOIRAC

In the valley of the Lot, lies the village of St. Pierre-Toirac. The rich, flat floor of the river valley, 250 acres of which are within the boundaries of the commune, strikes one as a kind of oasis. To the north and south stretch miles of *causses*, those eroded dry hills that remind one of the parts of the American southwest. Farming in many parts of the region is a harsh and grim struggle; but on the bottom land of St. Pierre, even the routine methods of the local farmers produce rich cash crops. Tobacco, sold to the state monopoly at a fixed price, is the chief moneymaker. Not only is St. Pierre prosperous, but it is open to currents from the outside world. An important railway line runs through the valley, so that St. Pierrians can easily visit Figeac, Cahors, or even distant Toulouse.

St. Pierre is a village of equals. The land is owned by forty peasants, none of whom holds more than thirty acres, and a few of whom hold less than five. Both cash tenantry and share tenantry are unknown. The only non-peasants are the local doctor, a few station employees, and a dozen retired railway workers or civil servants. Even the shops and *bistros* (such as they are) are kept by the wives of peasant owners.

Like so much of southwestern France, St. Pierre is leftist by long tradition. That tradition is vigorously anticlerical and individualistic; during the Third Republic, it was accurately translated into politics by the doctrines and leadership of the Radical Party. Prior to 1940, Anatole de Monzie, the district's favorite adopted son, always got his largest majorities at St. Pierre. The fact that he called himself an Independent Socialist probably gave him added glamor, especially since St. Pierrians knew as well as anybody else that de Monzie's socialism went no deeper than the label. When Marxist candidates appeared in the region, they were almost totally ignored by St. Pierre's voters. De Monzie's highly individualistic pseudosocialism was good enough for them. Then came war, occupation, and liberation. St. Pierre went to the polls in 1945 to choose among five tickets, all adroitly equipped with leftist labels and programs. The village, which had never before cast a single vote for an avowedly Communist candidate, went overboard for Communism. Sixty per cent of the voters chose that party's list, and they continued to do so in four successive elections from 1945 to 1951.

What produced this sudden transmutation of inveterate Radical smallholders into Communists? One factor, no doubt, was Radicalism's collapse in 1940, which left a kind of vacuum just to the left of center; another was de Monzie's tortuous attitude toward Vichy. But a more logical choice for St. Pierrians would have been the mild Socialism of Blum rather than the rigid Communism of Thorez. The explanation does not lie in the impact of some outstanding personality—a native son who suddenly espoused the cause, or led a resistance group in heroic fashion, or proved to be an organizer of genius. Instances of this sort did occur here and there in France; but in the valley of the Lot, the caliber of Communist leadership remained as low as it had always been. The only new source of Marxian ideas was the handful of retired

Reprinted from *Rural Revolution in France*, by Gordon Wright, pp. 189–192, with the permission of the publishers, Stanford University Press. ©1964 by the Board of Trustees of the Leland Stanford Junior University.

railway workers who settled down here during and after the war; and none of them was a leader.

Was there, then, a real change of heart among these violently individualistic peasants? Were they somehow converted into tough-minded sectarians, or utopian visionaries? A brief visit sufficed to destroy any such hypotheses. During my stay in St. Pierre in 1951, a government land survey was in progress, for the first time in a century. Hanging about the surveyors from dawn to dusk were four peasants, who turned out to be the leading Communists of the village. The surveyors were approaching their plots, and each peasant meant to make sure that no neighbor would gain a six-inch strip of soil at his expense. In a different way, the fellow-traveling mayor also showed a lack of the sectarian rigor that marks the true rural Communist; he went so far as to welcome an American visitor to his *bistro*, and to set up drinks on the house. True, his tolerance and credulity had their limits—as when somebody attributed expansionist tendencies to the Soviet Union, and referred darkly to the fate of the kulaks in Bulgaria. "Ça," he announced with finality, "c'est pour les poires." Only a sucker will swallow that stuff. Nobody, it appeared, was going to make *poires* of these hardheaded peasants of St. Pierre-Toirac.

If it was true that St. Pierre's Communism reflected nothing more than an old tradition of self-assertive individualism, when and how would that fact be demonstrated at the polls? The first indication came in 1956, when the impassioned demagoguery of Pierre Poujade (a native of the region) offered the St. Pierrians an alternative avenue of protest against all forms of external authority. The Communist share of the vote dropped from 60 to 39 percent; and about half of the party's deserters clearly went over to the Poujadist list. Two years later came an even more telling sign. In the 1958 elections that followed de Gaulle's return to power, the first day's voting ended in a stalemate between the Communist and the Socialist candidates. A week later, in the runoff ballot, St. Pierrians showed their true colors; they opted for the Socialist, 67 to 44. After more than a decade of pleasant and riskless flirtation with the idea of social revolution, the village found itself safe at home again.

Gordon Wright

POLITICS IN SAMAZAN

When one arrives in the village of Samazan (population 765), nothing seems to distinguish it from a hundred other sleepy towns of old Gascony, just north of the Pyrenees in southwestern France. True, it appears more prosperous than most; yet what brought me there was not its economic achievements but its political behavior. Forty years ago, Samazan and the surrounding district sent the first peasant Communist to parliament; and since that time, without interruption, Samazan's voters have never failed to back the Communist ticket. In 1935 they gave the party control of the city hall as well, and they have kept it there to the present day. Here is a clear example of rural Communism solidly implanted, and adopted by the free choice of its citizens.

Neither crushing misery nor class exploitation can explain the party's hold on Samazan. Two-thirds of the peasants are

Reprinted from *Rural Revolution in France*, by Gordon Wright, pp. 192–197, with the permission of the publishers, Stanford University Press. © 1964 by the Board of Trustees of the Leland Stanford Junior University.

small-holders; the rest practice that ancient form of share tenantry called *métayage*, which survives mainly in the southwest. Although *métayage* is widely regarded as a kind of feudal survival, the *métayers* of Samazan make out about as well as the small-holders, and in most cases they cultivate a larger acreage. These Gascon peasants, fiercely individualistic by nature, suspicious of aristocrats, Church, government, and even of their own neighbors, ought properly to be Radical Socialists of the purest tradition. And that is exactly what they were until they shifted brusquely to Communism, just after the First World War.

Why it happened, and what the results have been, were the things that first attracted me to Samazan. In a pleasant farmhouse on a ten-acre tract of his own I found the mayor, Renaud Jean, a tough and grizzled old figure with a twinkle in his eye and with the Gascon's ready tongue. I went in the hope he might suggest some reasons for Samazan's attachment to Communism; I came away convinced that I had found the reason in Monsieur Jean himself. The mayor was the son of Jean Jean, a local *métayer* who had managed, by a lifetime of hard work, to scrape together a nest egg big enough to buy his own farm. The son saw active service in the First World War, and returned from the trenches gravely wounded in body and intensely pacifist in spirit. During convalescence, he began the process of self-education that was to divert him from dirt-farming to Marxian politics. In 1920, he astounded the experts by getting himself elected Socialist deputy for his home district; and shortly afterward, when the French Marxians split, he became a charter member of the French Communist Party. The next two decades saw his steady rise in the Communist hierarchy. He crusaded persistently for a program of mass action among the small and middle peasants, who, he claimed, were ready to accept the gospel if it were properly presented to them. Although he met both active oppo-

sition and deep inertia in the party's ruling circles, he eventually began to get a hearing in the depression era. The party's rural successes in 1936 elections seemed to prove his foresight. By 1939 he was solidly established as Communism's expert and spokesman on peasant questions; and in the Chamber of Deputies he had risen to the chairmanship of the powerful committee on agriculture.

But throughout these years Jean was shrewd enough (and sincere enough) to keep his roots in Samazan. When, in 1935, he added the post of mayor to that of deputy, he was always on hand for village council meetings, whatever the pressure of business in parliament. No citizen's complaint was too petty to go unnoticed. While we sat talking in his parlor in 1951, an old peasant arrived, bowing and scraping, cap in hand: the postal authorities had chopped down one of his trees to put up a new telephone line. When he had departed, with assurances that his rights would be protected, I asked about the visitor. "Oh, he's not from Samazan," replied the mayor with just a touch of embarrassment. "He's from the village over that way. Somehow, when they don't know where to turn, they always seem to wind up here."

Jean's career as a top-rank Communist and as a deputy ended abruptly in 1939. The Stalin-Hitler pact outraged him, and he said so frankly. Besides, he played no part in the wartime resistance movement, but preferred to remain in quiet obscurity as a farm laborer in southwestern France, working under an assumed name. The party bosses did not forget; after the war they blackballed him as a candidate for his old parliamentary seat, and "parachuted" an outside candidate into his district. If Jean's pride was hurt, his loyalty to the Communist cause was unshaken; he backed the party's slate, and reconciled himself to a career of purely local scope. There in Samazan he was unchallengeable: at each municipal election his ticket of councilors far outdistanced all rivals, until at last no challengers even dared to enter the lists. And within the new farmers' syndicate, the FNSEA, Jean built himself a second career; he quickly emerged as secretary-general of the syndicate's departmental unit in the Lot-et-Garonne, and remained its dominant figure long after every other Communist had been dislodged from a position of leadership in the department.

When I returned to Samazan in 1960 after a decade's absence, it was clear that the years had been good to the villagers. There were ample signs of prosperity and progress: tractors droning in the fields; an occasional threshing machine maneuvering awkwardly past strips of vineyard, like a fat man trying to get into a Fiat; a modernized schoolhouse that might have done credit to an American town; a fine new tomato-packing plant; a surprising number of children, for a region that had almost invented planned parenthood. It appeared that village Communism had been a smashing success.

But an afternoon of renewing acquaintance with Mayor Jean left me far less sure of it. "You've certainly gone in for mechanization here," I remarked. "How many tractors are there now?" "You're right," Jean replied. "Fifty tractors for a hundred farms—and not a dozen farms big enough to support one." "But don't you have tractor cooperatives?" I asked. "After all, one finds them everywhere in France now." "Oh, they tried one," he said with a shrug, "but it didn't last long; peasants around here are too individualistic for that." "And the tomato-packing plant? Surely that's a municipal cooperative?" "No indeed; it's built and owned by Monsieur X." "What about organizations? Is there a unit of the young farmers' syndicate in Samazan?" "Not here; the young people are too busy having a good time." "You seem to have had your own population explosion since my last visit. Isn't that something new for this region—a sign, perhaps, of rising optimism and confidence?" "Frankly," said the mayor, "that's one of my biggest wor-

ries. School enrollment is up 60 percent over the last ten years. What are we going to do with all these youngsters when they finish their studies?"

Has the village, then, gained nothing from a generation of Communist control? To say so would, I think, be quite unfair. Renaud Jean could properly claim that he had given Samazan two things: a school and a priest. Of that model school plant he could speak with touching pride; his stubborn and persuasive action got it out of the villagers and the Parisian bureaucrats, and it may well stand as his monument. His more ironic achievement is the presence of the *curé*. Some years ago the long-time *curé* (who rejoiced in the name of Patrick Kelly) was transferred, and the living fell vacant. Like so many other rural parishes, Samazan was served sporadically by a priest from a neighboring commune. Although Samazan is anticlerical to the core, some parishioners complained: Didn't they have as much right to a priest as the next village? Mayor Jean's convictions did not stand in the way of his duty; he went to see the bishop. "Monsignor," he said politely, "my constituents want a priest. For several years the rectory in Samazan has been standing empty. If you don't send us a priest shortly, I intend to convert the building into a shelter for indigent families." Within a month, Jean recollected triumphantly, there was a new *curé* in Samazan.

Just before leaving, I raised the delicate question of the future. "Is there a vigorous new generation," I asked M. Jean, "raised in the Marxian faith and ready to carry on your work?" "Of course, of course!" came the impatient answer. "They'll carry on, they see how history is moving." Yet somehow there seemed to be more ritualism than conviction in his voice. The next day, in the regional metropolis of Agen, I expressed my doubts to a well-informed government official in the bureau of agricultural services. "You're quite right to be skeptical," he said. "Renaud Jean has run his commune for 40 years, and he has recruited and trained a remarkable number of young men who have gone high in national party councils. But in Samazan there's absolutely no one to take his place."

I thought of this comment recently when news came of Renaud Jean's death, at the age of 74. The obituaries in some of the non-Communist farm journals were even warmer than those in the party organs

—and perhaps rightly so. After forty years as a Communist fief, Samazan is scarcely more Communist in spirit than it was at the outset. It continues to vote Communist, almost by reflex; but whatever the election results, the village is likely to remain what it has been for a century: the epitome of Radical Socialism.

Laurence Wylie

A LOCAL ELECTION IN ROUSSILLON

The fact that the people of Roussillon are more interested in local situations and in each other as individuals than in political parties and national issues may be seen in a comparison of the participation of registered voters in the municipal and national elections in the village since the war.

NATIONAL ELECTIONS

May 1946	67 percent
June 1946	68 percent
November 1946	73 percent
June 1951	70 percent

MUNICIPAL ELECTIONS

April 1945	80 percent
October 1947	80 percent
April 1953	90 percent

Everyone told me that municipal elections were much more bitterly fought than national elections, but unfortunately, there was no municipal election the year I was in Roussillon. It would have been illuminating to witness the municipal election of April 1953, for people in the village wrote me that it was particularly hot. It had looked for a time as if the Communist faction, or rather the Chanon-Favre faction, would not even be able to put up a slate. The group had been badly split. They had

quarrelled over whether it was fair to hunt rabbits with ferrets. Pouget's zeal and lack of discretion had annoyed former friends of the party. Chanon had lost so much money when he was Mayor after the war that he insisted he would no longer accept the position if he were elected. In the last three elections the party had polled a smaller and smaller percentage of the votes—51 per cent in 1946, 46 percent in 1947, 45 percent in 1951. The outlook did not seem hopeful for the Communists. Then three things happened that improved the situation. The rabbit epidemic killed off all the rabbits and settled the ferret question. Pouget moved away from Roussillon. Jouve called on Chanon.

Jouve is the thirty-three-year-old son of a prominent ultra-conservative, ultra-Catholic family of Avignon. He intended to study medicine, but the war interrupted his education and by the time he would have been able to go to medical school he had decided that what he really wanted to do was to return to the soil. As a good Catholic, he felt it was his duty to live as a peasant, to help bring religious faith back to other peasants and to raise a large family.

For several years Jouve was kept busy learning to be a farmer, but little by little

Reprinted by permission of the publishers from Laurence Wylie, *Village in the Vaucluse*, pp. 233–239. Cambridge, Mass.: Harvard University Press, Copyright, 1957, 1964, by the President and Fellows of Harvard College.

he became bored and—according to Rivet's sharp tongue—decided that the people of Roussillon needed an intelligent well-educated man like him to run their commune. He talked the matter over with Ginoux, hoping to be given a place on the Moderate ballot in the municipal election. He even brought pressure to bear on Daladier so that the latter suggested to Ginoux that Jouve should be accepted as a candidate for the municipal council on the Moderate ticket.

Ginoux would have nothing to do with Jouve. Jouve obviously had no political future in Roussillon and would only be a liability on the Radical Socialist-Socialist ticket. Jouve was an outsider. He was a city man. He went to mass every Sunday. He kept his four little girls at home to be educated by his wife instead of sending them to the village school. He had living with him as a farm worker the son of an Avignon collaborator executed after the war. He could not be too serious a farmer since he tried any new modern method he read about. He worked actively for the Coop, which was threatening to ruin Ginoux's business. Ginoux resisted all attempts to foist Jouve onto the Moderate ticket.

Jouve then called on Chanon and proposed an alliance with the Communist faction. This action is not too surprising. Jouve was on good terms with his Communist neighbor, Raymond Laurens. Laurens was President of the local CGA (the Farmers' Union), and Jouve was Secretary. In this part of France the CGA is Communist-dominated. Jouve told me that he joined the CGA to bore from within, for he thought the Catholics could use this technique as effectively as the Communists. Jouve could justify his participation on the Chanon ticket on the grounds that he was boring from within.

Chanon and Léon Favre talked the matter over and decided that they were in no way frightened by Jouve's effort to bore from within and that his overture might give them the means to win. Their faction could normally count on about 45 percent of the vote. Perhaps Jouve could swing for them the three dozen votes of the devout Catholics, and with these extra votes they would win the election. It was true that Jouve insisted on being Mayor if their slate won the election, but that did not worry them. Chanon had no desire to be Mayor. He would be Assistant Mayor, and he would easily be able to control Jouve, because of Jouve's political ambition and, they believed, because of his stupidity.

Chanon accepted Jouve's offer, and a coalition slate was formed with six active members of the Communist Party (Chanon, Laurens, Vidal, Maurice Favre, Avenas, and Seignon), three members of the ultra-Conservative Catholic faction (Jouve, Joly and Gleizer), and four serious friends to add weight to the ticket (Borel, Jaumard, Mitifiot, and Fortias). This slate seemed strong to Chanon, aged thirty-eight, and to Jouve, aged thirty-three, because of its youth. Only two of their candidates were over fifty, while only two candidates of the Moderate slate were under fifty. Léon Favre pointed out that youth was not necessarily an advantage in an election.

The Ginoux-Aubenas slate was made up of seven incumbent municipal councillors and six new candidates. The latter were Gaston Jouvaud, and Julien Vincent, two of the most serious and successful men of the village, Madame Baume, the retired teacher who was disliked by some people but respected by most as their former teacher, le père Imbert, the father of a large brood of adult voters and the father-in-law of the postman, Brousse, a farmer who was supposed to be in with the devout Catholics, and Antoine Charial, a farmer only thirty-three years old who might serve as proof that the Ginoux Aubenas faction was not against young people as a matter of principle.

With these opposing slates, the electioneering began. The issues concerned the need for a sewage system, the erection of public baths (or rather moving the showers from the unused soccer field to a new structure near the public square), and the new school. Yes, the new school was still an issue. In spite of the promises made before the election of 1951 the school had not been built. The class that met in the upstairs room, the room which was immediately threatened by a cave-in, had been moved to Lataud's former café, but the other two classes still met in their rooms in the old building. But, of course, the most effective electioneering did not concern these issues at all; it concerned rather the *histoires personnelles* that I might have heard

if I had been in Roussillon. Unfortunately, my correspondents seem loath to put *histoires personnelles* in writing. When I press for details, they answer, "Oh, you know, these *histoires personnelles* that no one believes, but that everyone talks about."

The results were close. The majority necessary for election was 204 votes; no candidate received more than 217; and no candidate received less than 172. The results are shown below.

LIST OF REPUBLICAN UNION FOR THE DEFENSE OF COMMUNAL INTERESTS *(Socialist-Radical-Socialist).*

LIST OF PEASANT & WORKERS UNION FOR THE DEFENSE OF LOCAL INTERESTS *(Catholic-Communist)*

ELECTED

List of Republican Union		List of Peasant & Workers Union	
Marnas, Louis	217	Chanon, Raoul	216
Arnoux, Lucien	216	Mitifiot, Aimé	212
Jouvaud, Gaston	216	Fortias, Jean	206
Aubenas, Albert	213	Jaumard, Roger	206
Sanape, Marcel	213		
Vincent, Julien	210		
Ginoux, Laurent	210		
Baume, Geneviève	208		

DEFEATED

Laplace, Léo	203	Borel, Louis	202
Brousse, Paul	203	Laurens, Raymond	202
Charial, Antoine	202	Vidal, Guy	191
Massot, Georges	200	Gaston-Jouve, Henri	190
Imbert, Marcel	199	Seignon, Elie	180
		Favre, Maurice	177
		Joly, Paul	177
		Gleizer, Joseph	175
		Avenas, Maurice	172

It is obvious that party lines have little to do with local elections. This fact was even more apparent the following Sunday. Since only twelve of the candidates had received a majority of votes, a run-off election had to be held to elect someone to the thirteenth seat of the Council. After consultation, the moderates Laplace and Charial withdrew in favor of their friend Brousse. The Communist-Catholic group decided to run Borel against him. If the Socialist Radical group had been able to enforce party discipline, Brousse would have won the election easily, but when the votes were counted, it was found that he had lost to Borel, 224 to 160! A statistician knowing nothing of the

personalities involved in this election might sum up the results thus: The Moderates won 8 seats, the Communists 5. The Moderates got 52 percent of the popular vote, the Communists 48 percent. This is 3 percent more than the Communists received in 1951. Hence the Communists have gained strength in Roussillon in the last three years.

Obviously this is not the case. Even if we were to admit that Communism is an issue in this case, it would be necessary to point out that all the Communist Party members except Chanon were badly defeated. The only members of the Chanon-Jouve coalition who were elected were the *serious* men who were added to the slate to give it weight. Chanon himself was elected because he is a village hero. The regular Communist Party members like Avenas, Maurice Favre, Seignon, and Vidal were defeated along with the extreme conservatives Jouve, Joly, and Gleizer.

Rather than raise the issue of Communism in such an election, it would be wiser to seek other, more fundamental issues. We might say for instance, that the election was a victory for the farmers. This would scarcely be surprising in a commune in which three-fifths of the voters are farmers and farmers' wives. Seven of the thirteen councillors elected are farmers. Yet, this is certainly not a basic factor. In view of the high proportion of farmers on the ballot, they did no better than chance.

A more important factor is that of the origin of the candidates. All four of the candidates born outside the Vaucluse were defeated. It does not seem to have mattered to the voters, however, what part of the Vaucluse the candidates were from. Of the ten candidates born in Roussillon, five were elected. Of the eleven candidates born elsewhere in the Vaucluse, seven were elected.

Candidates living in the village itself seem to have been preferred to those living in the country, even though a majority of the voters live in the country. Seven of the eleven village candidates were elected, while only six of the fifteen country candidates were successful.

Still more important is the question of age. The median age among the successful candidates is fifty-three; among the unsuccessful candidates it is forty-four. This is scarcely surprising in a community in which the proportion of elderly people is unusually high. Jouve was wrong, as Léon Favre warned him he might be, in assuming that it was an advantage to have a "young, energetic slate."

Yet the factor of age is not the most decisive factor. The seventy-year-old Imbert and sixty-four-year-old Massot, both of

them farmers born in the Vaucluse, were defeated, while the thirty-two-year-old Fortias and the thirty-eight-year-old Chanon were elected. There must be still another factor which is more basic.

The one factor which correlates almost perfectly with success and failure in the election is simply a personality trait. If we make a list of all the candidates — regardless of their party label — who have the reputation of being *sérieux*, who mind their own business and seem indifferent to the affairs of other people, our list coincides with the list of successful candidates. There is the possible exception of Chanon, but even Chanon, though not considered *sérieux*, minds his own business. The relations of these men with other people are sufficiently warm. But they are the kind of men who are never accused of prying into what does not concern them.

This explains the curious victory of Borel over Brousse in the run-off election. When it was obvious after the first election that the Ginoux-Aubenas slate had won a majority of seats in the Council, the supporters of that slate did not hesitate to drop Brousse. He has the reputation of being a black reactionary and the unpleasant habit of telling people what they ought to do and think, which is never what they want to do and think. Borel, on the other hand, maintains cordial relations with other people, but he always gives the impression that he is indifferent to them. He has built up a profitable business simply by working hard and staying to himself and his family. He goes to the café but does not hang around. He plays boules now and then, but he does not have a passion for the game. He has been friendly with Communists but only as he has been friendly with everyone else. He is slightly *bien* with everyone and *brouillé* only with people detested by everyone, like Monsieur Martron. He is the kind of man the voters could count on to pry as little as possible into their family affairs and to be as fair as it is possible for a man to be when he is given power. Of the two candidates, Borel was the one that was less easily identified with the *ils* of the village and with the *ils* that lurk beyond the borders of the commune. Regardless of their party labels, Borel was elected and Brousse defeated.

Charles d'Aragon

MUNICIPAL OFFICE

Running a small commune is a thankless task. There are so few people that matters which would be considered commonplace anywhere else become special cases. The buildings are too big and there are too many of them, the roads too long for local income, which must constantly be supplemented by begging subsidies. Every decision one takes affects somebody who one meets every day, and consequently it raises a problem of personal relationships. There is a constant flow of official circulars, some of which must be put into force, all of which must be filed. Returns must also be completed for the central government— more often than not bearing the word "nil." All this must be done with derisory administrative resources. Add to this the fact that being first magistrate of a tiny commune will scarcely gild the brow with the smallest shaft of glory. How does one become mayor of such a place? Temper traditional squirearchy with the addition of ability, admit that a senator may have discovered a sympathizer and encouraged him to draw up a list of candidates with a view to improving the composition of the senatorial electoral college. Somehow or other a man emerges, and he draws the men who will figure on the electoral list with him from Right and Left, east and west. Geographical balance is as important, if not more important, than political balance. If the mayor comes from the south of the commune he would be wise to take his assistant from the north. Once the list is drawn up people vote, insert names from other lists, write in completely fresh names. When the ballot boxes are opened every member of the village, however obscure, discovers that he has his supporters— whether serious or facetious. Though the list was drawn up quietly enough the count is not without its excitement. Yet there are few surprises. Councillors are rarely defeated. After the election they soon forget that a few discontented neighbors struck out their names. The life of the commune continues on its normal course. Whether the mayor is highly energetic or a goodnatured idler his position is rarely threatened—though the latter is more conducive to stability than the former.

In larger places the lists are drawn up in a very similar manner but with a bigger population the leaders have more choice. The field of selection is nevertheless limited: political considerations of course count, but so too do hamlet and clan traditions. Heredity plays its part. A son often inherits his father's place. When an old councillor feels his end drawing near he is rarely refused the right to put his son or son-in-law on the list. Female suffrage has enforced this tendency. Since a country family is generally richer in widows and spinsters than males it is wise to ensure oneself of its continued benevolence. The degree of discretion surrounding the practice of reversion varies from region to region. In Tarn, where there is considerable turnover of population due to immigration from the

---

From J. Fauvet and H. Mendras, *Les Paysans et la Politique* (Paris, 1958), pp. 506–512. Reprinted by permission of Librairie Armand Colin. Editor's translation.

mountainous regions, a comparison of the 1952 and 1886 yearbooks fails to reveal a single case of prolonged inheritance of the office of mayor. On the other hand, where a commune has sufficiently stable families, "inheritance" of the office of councillor is common. In the Pyrénées a rural patriarchy maintains itself in many valleys, evidence of the voters' persistent preference for choosing their mayors and even their cantonal representatives from the same stock. Nevertheless, blood is not stronger than land. Whether one owns it or farms it, land has the power to make a man a "native," and the village community soon absorbs the newcomer unless his customs and behavior are an obstacle to assimilation.

Leisure and tact are two qualities which count heavily in the appointment of the leaders of the municipality. Leisure enables the rural mayor to show that personal devotion which makes him in turn public scribe, social worker and unpaid carrier. Tact allows him to carry through successfully all the approaches needed to push a matter forward or obtain a subsidy. These approaches are not always really necessary but they are thought to be necessary. The liberalism of the countryman will accustom itself to the open-handedness of the State, but he does not believe it is spontaneous. He believes it must be sought and he sets great store on the energy and persuasive ability of the man who must ask for it.

The debates of municipal councils show this. Whether they are left-wing, right-wing or both they are never so united as when something must be asked for. The municipal council of P . . . in Tarn provides a striking example. Wishing, reasonably enough, to obtain a state subsidy to accelerate the provision of water supplies, it issued strict instructions to the directors of the irrigation syndicate to invite the Premier, the Secretary of State for the Budget, and the Secretary of State for Agriculture to come and see for themselves the sixty communes' water requirements. In the introduction a reference was made to a previous ministerial journey at less exalted a level which was credited with the grant of a subsidy. In sum, the State is thought of as a good prince whose attention is inclined to wander, but who does good things if one takes the trouble to suggest them to him.

This outlook is neither Right- nor Left-wing. It is a common conception, at least in the generation currently holding municipal office. It is evident that stability in office implies ageing. The only place where a man of 45 can enjoy the illusion of being young is at a meeting of the mayors of his department . . .

The really rural mayors rarely represent a party. This can be seen by looking at the details given by prefectures of the political affiliations of the mayors and candidates at local elections. Socialist Republicans, Republicans for Communal Action, Lists for the Defense of the Family abound. Though these are vague terms, in the last resort they mean what they say, and their vagueness is taken as a commitment to genuine independence. The same is true for the departmental councillors. A little haziness is thought not inappropriate . . . In politically organized cantons where one particular tendency is clearly dominant, a label is welcomed. This is the case in communes with mixed economic activity, where peasants and workers live side by side. On the other hand, in strictly rural communes where political and personal contests often coincide, imprecision is well thought of. At bottom, people know which senator or president of the departmental council a man will vote for, and that is enough to give the election the political flavor it needs and to increase interest in it. . . .

There are several kinds of departmental councillor, just as there are several kinds of canton. Where the chief town of the canton is one of the most important towns in the department the rural communes look like poor relations. They supply only a few additional votes. With an electoral college of this size every party wants to try its chances. The contest becomes intensely political, losing much of its savor. At all events the person who is elected will be busy and distant, separated from his rural electors by the numerical importance of his urban sponsors and by the demands of his party comrades. Obliged to defend his seat at each election, his role is quite different from the peaceful tenure of the familiar figure with a small, homogeneous population in the rural cantons. Sometimes the latter is a Socialist Republican or a moderate who is obliged to win a certain victory at each election. At other times it is that rare bird a Socialist Republican with spiritual leanings whose very name puts teachers and priests, peasants and traders, landowners and tenants at ease. Such a man is attractive and useful, rather too much of a Santa Claus perhaps—but in this job who isn't?

Personality counts, but so does the pull of particular occupations. Some open the doors of the departmental council more readily than others. It varies between departments. In Haute Vienne the medical professions are well in the lead. Of 26 councillors, eight are doctors, two are vets and one a druggist—the latter being the third of his family. On the other hand there is only one notary—an exogenous one at that. This solitary notary is evidence of the decline of the office of notary as a vehicle for political success. Rural notaries have climbed a rung in the hierarchy of those with possessions, a phenomenon which is rarely accompanied by popular favor. Further, his robe does not confer the almost religious prestige attached to medicine or education. One can discuss matters with a lawyer but not with a doctor—an attitude which creates a predisposition to electoral loyalty. One should add that gratitude is not an empty word and that a medical ministry offers a thousand occasions for praiseworthy devotion. A doctor's visits at critical moments are the only ones many people receive; they are full of prestige, unforgettable. With antibiotics they have become more effective. Devotion more frequently brings relief—but less heroically. May it be that the doctor commands less of an audience now he heals more? Things have not yet come to that.

The teaching profession is an aid to success in cantonal elections. In Tarn primary and secondary teachers are as numerous as doctors. They also have a prominent place in Ariège. The primary teacher usually gets himself elected in left-wing politically organized cantons. The only idea which really stirs the active socialist and his unorganized left-wing neighbor is the defense of laicity. It is quite understandable that the man who embodies this should receive their vote. In our region of Languedoc, having counted the doctors and teachers on the general council, other professions can be grouped simply as "others": farmers, industrialists, wholesalers or lawyers—almost all of whom give us the occasion to employ the term "squirearchy" yet again—it has the advantage of emphasising yet again the nineteenth century side of provincial life.

Watch our departmental councillor confronting his village public. Let us take an author who knows his subject: M.R . . . writes in his election address "For thirty years you have shown your confidence in me with ever-increasing majorities. . . . I am not going to offer you a programme for the future, my past action being the proof of my devotion to the interests of the canton which is dear to me." An imposing list follows this declaration: for this commune 1,460,990 francs for road repairs, for that one 400,000 for school hall, for another 1,300,000 for roads; 638,000 for various useful works. There is a detailed list for the eight communes in the canton. The division is so fair that none of them can feel it has received less than its due. I have quoted this declaration because of its electoral wisdom. It is better to render an account of one's stewardship than to make promises. Promises are simply a form of words of which the countryman is suspicious. As for the candidate's political opinions, they are these: "A lifelong republican, I will be as I have been for thirty years, a ferocious defender of our institutions." Fifty lines of subsidies, two lines of doctrine. Though it is short this declaration says all that really needs saying

.... But in the last resort this proclamation, like thousands of others, is a sign of the "subventionism" which is the basis of political life in the countryside. You know a man by what he can get. People's mentality is such that one must appear to have obtained by skill or intrigue what would have been given in any case.

Jean Couvreur

THE MAYOR

Is any man more celebrated yet at the same time more unknown among his fellow citizens than the mayor of a big city? Because of his eminent position he is all too often believed to lead a wholly enviable existence: honours, invitations, a private box at the Grand Theatre, use of the mayoral limousine . . . Really these are slender delights — as the man receiving them rapidly realises. His assistants and friends apart, few people have any accurate idea of his life, packed as it is with work and commitments of every kind.

It has, of course, its satisfactions. Many of the tasks are challenging (the safety and well-being of others, the whole future appearance of the city) but the responsibilities are overwhelming (the slightest error could have repercussions for generations). "If he's there it's by his own choice," people say. They often forget that there must be *somebody* who is strong enough to carry the burden and who can settle down day in, day out, to a life which demands, both literally and metaphorically, that he has the heart, nerves and stomach for whatever may come.

The (conservative) mayor of Nantes is at present M. Henry Orrion. At present. For in a few days the seventh city of France will have a new master. After some twenty years of office M. Orrion has decided not to stand again. Here is the life the first citizen of Nantes has led for those twenty years. Firstly a very strict timetable. He reaches his office at 9:30 every morning and leaves at seven in the evening. Up to eleven in the morning he is simply finishing off matters held over from the previous day. The municipality's day really begins with the arrival of the mail, which is sorted out by the secretariat which has put aside the most important matters for the mayor. He reads about forty letters, annotates them, then passes them on to the appropriate sections, whose heads prepare draft replies for him.

Nantes has a very compact municipal organization. As in all town halls there is a secretary-general who has general charge of all sections. Under him is an assistant secretary-general with special responsibility for administrative matters (staff, financial questions, economic services etc.) and a director-general of works, head of technical services (roads, cleansing, buildings, transport etc.). Each division is divided into *bureaux.*

After the "wave" of mail a second wave breaks over his desk: files. These usually take up his afternoons. Cardboard folders such as you would find on the desk of the head of any firm. But these files contain the present and the future of the city of Nantes. Every day brings its problems and swells the files still further. Today it is the maintenance of the buildings for which the commune is responsible, questions of administrative by-laws, school canteens. Tomorrow there will be general finance, public baths and wash houses, the city bus system and a matter involving compulsory purchase. Everything which makes up the

Le Monde, 7–8 March 1965, by permission. Editor's translation.

life of a great city—its glandular and nervous system, its muscles and circulation: from the legal department to the fire brigade, the art school to the fish market, the veterinary service to parks, gardens and floral decorations.

Towards the end of the day comes the third wave—letters to be signed. The mayor signs a sizeable fraction of the town hall's voluminous mail personally; the rest is shared among his assistants depending on the function delegated to them. As for the rest—certificates, documents relating to births, marriages and deaths etc., an assistant initials over five hundred of these daily.

Yet all this, which is substantial enough, and in the popular imagination takes up most of the mayor's time, in reality takes up only a fraction of his working day. His day often begins much earlier and ends much later, broken up or overburdened with such interludes as political, civic or social duties, receptions, meetings, visits, openings, cocktail parties, dinner-concerts, speeches, which make a mayor's daily round almost as crowded and varied as a Chief of State's.

To begin with, the stream of visitors. "I believe," M. Orrion told me, "that a mayor must be available to the people he is administering. I have always put human relations first, and I have seen practically every delegation that has come to see me: veterans, students, sportsmen, shopkeepers, young people, sailors, artists, workers, unemployed, strikers. . . . The door of the community's house must never be closed. At moments of crisis and danger this is where people turn."

Everything must come to his ears. There are people who insist on seeing "the mayor and nobody else" to tell him their problem, to confide a secret, to ask a favor or simply to seek advice. He must be everywhere, appearing at four or five different places on the same day for the most varied reasons. M. Orrion opens his desk diary: "This afternoon at three I will be at the university. At five I am presiding at the reopening of a

museum. Tomorrow morning some television people are coming, and I will be visiting the Shakespeare exhibition at the university library. This afternoon I will be welcoming the English lady who has organized this exhibition. I am going to a lecture by a departmental councillor who has just come back from China, and in the evening I will be going to the France-Great Britain dinner.

He showed me his appointments list for 1964. It ran to no fewer than twenty-six pages and I counted 375 different engagements. Here are some examples. First, meetings: of the university council, the fine arts commission, the town sports office, the committee for the protection of children, the special section for building permits, the Nantes committee against atmospheric pollution, etc. Lunches and dinners which the mayor presides over: lunch at the competition for wine-waiters; the banquet of the local union of automobile traders; lunch at the fourteenth national tuberculosis congress; at the congress of the national federation of building workers; at the fifty-eighth congress of the French chrysanthemum society; at the regional committee for gas distribution etc. Openings and receptions on the invitation of the mayor: a reception for the Japanese handball team, for the mid-Lent Queens, a reception marking the French billiards championship, the opening of an "Aspects of Botany" exhibition, and so on.

Miscellaneous occasions range from the launching of the dredger *Mer-Noire* to a performance of Molière's *Monsieur de Pourceaugnac* by the Comédie de l'Ouest; from the doctors' annual ball to the School of Commerce's gala night; from the football match between the French and Portuguese army to the floral ball: from the concert by the Philharmonic Union of Nantes to the opening of the Le Corbusier exhibition, invariably accompanied by much formal ceremony—*vins d'honneur*, Christmas trees, requiem masses, laying of wreaths, processions, military parades, speeches long and short (to be given or listened to) which, when one adds them up, amount to a tidy number of memories and words.

I asked, "In your opinion can the mayor of a big city hold another job—for example a professional practice or management of a factory?" He replied, "I think it would be very difficult. One really cannot have a private activity and at the same time meet all the commitments of being a mayor. This is doubtless why so many young men hesitate to go into local government: an extremely modest honorarium is no substitute for a normal salary. The "first citizen" of the city has not even a pension or a social security coverage, unlike the humblest of his employees."

The mayor of Nantes who is also a member of the jury in competitions to recruit the commune's employees (of which there are some 35 to 40 each year)[1], of social welfare committees (20 to 25 per year); disciplinary boards (about six annually); the governing bodies of lycées, technical schools, institutions of higher education (25 to 30 meetings per year); who is present at the awarding of contracts by tender (20 to 25); officiates at marriages (admittedly his assistants take most of this burden off his shoulders); who calls the town council into session about ten times a year and his steering committee (of his assistants) every Monday, is still president *ex officio* of the hospital and university center's administrative commission, the social welfare bureau's administrative commission, and the administrative council of the Municipal Credit Fund, which adds up to another 25 to 30 meetings each year.

Another job. Clearly it looks difficult. M. Orrion quoted his own case. He has a law degree and after the first world war he became a partner in a chemical and drug business. On becoming mayor he sold his share to give himself full-time to municipal business. He even doubts whether the jobs of mayor and deputy can be combined satisfactorily. When he sat in the National Assembly he left for Paris on Tuesday

[1]Most public posts in France are filled by competition. [Editor's note.]

mornings and returned on Friday evening to steep himself in the town hall's files for the three remaining three days of the week.

The compensation is that it is absorbing work. One gets caught up in it, gripped by what is at stake in this city which, like all cities, is growing rapidly owing to births and people coming in from elsewhere (the population of Nantes, now 250,000, will be 280,000 in 1975). All mayors have the same preoccupations: how to house and feed, find work, modernize, build, clear, protect, and above all see far and see big, to project the city into the future, 20 to 50 years ahead "when we will no longer be here."

When he is an ordinary citizen again and he walks the streets of Nantes, M. Orrion will be able to stand in front of this housing project or that school, or that old street which has been straightened and widened, and say, "That was planned and carried through in my time." Beside his office there is a huge map of Nantes with its Zones for Priority Development: the Saint-Herblain zone which is to contain 5000 to 6000 housing units, the Beaulieu zone (6000 to 7000), the Eradière zone opposite the university. After the housing, the jobs. The plan shows several industrial areas, chiefly around Carquefou, Razé and Saint-Herblain. A mayor has to think of both business and learning. The university will be here on one of the finest sites in the city, while the proposed produce market will be there . . .

M. Orrion is going. Goodbye to his mayoral sash, to his town hall. Somebody else will be sitting in his place in what was once the Hotel de Derval, behind his Empire style desk with its engraved gilt bronzes, between the portraits of Graslin, Louis XVI's *receveur général des fermes*, who built the central quarter of the town, and of Daniel de Kervégan who was mayor of Nantes after the Revolution and represented it in parliament. As a legacy . . . he will perhaps find this recipe which M. Orrion considers an essential condition for a career in local government: good health, good digestion, and steady nerves.

François Goguel and Alfred Grosser

THE CRISIS IN LOCAL GOVERNMENT

In recent years French local government has all too frequently been incapable of providing a satisfactory solution to the problems confronting it. It has certainly not been overdramatic to speak, as Goguel and Grosser do here, of a crisis in local government. Here they discuss the principal reasons for the chronic disparity between the demands on local authorities and their ability to respond successfully.

The physical boundaries of the communes and departments of France were laid down at the end of the eighteenth century, while the principles by which they are administered date from the beginning of the Third Republic. But communes really go back much further. Most of them correspond to the parishes of the Ancient Régime; the great variety of forms taken by ecclesiatical organization in the various dioceses explains the great differences between the areas and populations of communes in different departments today. To quote only two examples, both from areas of scattered population in Western France, the department of Calvados has 480,686 inhabitants who live in 759 communes, whose average population is 633, while the 530,833 inhabitants of the department of Morbihan are shared among 263 communes whose average population is 2,018 — more than three times greater. At the time of the Revolution many more communes were established than exist today, but it was soon realized that many were too small to be viable. After the short-lived experience of cantonal local government during the Directory, the Consulate, the Empire and the Restoration carried through many re-

groupings. The present map of the communes is therefore, with a negligible number of exceptions, almost a century and a half old. That is, it dates from a period when the great majority of people in France lived in rural communes, which today account for a small section of the population, while the population of the country as a whole has been steadily rising.

The boundaries of the departments with a few exceptions were laid down by the Constituent Assembly in 1790. Contrary to a regrettably widespread belief this was not done in the abstract but was based on thorough local enquiries, employing the techniques of social geography before the letter: "How many of our departments and arrondissements," Jean Brunhes has written, "represent genuine links between the land and the activities of the population?" Of course, many of these connections have now lost much of their old importance. Yet almost two centuries of living within the same administrative framework have given birth among the people living in the various departments to customs and traditions which have led to the development of genuine departmental temperaments. The psychological and human reality of most of

From F. Goguel and A. Grosser, *La Politique en France* (Paris, 1963), pp. 47–48, 50–54. Reprinted by permission of Librairie Armand Colin. Editor's translation.

these administrative constituencies, which it would be a grievous error to consider purely artificial, is today very deep. . . .

INCOME AND EXPENDITURE

The problem arises today in completely new terms, both in relation to income and expenditure. The difficulty with the former goes back to the first world war when the State replaced the old direct taxes with a system based on checked declarations of taxpayers' incomes. This dissociated the system of "State" and local taxation. The "principles" of the old direct taxes were fictitiously maintained, that is the sum that they would have raised for the State had they remained in force, and the [property] taxes raised for local authorities and calculated on the basis of "additional centimes" voted by municipal and departmental councils continued to be based on these "fictitious principles." But very quickly, inflation led to a tremendous increase in the number of additional centimes, and the foundation of direct local taxes became more open to attack than ever because the bases, which went back to the nineteenth century, had progressively lost almost all relationship to the ability of the taxpayers to pay. So far this situation has not been remedied — which is all the more inconvenient for local government because the number of centimes assessed on entirely fictitious principles cannot be raised beyond a certain limit.

Communal and departmental taxes of secondary importance, authorized by several laws adopted between the wars, have not been sufficient to remedy this situation. It was only in 1942 that the introduction of a local sales tax provided the communes with a source of substantial revenue which had the advantage of rising automatically either with rises in prices or with the expansion of the local population or the economy. But the value of this tax varies greatly from commune to commune; sales increasingly tend to be concentrated in the

larger cities. However, the "dormitory communes" in the suburbs, where the population works and does most of its shopping away from where it lives, are almost as severely hit as the small rural communes. This made it necessary to develop complicated equalization procedures, a proportion of the local tax raised in certain communes being turned over to others. But this has not been enough to provide all local authorities with sufficient income to meet their obligations. The State has had to grant them subsidies over and above their own income, and these subsidies are a constantly increasing proportion of local budgets, while the way in which they are shared naturally gives rise to a great deal of criticism. Their existence threatens the local assemblies' freedom to run their own affairs, since naturally the State tends to try and control the use of the subsidies it grants.

But it is not only inadequate income which makes the problem of local finances extremely difficult. Local authorities have to face a constant rise in expenditures, due less to rises in prices and salaries than to the extension of the field where departmental and communal assemblies are nowadays bound to intervene.

THE PROBLEM OF PLANNING

The generally accepted view of what services should be provided by local government has been steadily widening; nowadays there is a tendency to think that all citizens should have the same administrative services available to them regardless of the size of place they live in. To give just one example: thirty years ago it was considered normal or at least inevitable for country children to be obliged to walk long distances to and from school. This is no longer acceptable today, and in many regions the organization of school buses is a major problem for the local authorities. The supply of piped water and electricity, the organization of school meals, the improvement of the hospital system and the social welfare services, street lighting in built-up areas, the removal and destruction of refuse are other tasks which are now considered normal activities for local authorities.

Apart from these public services which benefit individuals directly, during the last few years local authorities have been called on increasingly to play a part in economic policy-making, for which the State cannot assume entire responsibility. The days have gone when this economic policy consisted essentially of tariff adjustments which could only be decided by the central government. Many communes, threatened with seeing part of their population compelled to emigrate in search of work as a result of technical change in agriculture, are seeking ways of attracting factories by creating "industrial areas". But it is absolutely essential that such local initiatives should be coordinated, and accordingly local councils cannot take the final decisions, particularly since such projects almost always depend on State aid.

But many difficulties militate against the participation of the departmental authorities in the preparation of these programmes going completely smoothly. The departments are simply not large enough to be meaningful units for such programmes, which invariably tend to establish economic systems which are too complex for their limited population and area. This is why the "planning regions" which were set up in 1956 and given their present organization in 1964 included a regional prefect and a regional administrative conference comprising the prefects of the departments concerned and a number of civil servants. A beginning has also been made with a system of representing the people at regional level: every planning region except Paris has a Regional Economic Development Commission with between twenty and fifty members depending on the number of departments involved. At least a quarter of the members are appointed by departmental councils either from their own ranks or from among the mayors in

the department—the mayor of the main city in each region sits on the Commission ex-officio. Half represent the Chambers of Commerce and Industry, the Chambers of Crafts, the Chambers of Agriculture and organizations of employers and workers, the rest being appointed by the Prime Minister from people with special qualifications.

The Regional Economic Development Commissions are consultative bodies: they give their opinions on questions concerning economic or social development and regional planning, particularly on regional aspects of the national plan. The planning region is not a "local authority;" it has no budget and no staff of its own . . . The Commissions' advice relates to the expenditure of State rather than departmental funds: in principle their existence does not impinge on the powers of the departmental councils. But in fact departmental and State investments must be coordinated. It is therefore understandable that though the Regional Economic Development Commissions are a step forward in enabling representatives of the people to take part in the planning policy process, the departmental councils consider their representation inadequate. But it must be admitted that the system by which departmental councils are elected, which rests on the principle of the equality of all cantons irrespective of their population, makes them bodies which represent almost exclusively a rural society. While they are quite capable of providing the departments with roads and hospital services, departmental councillors might perhaps be less at home in helping to draw up programmes of regional economic expansion, the problems of which are primarily industrial. Many departmental councillors have no qualifications at all for such a rôle. It is to be feared that were they called on to do this their preoccupation with agricultural problems would steer them towards solutions which would scarcely be favorable to the long-term interests of the communes to which they belong. This is why the 1964 reform granted the elected representatives of the people so little responsibility in planning policy. But here as in other fields it is not easy to find the right balance between the power of the technocrats and democracy, perhaps because democratic institutions have not been adapted to the changes which have taken place in society since the beginning of the twentieth century—particularly their electoral system in the case of departmental councils.

Maurice Duverger

LOCAL COUNCILLORS IN A CHANGING FRANCE

The note on which Goguel and Grosser concluded their analysis of the causes of the crisis in French local government is taken up and amplified by Maurice Duverger in this comment on the composition of the *conseils généraux* which are responsible for the affairs of the departments. In doing so he puts his finger on a wider problem of adapting the political system to the needs of a modern society.

Departmental councillors, like senators, represent the mental outlook, preoccupations and interests of a France which has been left behind by change. The under-representation of the towns is even more striking at departmental level than in the upper house. More than 60 percent of departmental councillors are elected in cantons of under 10,000 inhabitants; only 9.9 percent of them are elected by cities of over 30,000 population—in which 28.5 percent of the population lives. Within each council the urban population is practically powerless. This is particularly shocking because most often they pay the lion's share of departmental taxes. This explains a considerable difference in voting turnout between the towns and the countryside (in 1964 over 40 percent of the electors abstained at Toulouse, over 45 percent at Marseille, 58 percent at Brest and 69 percent in the third canton of Bordeaux, while in the rural cantons of the same departments abstentions were far fewer).

The social composition of the departmental council is noteworthy for the very low proportion of wage-earners. At present farmers hold 18.3 percent of the seats (they are 15.7 percent of the active population); industrialists and shopkeepers, 20 percent (against 10 percent in the population), white and blue collar workers and supervisory grades, 11.7 percent (compared with 62.5 percent in the population as a whole). The social composition of the National Assembly has more or less the same defects, though in less acute form (but the position has deteriorated under the Fifth Republic because the electoral system has cut the strength of the Communists, many of whose deputies were wage-earners). At all events the contrast is more shocking at the local assembly level because this is precisely where one would expect popular participation to be greater.

The age composition shows similar characteristics. The average age of departmental councillors is currently 56 years 7 months. It was 55 years 11 months in 1959, and 51 years 11 months in 1945. It is clearly higher than that of the National Assembly (51 years 2 months at the moment, 43 years

Le Monde, 9 June 1966, by permission. Editor's translation.

11 months in 1945). The opposite would be more normal, since the departmental council is a lower grade in the *cursus honorum* of public life. In several departments the average age of the councillors is over sixty. This scarcely predisposes them to make innovations.

Two years ago another doctoral thesis studied the departmental councils in 1840–8. A comparison of the two theses shows that there have been no basic changes. The councillors of 1966 are almost the same types of men, from the same sections of society, with the same ways as their nineteenth century predecessors. But in the interval France has changed profoundly. One hundred and twenty years ago these rural bigwigs, doctors, notaries, lawyers, vets, shopkeepers and landowners who were the backbone of the departmental assemblies were something like an image of France. They are not so in the same degree today.

André Passeron

A SUCCESSFUL MERGER AT SAINT-CHAMOND

There has certainly been no lack of attempts to find solutions to the problems confronting every level of French local government. The last few years have brought new regional economic development councils, reorganization of the Paris area, the introduction of "urban districts" or "urban communities" in conurbations, and schemes for encouraging communes to merge and form more viable entities. So far success has been extremely patchy; one can scarcely speak of a national trend. While this and the following extract are untypical "success stories," they show the ways in which some local authorities are struggling with their difficulties, and also some of the resistances that must be overcome.

Saint-Chamond has a very old industrial tradition, going back to the establishment of the Forges de la Marine beside the lively waters of its river as early as 1600. The town grew up between the three rivers which converge at its center: the Janon, the Laugonaut and the Gier. The town rapidly expanded until it reached its boundaries, with houses, factories, workshops making ribbons, dyeing and tanning all packed together cheek-by-jowl. The commune's 246 acres were rapidly saturated and overpopulated by the 17,000-odd people living there. Even before the war M. Pinay, who has been mayor since 1929, tried to get more space. To do this he had the rivers, which pass through the town, and which had been turned into open sewers by industrial effluents, culverted and made into broad streets. Even that was not enough.

The economic life of the city progressively spilled over the obviously inadequate area of the commune and made considerable inroads into the neighboring communes. The winding frontiers of Saint-Chamond penetrated deeply into the three villages which had become its suburbs. Even the mayor could no longer tell exactly where his town ended. Some inhabitants moved from one commune to the next every time they walked from their living room to the kitchen. Others claimed that they slept with their heads in Saint-Chamond and their feet somewhere else. M. Pinay likes to

Le Monde, 5 March 1965, by permission. Editor's translation.

demonstrate just how tightly dovetailed the various places are by picking up a stone in Saint-Martin-en-Coailleux and throwing it a few yards into Saint-Chamond, it having passed through Saint-Julien-en-Jarez on the way.

All this would be of merely anecdotal interest were it not for the grave inconvenience that results from it. In fact Saint-Chamond remained the real center of everything. Local trade is concentrated there, all the canton's financial offices are housed in a vast building there; one railway station serves all four places. The three neighboring communes benefit from the services of many bodies created by the municipality of Saint-Chamond alone: the tax office, the hospital, the HLM office[1], the lycée, the fire-brigade, the water supply. Even so they must pay for highway maintenance, street lighting, schools, administration of births, marriages and deaths, at a time when industrial plants were developing on their land. The lycée—over half of whose pupils do not live in Saint-Chamond—the hospital and other installations which were widely used by the inhabitants of the surrounding area were paid for by the inhabitants of Saint-Chamond. On the other hand, since trade was concentrated in the town, it took the lion's share of income from local taxes and licences.

The three riparian communes found themselves in financial difficulties from a combination of low income and costly commitments, particularly the maintenance of a large network of country roads. Some made a little extra income by reselling services received from Saint-Chamond. Thus water sold to them by M. Pinay's town at 18 centimes per cubic meter was resold for as much as 175 centimes to some consumers.

Artificial disparities developed. The amount people paid in taxes sometimes varied according to which side of a street they lived on. Further economic expansion in Saint-Chamond became impossible. That of the other communes developed in a

[1] A semi-public body providing housing at relatively low rents. [Editor's note.]

completely unorganized manner quite unrelated to the needs of the area as a whole. The neighboring places lacked the funds to carry through a number of essential developments, and the inhabitants of Saint-Chamond were extremely reluctant to pay for their neighbors. Yet this was inevitable: how, for example, could inhabitants of Izieux or Saint-Martin be charged more for swimming in the municipal bathing pool? The ultimate in disputes arose when everyone wanted to be buried in Saint-Chamond because it had the lowest charges for cemetery plots.

Having thought at one time of setting up a Multi-Purpose Inter-Communal Syndicate, the four mayors finally decided on a merger, and this took formal effect with the prefectoral *arrêté* of 14 March 1964. A new municipal council has replaced the four old ones. Out of 27 councillors from Saint-Chamond, the thirteen with the fewest votes on M. Pinay's electoral list have given up their seats, and their places have been absorbed—one from Izieux, four from Saint-Julien and four from Saint-Martin, making 31 councillors in place of 27.

The outcome is that the population of Saint-Chamond has more than doubled, rising from 17,107 to 35,860 . . . The city has become the third largest in the department . . . But, most important, the new Saint-Chamond has a greatly increased area, rising from 346 acres to 13,531, making it the largest commune in the department.

The municipal council of Izieux, however, only gave its support by twelve votes to nine; the minority felt that their town already had a sizeable population and many factories and could continue its separate existence. But local chauvinism was not so intense as to lead to a list of anti-Pinay candidates fighting the local elections. The Popular Front (Communists, Socialists and PSU) which formed against M. Pinay, led by M. Ferraz, a Saint-Etienne architect, will campaign in the many factories of the area, with their almost 10,000 workers, on the issue of threats of recession which are beginning to make themselves felt.

The merger has had immediate spectacular consequences. In the most urgent field, housing, a coherent development plan has been drawn up and some work has already begun. A Zone for Priority Development has been created at Fonfala in what used to be Saint-Julien, to build three thousand houses. At Saint-Chamond itself 1200 houses are under construction, replacing the slums which could not previously be demolished. Several groups of a hundred houses are planned for Saint-Julien, Saint-Martin and Izieux, which their old councils could not have undertaken by themselves. The main effort will be made in these communes, so as to relieve the congestion of the urban core, and it will also try to improve the at present inadequate facilities of the outlying areas.

The merger has also made it possible to unify many by-laws, particularly those dealing with parking and traffic. But above all a number of taxes and dues have been brought into line. The price of water has been fixed at 22 centimes everywhere, double taxation — chiefly relating to licences — has been abolished. The high taxes levied on the inhabitants of the old suburban communes will fall while those in the town will rise: 31 additional centimes will be levied in Saint-Chamond, but 6 percent less in Izieux, 28 percent less in Saint-Julien and 28.4 percent less in Saint-Martin. From a tax point of view, it can be seen, the merger brings greater benefits to the taxpayers of the old communes than to those in Saint-Chamond. But everyone realizes that the price had to be paid if the town was to keep its privileged position as the center of urban development and to ensure its future progress.

André Passeron

REFORMING LOCAL GOVERNMENT AT TOURS

Practically every week the government issues statements calling on the communes to merge and form larger units. Turning from mere encouragement to active help, it is preparing a decree . . . providing financial incentives to regrouping. However, a number of places have already done this, sometimes a number of small rural cantons, and at other times a city and the surrounding places which have gradually become its suburbs. A merger of this second type has just been carried through at Tours, where the main town of Indre-et-Loire has absorbed the communes of Saint-Symphorien and Sainte-Radigonde.

Squeezed into its "Mesapotamia" between the Loire and Cher rivers, Tours had been suffocating for some twenty years. Its 96,000 inhabitants were cramped into the

communes 3,680 acres and the city had one of the highest population densities in France. With a population growth above the national average Tours no longer had any land left for housing and schools, for new industries or for development.

The first move came when the deputy-mayor of Tours, M. Jean Royer, took some liberties with customary administrative procedures and acquired several acres of land ceded by the communes lying to the south of the city, which pushed its boundary across the Cher. But this ground was subject to flooding and required extremely expensive development — in filling, dredging, construction of dykes to hold back high waters, sanitation and construction of roads. After many difficulties an industrial zone was laid out. Today it covers 67 acres

---

Le Monde, 29 July 1964, by permission. Editor's translation.

and looks like one enormous building site. But from the beginning everyone was aware that this was merely a temporary palliative, and that the solution lay elsewhere.

Meanwhile, in 1960, a decree set up an "urban district" comprising Tours and the eight communes surrounding it. Was this a first step towards a merger? Very rapidly experience showed that the new system created more difficulties rather than solved any. The municipal councils did not delegate to the district the powers it required; the entire financial burden fell on Tours; state aid was nonexistent; personal antagonisms and clashes of personality dogged it constantly. To all intents and purposes the district was never operative. Its council, whose chairman is the mayor of Tours, has ceased to meet. Its budget remains symbolically fixed at $25.

What was the answer? M. Royer, strongly supported by the prefect of Indre-et-Loire, M. René-Georges Thomas, regional prefect for the Tenth Region, reached the conclusion that the only solution was a complete merger of the city and several of the communes surrounding it. Two municipalities, Saint-Symphorien and Sainte-Radegonde, were in financial difficulties, and were unable to carry through their development plans or build a lycée. As dormitory areas these communes were very short of tax revenue. M. Royer actively propagated the idea of a merger among their leaders and voters. He held many public meetings, contacted many people and had preparatory studies made, so as to demonstrate that everyone who lived north of the river would find it to his advantage to belong to a larger unit, which alone would be able to carry through the essential capital program. Agreements were drawn up, the municipal councils voted, and the merger of the three communes was carried through, culminating with the prefectoral arrêté of 1 June 1964.

However, at Saint-Cyr-sur-Loire a pro-merger list at a by-election, which M. Royer supported with perhaps a trifle too much force, was defeated. But M. Royer says that this is just a pleasure deferred, since even these voters gave his list little short of 50 percent of the votes.

But from the administrative and economic points of view, how does the new Tours function? Legally Saint-Symphorien and Sainte-Radegonde no longer exist. However, the transition was carefully handled and traditions were maintained. The two former mayors are now members of the municipal council of the new Tours, with the rank of special assistant-mayors. The members of the municipal councils of the suppressed communes are consulted about decisions concerning the areas they once represented. The old town-halls have become "town hall extensions" for the convenience of the public, and continue to deal with births, marriages and deaths, social welfare and a number of other matters —particularly relating to agriculture. All the employees of the dissolved municipalities have been re-employed by the city of Tours.

The prices of certain services supplied—such as the cost of water—to the inhabitants have fallen. Local taxes have been cut slightly: the old tax assessment was as high as 40,000 "additional centimes" at Saint-Symphorien and Sainte-Radegonde against only 28,000 at Tours. The Local Tax raised 140,000,000 francs in Tours, to which should be added 700,000 at Saint-Symphorien and 100,000 at Sainte-Radegonde. Tours is now a city of almost 120,000 people, its income is higher and its area has more than doubled, now reaching 7,546 acres.

To convince his new fellow-citizens of the benefits of the merger M. Royer has been careful to order a number of spectacular moves: road maintenance and street-cleaning crews and the city's buses ostentatiously run through and serve the new quarters. But other important measures have been taken. The "trench" which goes through Saint-Symphorien, and which forms the National 7 linking Paris and Bordeaux will be widened from two lanes to four. An industrial zone of 310 hectares will be created alongside this highway; the infrastructure will cost $2,000,000; a number of industries have already decided to set up there—since the zone on the banks of the Cher is now full. A collège d'enseignement secondaire and a technical lycée are to be built there; huge sites have been made available for house building. Until now Tours has had 7,500 requests for housing each year which it could not meet because space for building was so short that building permits could be granted to only about half of those who asked for them. An original plan has been drawn up; in one month 1500 prefabricated houses are to be erected on 100 acres of the new municipal lands in the north of the city, and they will be sold for $5000 – $7000.

But M. Royer is already looking ahead to the next stage, a further extension of the city. He has decided that at the 1965 election he will support pro-merger lists in the surrounding communes. He also thinks that "the State should give more active encouragement to mergers by passing a law to allow local referendums. I do not see why they have any hesitations. It is quite normal for the people involved to decide their own fate. . .

The deputy-mayor dismisses the objections his proposals raise. "Country-dwellers are afraid the merger of communes will lead to their losing their land. Then we must find zones for them to move back to and this means we must draw up an over-all long-term plan for the whole area. If councillors are reluctant to sacrifice their seats, they must be kept on for a fairly long term, as consultative members of the new municipal council. "He is sceptical about the real importance and breadth of the financial and tax incentives envisaged by the government, and advocates a different approach. He says, "When a big commune decides on an important capital project it should be included automatically in the national Plan. Then people would see results—otherwise they will not give their support and mergers will fail."

Epilogue

"France is bored". So ran the headlines over a feature article in one of France's most respected newspapers early in 1968. The years when the Fifth Republic lived dangerously seemed to have ended with the Algerian war in 1962. De Gaulle had won the 1965 presidential election, even if the majority was less imposing than had been foreseen, and the Pompidou government had succeeded in dominating the Assembly despite its theoretical lack of a majority after the 1967 elections, thanks to both the immense procedural advantages governments now enjoy in Parliament, and to the divisions, fears and incompetence of its opponents. True, de Gaulle's foreign policy was widely criticized, and many regions were discontented over hardships arising from economic stabilization measures; and for some time the rather self-righteous complacency of the mid-sixties had seemed to be giving way to apprehension about the future. Yet despite uncertainty about whether the Fifth Republic would long survive the General's departure, it was generally accepted that, as long as he was at the helm, a major upheaval was unlikely.

But abruptly the leisurely speculation over post-Gaullism was shattered, and the regime's ability to survive even its founder hung in the balance. The first phase began mainly in the universities, sparked off by the rector of the University of Paris calling in police to clear the Sorbonne courtyard of students protesting disciplinary action against several of their leaders, and by the harsh police treatment of those who demonstrated at this violation of the University's traditional sanctity. As so often in history, a relatively minor incident sparked a conflagration fed by resentments and frustrations which had been mounting quietly for months and years. Night by night students and riot police clashed across barricades in the Latin Quarter, thousands were injured or arrested, while throughout the country institutions of higher education were peacefully occupied by students demanding greater autonomy from central government control of the universities and more student participation.

Next the contagion spread to the workers, whose patience over delays in meeting their demands suddenly snapped. In a few days more than half the industrial labor force was out on strike, and hundreds of factories had been occupied by their workers. There was none of the naked violence of the Latin Quarter in the factories, but the country's economy was steadily approaching paralysis.

By mid-May the much-vaunted solidity and stability of the Fifth Republic had been brutally and derisorily brushed aside. Ministers vacillated between concession and repression, with little feel for which moment was appropriate for each. Even de Gaulle, belatedly addressing the nation, appeared for the first time as an uncomprehending and querulous old man uncertain of his ground. He announced a referendum for June. Formally the people would vote on economic and university reforms. But the terms in which these were described were negligently vague. In practice, more overtly even than in the referenda discussed earlier by Henry Ehrmann, the real choice was to lie between de Gaulle or chaos. The proposal was frostily received, and the crisis deepened. When negotiations between government, unions and employers produced a package of concessions which in normal times would have been highly advantageous, the militants rejected it. They had the bit between their teeth. The cry now went up for a government of all the left, Communists included. The existence of the regime itself was now in question.

As the month drew to an end, the economy was grinding to a halt; the government's ability to hold its referendum in conditions of incipient anarchy was increasingly in doubt (and word had leaked that the Conseil d'Etat viewed the whole proposal as unconstitutional). More important, although the Communist leadership in the party and the main trade union federation had so far held to a parliamentary and reformist line, castigating extremist students and revolutionary-minded workers, it was thought they might be wavering under pressure from below. The government itself seemed increasingly impotent and irrelevant. When news came that de Gaulle had left Paris, such had been the impression of drift and decay that even highly placed Gaullists believed that the end of the Fifth Republic was a matter of hours.

But de Gaulle returned from a symbolic sojourn at his Colombey retreat in fighting mood; he had assured himself of army backing, and he probably knew now the Communists were not going to risk revolution. Decisive, every inch a leader again, he declared his refusal to resign or dismiss the Prime Minister and dissolved the Assembly, precipitating a general election. The Assembly had in fact been almost blameless during the crisis; demonstrators had passed it by with barely a passing glance, for it seemed irrelevant. An opposition censure motion against the government had failed. But in calling for elections de Gaulle was gambling that his countrymen were weary of disorder and inconvenience and alarmed at the spectre of civil war. The gamble worked. The Gaullists recovered their nerve; the slow return to something akin to normalcy began.

The ensuing campaign was the shortest and one of the crudest in French history. Swinging sharply to the right, the Gaullists fought as defenders of the Republic against the Red peril and civil war. No matter that the argument was a travesty, and that the Communists' very absence of revolutionary zeal had helped save the day for the regime; the tide of exasperation and fear ran strongly to de Gaulle. The Gaullists romped home to the largest parliamentary majority in the history of the Republic, with 358 seats out of 485. (Casualties included Pierre Mendès-France, narrowly defeated at Grenoble.) Although all the Gaullists' opponents suffered, the havoc was greatest on the left; the infant Federation of the Left, which had been rent asunder by the crisis suffered particularly heavy losses. Clearly the emergence of a simple and more coherent party structure now seemed more intractable and problematical even than when Stanley Hoffmann discussed the problem earlier.

Before the new Parliament had even met, de Gaulle reacted characteristically. On May 30 he had paid striking tribute to M. Pompidou's conduct during the crisis; he had praised the solidity and determination of the government. Now, on July 11, with M. Pompidou looking more than ever the heir apparent, having led the Gaullists to their unprecedented victory, de Gaulle dismissed him in as summary a fashion as the eviction of M. Debré described in an earlier chapter.

He installed as head of a new government Maurice Couve de Murville, a career civil servant who had served as Foreign Minister since 1958 until his move to the Finance Ministry only a few weeks earlier, and who was now entering Parliament for the first time. At the same time the nominee of the Elysée was dutifully elected chairman of the Gaullist parliamentary group (rebaptized yet again UDR—Union des démocrates pour la République).

De Gaulle thus emerged from the immediate crisis more than ever at the helm. The cabinet seemed more even than in the past his personal instrument, in tackling the economic fallout of the crisis and the promised program of reform. Whether or not acceptable solutions would be found remained to be seen, but some of the wider political implications were already clear. Most important of all, the political stability the Gaullists claimed as one of their principal achievements, the stability in which so many non-Gaullist Frenchmen took such pride, was brutally revealed as only skin deep. The traditional anarchic and violent strands in the French political culture had lost none of their vitality. If anything, the mistrust of authority and the "forces of order," which Laurence Wylie explored earlier, must have been reinforced in many Frenchmen. Determined revolutionaries during the crisis were few, though events frequently lapsed into a nostalgic attempt to recapture revolutionary style—a feeling for which seems part of the socialization process in every French child. The students in the Latin Quarter erected their barricades just as their predecessors in 1848 and 1870 had done; the workers occupied their factories in imitation of the earlier occupations of 1936. Throughout, in the heady excitement and fervent oratory in Paris (for major incidents were few elsewhere), there were constant echoes of all the previous *glorieuses journées* of French history.

More important than the superficial style of the crisis, the underlying problems of the relationship between society and the state, as described by Philip Williams in the first chapter, plainly remain unresolved. When tested, the political institutions of the Fifth Republic had little vitality of their own. The regime was thrown back for revival on the ultimate political sanction of military force, and on de Gaulle himself. Inevitably, therefore, the ability of the Fifth Republic to survive him looked increasingly problematical. De Gaulle's handling of events if anything emphasized the strikingly provisional air that the political system retains at the end of its first decade. He proposed a referendum of highly dubious constitutionality; he treated Parliament as little more than a pawn in the power struggle; he raised again the old idea of reforming the Senate to provide greater "participation" for major interest groups in the policy process; he dismissed his Prime Minister summarily with only the barest genuflection to constitutional proprieties. "Mutation" and "participation": such were the two watchwords de Gaulle advanced to cure the *malaise*. But whatever the content of these slogans might be in the universities and industry, it was clearer than ever that they were not to apply to the political process. M. Pompidou was dismissed without the slightest attempt at credible public explanation.

It was clear that de Gaulle was determined to stay on, more assertive in his monarchical style of rule than ever, choosing as Prime Minister a man whose faithful execution of the General's policies had never wavered—but with little apparent endowment in the basic skills of the democratic politician. Yet one of the underlying causes of the crisis had almost certainly been the lofty way de Gaulle treated policy-making as his private preserve. On several previous occasions the lack of adequate intermediaries and communications channels within the system had resulted in frustrations building up to such a degree had led to such groups as the farmers taking direct action to compel the government to pay attention. It was not really surprising that eventually a major crisis blew up. Plainly the whole style of Gaullist view was a contributory factor in the events of May; yet it was just this style that the General was probably incapable of altering, and was even reasserting more vigorously than ever. For a man of seventy-seven it was a striking performance, but as a solution to the longer-standing problems of how eventually democracy and effective government can be reconciled in France it was highly questionable. Were these really the means by which the institutions of the Fifth Republic might gain the vitality required to survive the passing of the General? In the short run there was de Gaulle—but all the uncertainty about what might come after him was now enhanced.

Suggestions for Reading

There is no lack of books providing the general historical background to the problems of contemporary France. Among the best introductions are Alfred Cobban *A History of Modern France*, (Penguin Books, 1965) and Gordon Wright *France in Modern Times* (Rand McNally, 1960). Also useful is David Thomson's essay in historical analysis, *Democracy in France* (Oxford U.P., 4th edition 1960). Among the more detailed studies of the pre-war and wartime periods are Sir Denis Brogan *The Development of Modern France* (Harper, 1940) and Alexander Werth's *The Twilight of France* (Harper, 1942), written with splendid journalistic panache. Also four books by Robert Aron *The Vichy Régime* (Macmillan [N.Y.] 1958), *De Gaulle Before Paris* (Putnam 1963), *De Gaulle Triumphant* (Putnam 1964) and *France Reborn* (Scribner 1964).

For the complete beginner the best introductions to the Fourth Republic are François Goguel *France Under the Fourth Republic* (Cornell U.P., 1952) and D.M. Pickles *France: The Fourth Republic* (Methuen 2nd ed. 1958), while among more journalistic works there is Alexander Werth's *France 1940-56* (Holt, 1956). However, the outstanding work on this period is Philip Williams *Crisis and Compromise* (Longmans, 1964; paperback edition, Doubleday 1966), which also includes an excellent critical bibliography.

The decline and fall of the Fourth Republic and the circumstances in which the Fifth Republic was born are described in Philip Williams and Martin Harrison *De Gaulle's Republic* (Longmans, 1960). Edward Behr *The Algerian Problem* (Norton, 1962) gives the best account of the problem which killed the Fourth Republic and dominated the early years of the Fifth.

A most useful description of the sources of the Fifth Republic's constitution and the way it was drafted can be found in an article by Nicholas Wahl in *The American Political Science Review*. Wahl has also written the best brief account of the institutions and politics of the Fifth Republic in his section in S. Beer and A. Ulam *Patterns of Government* (Random House, 2nd edition 1962).

For discussion of the relationship between France's recent economic and social development and her political evolution see Raymond Aron *France: Steadfast and Changing* (Harvard University Press, 1960), Edward R. Tannenbaum *The New France* (University of Chicago Press, 1961) and Stanley Hoffmann (ed.) *In Search of France* (Harvard U.P., 1963), also known under the title *France, Change and Tradition*.

Regrettably there are no really good biographies of de Gaulle. In a poor field François Mauriac's hagiographical *De Gaulle* (Doubleday, 1966) is to be avoided at all costs, while Alexander Werth's *De Gaulle* (Penguin, 1965) is reasonably reliable but displays his characteristically expansive style without his customary idiosyncratic insights. The best source on the General remains the General himself in the three volumes of his *War Memoirs* (Weidenfeld and Nicolson, 3 vols., 1956-60).

His earlier work *The Edge of the Sword* (Faber, 1960) also provides many insights into his character.

For the style of gaullist rule there is Pierre Viansson-Ponté *The King and His Court* (Houghton, 1964). Studies of decision making in the Fifth Republic are rare, but some light is thrown on de Gaulle's methods in D.M. Pickles *Algeria and France* (Praeger, 1963), and in Bernard E. Brown's contribution to J.B. Christoph's *Cases in Comparative Politics* (Little, Brown, 1965) as well as in the same author's "Pressure Politics in the Fifth Republic," *Journal of Politics* 25 (3), August 1963. See also J.S. Ambler *The French Army in Politics 1945-1962* (Ohio State U.P., 1966) and P.M. Williams, *The French Parliament* (Allen & Unwin, 1968).

Though slightly overtaken by events, Henry W. Ehrmann *Organized Business in France* (Princeton University Press, 1957) still remains a valuable source on pressure groups, as does Georges Lavau's contribution on France to H.W. Ehrmann (ed.) *Interest Groups on Four Continents* (Pittsburgh U.P., 1958). This is also J.E.S. Hayward's most useful monograph *Private Interests and Public Policy* (Longmans, 1966) on the Economic and Social Council and the same writer's study of policy making. "Interest Groups and Incomes Policy in France" *British Journal of Industrial Relations*, IV. One of the most systematic critics of the present system is Pierre Mendès-France, *A Modern French Republic* (Hill and Wang, 1963).

The literature on the political parties is patchy. For the left there is David Caute *Communism and the French Intellectuals* (Macmillan N.Y. 1964) and George Lichteim *Marxism in Modern France* (Columbia, 1966) and C.A. Micaud *Communism and the French Left* (Praeger, 1963), and also Hadley Cantril *The Politics of Despair* (Basic Books, 1958). The Radicals are covered to nearly the close of the Fourth Republic by Francis de Tarr *The French Radical Party* (Oxford, 1961). On the MRP there is R.B. Capelle *The MRP and French Foreign Policy* (Praeger, 1963), and L. Bosworth *Catholicism and Crisis in Modern France* (Princeton U.P., 1962). Little has so far appeared in English on the conservatives and gaullists; René Rémond's admirable *The Right Wing in France* (University of Pennsylvania P., 1966) is primarily historical.

The electoral system is described succinctly in Peter Campbell *French Electoral Systems* (Faber, 2nd ed, 1966). For a lively and anecdotal description of the 1958 campaign see P.M. Williams and M. Harrison in D.E. Butler (ed.) *Elections Abroad* (Macmillan [London] 1960). For descriptions of succeeding elections and referenda see *Parliamentary Affairs* XIV (3) Summer 1961; XV (3) Summer 1961; XVI (2) Spring 1963; XIX (1) Winter 1965-6; also *Political Studies*, II (3) October 1963 and 14 (2) June 1961.

For local government and administration there are two good formal works by Brian Chapman *Introduction to French Local Government* and *The Prefects and Provincial France* (Allen & Unwin, 1953 and 1955). (The best recent general description of the French administrative system is F. Ridley and J. Blondel *Public Administration in France*, [Barnes and Noble, 1964]). Two excellent accounts of rural France based on personal observation are Laurence Wylie *Village in the Vaucluse* (Harvard University Press, 1957) which is followed up in his contribution to the Hoffmann symposium mentioned above—and Gordon Wright *Rural Revolution in France* (Stanford, 1964).

123456789